THE
GREAT BOOK
OF JEWELS

ERNST A. AND JEAN HEINIGER

THE GREAT BOOK OF JEWELS

With contributions by EDUARD GÜBELIN

ERIKA BILLETER

GUIDO GREGORIETTI

R.A. HIGGINS · HUGH TAIT

CHARLES LEDIT

R.W. LIGHTBOWN

RENÉE S. NEU

GEORGE S. SWITZER

EDITA LAUSANNE

First published in Switzerland 1974 by Edita S.A., Lausanne
Copyright © 1974 by Edita S.A. and Ernst and Jean Heiniger

Library of Congress Catalog Card Number: 82-84585
ISBN: 0-517-181320

Printed in Italy and bound in Switzerland

CONTENTS

PREFACE

To undertake a book of this kind is to undertake a study of the history of mankind. Had we realized this awesome fact some five years ago when we started our work on The Great Book of Jewels, *we might never have begun it. In that case, we would have missed the greatest adventure of our lives, for the jewels exist virtually all over the world – in museums, in bank vaults, and in private collections; in 1972 and 1973 we journeyed through twenty countries studying and photographing some of the most dazzling jewelry and gems in existence, and had the opportunity to meet their equally fascinating owners or custodians. It is our hope that after leafing through this book, readers will sense some of the romance and adventure connected with jewels and will begin to understand why wars have been waged, cities sacked, men tortured and even assassinated for the sake of a glittering gem.*

In studying the jewel collections in the great museums, we found that with few exceptions – such as in the Schmuckmuseum at Pforzheim – the jewels were poorly displayed or neglected, while such larger objects as sculptures and paintings were well presented and publicized. We therefore decided to create a book whose exceptional illustrations and distinguished text would bring some of the world's finest jewels to a wide audience, since very few people would ever have the opportunity to see those treasures at first hand.

From the beginning, we realized that it would be necessary to make new photographs of the jewels. Studying the existing books on jewels and the museum archives, we found the photographs generally to be static and uninspired – mere records, so to speak. This is understandable, for the photography of jewels is perhaps technically the most difficult form of camera work.

In photographing the jewels, we tried to capture not only the physical qualities of each jewel – its material and structure – but also the subtle essence, often exotic and inscrutable, that emanates from each of these gems. If a jewel has traveled from one owner to another, from one country to another, and has been associated with varied personalities, it acquires a character all its own. Therefore, for the most part, we have not photographed the jewels against distracting backgrounds, since each should speak for itself. Personally, we feel there is really only one way to elicit an understanding of jewels and gemstones, and that is by touching them — by holding them in the hand. Before making a photograph, we always tried to hold the object, to study it from every angle, to recall its history, so as to establish a rapport with it.

How to approach the museums and collectors for permission to photograph their famous jewels was a problem of the very first order, since it is forbidden to photograph a large portion of these treasures. We finally worked out a rather mysterious letter stating that we were planning to be in a certain city on a particular date, that we were preparing a publication, The Great Book of Jewels, and would like to meet with the owner to discuss his jewel collection. We did not ask for permission to photograph. Thus, although we were always received by the collectors, we could never be sure in advance that we would be able to take a single photograph. This was a rather risky and expensive way of operating. However, we felt it imperative to have personal contact in order to secure permission to photograph the jewels. We prepared a dummy which gave a fairly accurate idea of the book we wanted to create; after glancing through it, each collector wanted his jewel to be included.

Before starting our travels, we made an extensive study of light and camera equipment. We finally assembled a complete studio outfit, portable and light in weight (including a collapsible light table for illuminating the gems), which provided everything necessary for shooting the best photographs under the most difficult circumstances. The whole outfit was designed to fit into the trunk of our automobile. We often had to take photographs in the vaults, surrounded by guards, with barely enough space to set up our equipment, because to our great surprise we found that most world-famous gems never see the light of day. They spend their lives in the vaults of the great banks in New York, London, Paris, Munich, Geneva, and so on. When we left our studio in Zurich we usually left no word as to our destination, since we were reluctant to risk publicity and the possibility of a robbery.

One of our early photographic journeys was to New York, where we lost no time in calling on the renowned jewelry houses on Fifth Avenue. At Tiffany's, we made arrangements to photograph the world-famous Tiffany Diamond, the finest and largest yellow diamond in the world. After completing our work there, at the Metropolitan Museum of Art, and at the Museum of Natural History, we went on to Washington, D.C. There we contacted Dr George Switzer, curator of the Division of Mineralogy at the Smithsonian Institution, which houses the celebrated Hope Diamond, the extraordinary sapphire called the Star of Asia, and the Rosser Reeves Ruby (the largest and finest star-ruby on earth). These, as well as many other gems from the Smithsonian's collection, were photographed for inclusion.

Of all the great gems, the Wittelsbach Diamond, also known as the Haus-diamant or the Great Blue Diamond, was the most elusive. Once a Crown Jewel of Bavaria, it remained in the Wittelsbach family until 1931, when it disappeared mysteriously. It reappeared in Belgium in 1961 and was bought by the well-known diamond dealer I. Komkommer of Antwerp. In 1964 the Wittelsbach Diamond changed hands again, but the name of the purchaser was guarded with utmost secrecy. We could obtain no definite information concerning its whereabouts. Finally, after three years of searching, we learned partly by chance that the famous gem was in a Swiss vault not far from our studio.

Costly insurance and a lengthy period of negotiation were required, however, before we were able to photograph the diamond. Also, before being told the name of the owner and the precise location of the jewel, we had to affix our signatures to a document stating that we would never reveal either fact.

The discovery of the Wittelsbach Diamond was one of the most exciting moments in the making of the book, but there were many other challenging and satisfying episodes, and some disappointments as well. The crisis in the Middle East prevented a trip to Cairo to photograph pieces from the Treasure of Tutankhamen – but fortunately this jewelry has been adequately published in recent years. Many important jewels could not be included for lack of space or other reasons. Except for Chapter V, "Sacred Jewels," we have concentrated on jewelry for personal adornment, which meant excluding many extraordinary objets d'art. Unlike almost all the other jewelry represented, the contemporary pieces selected are not necessarily of high monetary value; they were selected to show the great diversity and inventiveness of the jewelry being created today.

*

It would require many pages to thank each person who assisted us in the creation of The Great Book of Jewels *and we can mention only a few. In particular, we should like to express our gratitude to Dr Henry Fischer of the Metropolitan Museum of Art, New York; Dr George Switzer of the Smithsonian Institution, Washington, D.C.; Dr Henry Higgins of the British Museum, London; Dr Erwin M. Auer of the Kunsthistorisches Museum, Vienna; Dr Herbert Brunner of the Schatzkammer, Munich; Dr Hermann Wahl, Dr Fritz Falk, and Mrs H. Senner of the Schmuckmuseum, Pforzheim; Dr Kemal Cig of the Topkapi Museum, Istanbul; and Her Imperial Majesty, Empress Farah of Iran. We should like also to thank the eminent authors of our text for their untiring efforts; our publisher and his associates for their confidence and understanding throughout the project; and the great museums, private collectors, and galleries throughout the world for their cooperation in making this book possible.*

Ernst A. and Jean Heiniger
Zurich, Switzerland

THE ORIGIN
OF GEMSTONES

EDUARD J. GÜBELIN GEMMOLOGIST, LUCERNE

When man's earliest ancestor picked up a particularly pretty pebble, rubbed shiny by the sea, and carried it around, he was responding to the same attraction, with the same wonder and delight, that we feel today when we twist and turn a gemstone in the light to enjoy its luster and color.

It is therefore not surprising that these aristocrats of the mineral kingdom were collected and hoarded from the beginning. Gems and seal rings beautifully made from precious stones have come down to us from the Babylonians and the Sumerians. Men wore gems as decoration and as symbols of might and riches. They also offered them to the gods, decorating their idols and altars with them, aware that only the gods could have created them. Kings adorned their crowns and filled their treasure chests with jewels, for they provided a ready form of capital. Only much later, as societies became increasingly humanized and "democratized," were gemstones used as ornaments for women.

The fact that gemstones are idiosyncracies of nature – durable, beautiful, and yet so rare that they are difficult to find and acquire – led man time and again to ascribe supernatural power to them, just as he attributed wonderful and miraculous effects to many other phenomena that seemed to him magic and inexplicable. He looked to gems for victory in battle, fruitfulness, personal protection, and much else.

Specific properties raise a mineral to the rank of gemstone: beauty, rarity, and durability. The old label, still in use, of "semiprecious" stone should be forgotten, because it is misleading. Every stone has its particular character, and valuable and very attractive stones are slighted when they are referred to by this outmoded term. Opaque gemstones are sometimes distinguished as "ornamental" stones, but an overwhelming majority of contemporary experts agree that all gemstones endowed with beauty, rarity, and durability should be regarded as precious.

Beauty as a Property of Gemstones

It is a particularly attractive and perhaps typical idiosyncrasy of the science of gemstones – called gemmology – that unlike most other rational disciplines, it employs the criterion of beauty. Beauty, which must of necessity escape sober reasoning, is a thoroughly delightful concession to humanity in what passes for a very prosaic and factually exact science.

The first aspect of beauty that strikes the observer is the color, which is an outward manifestation of light. The deep green of the emerald, the play of color in the opal, is produced by rays of light falling upon the gemstone. Light of different wave lengths is perceived by the human eye as different colors; as the waves which enter a gemstone as white light pass through the stone, they are affected by the chemical and structural nature of the mineral. Some wave lengths are absorbed; only those that are not absorbed – and are therefore visible to the eye – are reflected. Thus, a combination of different wave lengths radiates from the stone: white light becomes colored light.

Certain elements of gemstones absorb portions of white light and thereby reveal colors. We must distinguish between idiochromatic (self-colored) gemstones, whose color-inducing substances are part of the chemical composition, and allochromatic (extraneously colored) stones, which become colored only by the accidental presence of a foreign element in the chemical composition. The element – usually present in only microscopic quantities – is enmeshed as an impurity in the crystalline structure; its presence can transform the colorless and transparent stone, otherwise worthless, into the most valuable of nature's creations. In this context it is interesting to note that the same element may produce different colors, depending on the host mineral it has invaded. Thus, a minute trace of chromium imparts the green color to the emerald. Chromium in the ruby, on the other hand, absorbs the entire green portion and the greater part of the blue portion of the light spectrum; the remainder is a mixture of red, orange, and yellow, with a trace of blue, which together produce the beautiful carmine red of the precious ruby – a color described as pigeon's blood.

But the luminous colors of the stones tinted by their chemical composition are not as amazing as the behavior of the so-called phenomenal stones. Even though contemporary gemmology, utilizing modern optics, has identified the cause of such unique light phenomena as chatoyancy (cat's eye effect), asterism (star formation), adularescence (moonstone effect), and opalescence, these effects of light can still make us forget sober explanations. Seeing a star of light sweeping over the stone, the observer reverts to the same state of awe tinged with mysticism and enchantment induced in our ancestors at the sight.

The explanation sounds prosaic: "Light is reflected by microscopically fine arrays of hollow tubes or mineral fibers." If the stone is cut so as to create a curved surface above these reflecting inclusions, the broad sheen of reflected light becomes concentrated into a ray of light which appears to float above the surface and, when the stone is moved, to roam over the surface; this produces chatoyancy, the "cat's eye" effect. Asterism (as in the star sapphire) comes from a multiplicity of parallel tubes or fibers crossing each other at angles of 90 or 120 degrees, producing the impression of a four- or six-rayed star.

Other phenomena of gems are just as easily explained, and just as marvelous. In the ornamental gems – especially the many kinds of agates –

additional effects of light and color are caused by macroscopic elements –
that is, particles visible to the naked eye. They consist primarily of iron
or manganese compounds deposited in cracks or fissures, where they
crystallized. This has led to enormously varied specialization among
connoisseurs, who collect the unique designs of dendritic, fortification,
moss, and landscape agates.

The other ornamental stones also owe their beauty to their splendid
colors, and often to the charming contrasts formed by the host stone and
its encapsulated mineral traces. The sky-blue turquoise with its velvety
brown veins belongs in this group, as do the rose-colored rhodochrosite
with its blossomlike patterns and the deep-blue lapis lazuli with its golden
flecks of pyrite.

The sparkle of a precious stone is as important as its display of color.
If a well-cut ruby is held in one hand and a similarly cut piece of glass of
the same color in the other, the difference is immediately apparent even
to the layman. No matter how cleverly color and transparency are imitated,
there is no way to duplicate the luster and sparkle that characterizes a
gemstone. This sparkle is the result of several optical properties peculiar
to gemstones – primarily refraction, double refraction, dispersion, luster,
brilliance, and "fire." When a ray of light enters a gemstone, the velocity
at which the light travels is affected by the close atomic packing. This
occurrence becomes visible as so-called refraction of light: the ray of light
is deflected from its original path by the denser medium. The angle of
deflection, or "index of refraction," as measured by special instruments,
is one of the important diagnostic tools used by gemmologists in identification. In general, the higher the refractive index (that is, the slower
the speed of the light in the stone in relation to its velocity in air), the
greater the sparkle of a gemstone.

In most precious stones, moreover, the index of refraction differs
markedly in the various directions of the crystal. This phenomenon is
called double refraction. In some gemstones, such as the zircon, double
refraction is so high that the facet edges of the pavilion appear doubled
when viewed through the table of the cut stone. (See diagram P. 47).

Nor is the degree of refraction identical for all wave lengths. A particular crystal will impose a different speed on the red portion of the day-
light spectrum than it does on the blue. This property, which differs from
mineral to mineral, can be measured as "dispersion" and used in gemstone
analysis. For the observer, dispersion has the effect of separating the
colors. It accounts, for example, for the peculiar feature of diamonds:
the light, subjected to a high degree of dispersion, splits into its components
and emerges as the colors of the spectrum. This property of diamonds is
valued as "fire."

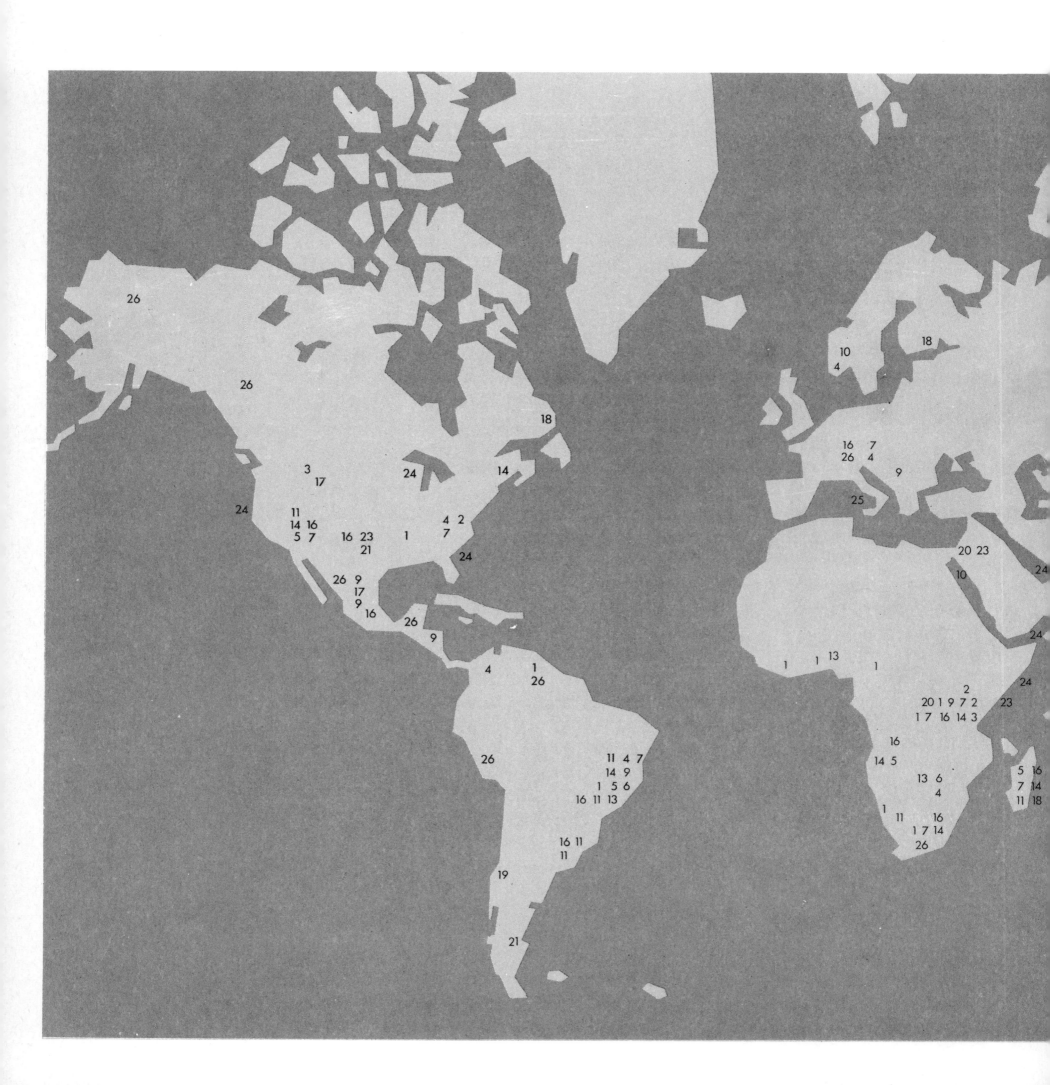

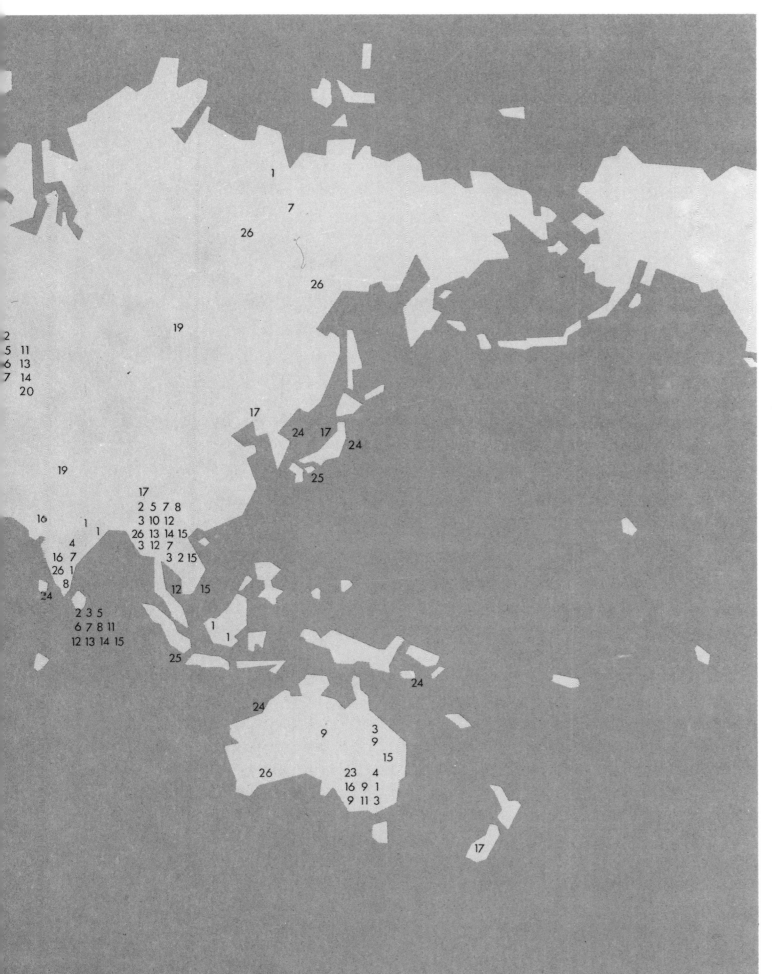

Geographical distribution
of precious stones,
pearls, coral, and gold.

1 Diamond
2 Ruby
3 Sapphire
4 Emerald
5 Beryl
6 Chrysoberyl
7 Garnet
8 Moonstone
9 Opal
10 Chrysolite
11 Quartz (amethyst, rock crystal,
    smoky quartz, rose quartz,
    citrine)
12 Spinel
13 Topaz
14 Tourmaline
15 Zircon
16 Agate
17 Jade
18 Labradorite-spectrolite
19 Lapis-lazuli
20 Malachite
21 Rhodochrosite
22 Rhodonite
23 Turquoise
24 Pearls
25 Coral
26 Gold

The luster – the ability of the mineral to reflect light from the surface without allowing it to penetrate – also contributes to the stone's sparkle. But such external reflection is only a minor element. Reflection from penetrated light – described as brilliance – plays a much larger role. A clever design for the cut and optimal arrangement of the facets can cause the greatest possible amount of the light striking the stone to be deflected in such a way as to reappear visibly at the surface. It makes sense, therefore, to consider the index of refraction when planning the best cut for any particular stone.

Practically speaking, every cut gemstone exhibits some brilliance. But this property has been developed to near perfection in the so-called brilliant cut in diamonds. Its fifty-eight facets direct the incident light in such a way that, at best, "total reflection" results – that is, all the light entering the surface emerges again through the large top facet called the table. All these optical-physical properties are thus responsible for the flash and sparkle that have always captivated lovers of gems. Gemmology's prosaic explanations of these spectacular displays have not been able to rob gemstones of the magic with which they were and are surrounded, nor to diminish the pleasure and admiration a well-cut stone evokes.

The beauty and character of a gemstone are not determined by its color and "fire" alone. A very considerable role may also be played by foreign matter embedded in the stone – so-called inclusions. Anyone who has ever bought a diamond knows that its value is significantly determined by the presence of inclusions. (The presence of inclusions, in fact, is very important in evaluating most gems.) Here we are concerned with the *beauty* of inclusions. Most gemstones still carry the marks of enormous geological processes which go back much further than the earliest artifacts we admire so greatly. The study of inclusions can not only enlighten us about the origin of the gemstone; it can also provide us with a glimpse into the history of the earth.

Inclusions come about through elimination or settling of foreign components in the host solution, through developmental imperfections, through chemical or physical changes in the process of crystallization, or for other causes. Depending on their characteristics, we can distinguish among solid, liquid, and gaseous inclusions; it can be assumed that every gemstone contains a clue to its origins in the form of one or more inclusions, even though present technology cannot always isolate them. Solid inclusions generally represent foreign minerals; frequently the faces of fully formed tiny crystals can be seen under the microscope. Liquid inclusions are the most beautiful and, to the gemmologist, the most interesting. Depending on their shape, they are described as flags or as cavities. Cavities, in which the outer crystal faces follow the shape of the host crystal, are called "negative crystals"; many of them contain the residue of a million-year-old mother liquid, such as water, carbonic acid, or salt solutions. The so-called three-phase inclusions – in which a liquid-filled cavity holds both a gas bubble and a small crystal – are particularly interesting.

This brief sketch of the heart of sparkling gemstones is intended to stress two points. First, an inclusion in a stone need not be considered a "flaw" or regarded as a detriment to its value or beauty, for inclusions may frequently make a positive contribution to the inner beauty of gemstones. Second, inclusions provide the careful observer, who takes the trouble to study them, with clues to the origin and history of his gemstone.

Inclusions in gemstones can also be identifying marks. Though the cutter's skill can alter the form and possibly the color of a stone, the intrinsic features – the pattern of the inclusions – is unchangeable if the stone's splendor is not to be destroyed by brute force. The connoisseur of precious stones, therefore, does not consider inclusions as flaws of nature, but welcomes them as an attractive addition.

Rarity as a Property of Gemstones

The second characteristic of gemstones – rarity – is related to their development rather than their composition, for most are composed of common chemical elements, found in abundance throughout the world: carbon, aluminium, silica, and lime, among others. Most gemstones are minerals, but some are rocks. (Minerals are physiochemically uniform, structurally separate, natural components of the earth's crust; rocks, on the other hand, are aggregates of disparate solids belonging to one or more mineral varieties.)

Most gemstone minerals are crystals – that is, structured matter in which the individual atoms are arranged in a fixed order which is discerned as the regular architecture of the crystal. Most often two atoms are linked when one has a positive electric charge, the other a negative one. The mutual attraction of these electrically charged atoms – called ions – results in a bonding, called cohesion. Special conditions are necessary in nature for ions with opposite charges and complementary to each other to appear in gases or molten liquids; further, the proper conditions of pressure and heat must occur to enable them to form atomic aggregates of space-filling lattices, whose scheme and structure are expressed outwardly in a symmetrical arrangement of multiple faces: the crystal.

How, then, were gemstones formed? What conditions of earth history made possible the anomalies leading to the formation of these rare treasures?

There are three main cycles of rock and mineral formation:

1. the magmatic cycle (*magma* = viscous mass)
2. the metamorphic cycle (*metamorphosis* = change of state)
3. the sedimentary cycle (*sedimentum* = deposit).

1. The *magmatic cycle* is named for the molten rock material within the earth, the magma. Magmatic minerals were formed either at some depth in the earth or in eruptions near the surface. The solidification of the magma and crystallization into minerals is an extremely complex process lasting millions of years; it can only be briefly sketched here.

In the first stage of the magmatic cycle, the liquid-magmatic phase, at temperatures from 1,500 to 700 degrees centigrade, the primary formation of rocks occurred. The igneous rocks (granite, dolerite, gabbro) were formed at this time. With the exception of the diamond, only a microscopically small quantity of gemstones was formed, so generally the commercial value of magmatic gemstone deposits is small.

Further cooling of the magma left residual molten matter in which the "volatile" constituents became increasingly concentrated: water, boron, chlorine, fluorine, carbonic acid, phosphorus, sulphur, and the like, as well as a number of rare elements. There was considerable pressure within this residue, and the residual solutions oozing from the solidifying magma created a further rise in pressure, until the liquids forced their way into cracks and fissures where the chemical and thermal effects changed. In this pegmatitic phase (*pegma* = texture or framework) the most beautiful and the largest gem crystals were formed. The quantity of water in these residual fluids, still at temperatures between 700 and 500 degrees centigrade, rendered them particularly motile, and the abundance of volatile residual constituents favored the formation of large crystals. It was this phase which gave rise to apatite, beryl, chrysoberyl, euclase, kunzite, moonstone, sapphire, spodumene, topaz, tourmaline, and many others.

As the molten rock mass continued to cool, it was further enriched with additional volatile constituents; new solutions containing gas and steam penetrated even more deeply into the surrounding strata, causing chemical alterations. The pneumatolytic deposits (*pneuma* = breath; *lyein* = to dissolve) emerged during this phase. While the solutions were still hot (500 to 400 degrees centigrade), their chemical interaction with adjacent rocks formed new and stable minerals. The extremely potent chemical activity and the motility of these residual solutions resulted in mineral assemblages. The great variety of gemstones formed in this way (in Burma, Ceylon, the Urals, and other areas) include alexandrite, ruby, sapphire, spinel, emerald, and lapis lazuli.

The last part of the magmatic cycle was the hydrothermal phase (*hydro* = water, *thermos* = hot). While temperatures ranged from 400 to 100 degrees centigrade, the watery solutions of those elements that so far had formed no compounds were under sufficient pressure to extrude through cracks and fissures, crystallize as cooling continued, and fill cavities in the rock. This phase accounts for the formation of the large family of quartzes, as well as the tourmalines and topazes (formed also in the pegmatitic phase). The emeralds of the calcareous shales of Colombia are also of hydrothermal origin.

2. The *metamorphic cycle,* another rock-forming process, has little significance in gem formation. Thrusting, faulting, and circulating residual solutions subjected rocks already existing in the magmatic phase to increased pressure or temperatures. Previously formed rocks and minerals evolved into new minerals of a different kind. Almandine, jadeite, and nephrite developed during this phase.

3. The *sedimentary cycle,* the last cycle of rock formation, is also of minimal importance for the creation of gemstones. When formation has been completed, weathered rock, exposed to water and wind, can accumulate dry deposits which in turn become compressed. An interesting ornamental stone of this sedimentary cycle is rhodochrosite, found as stalagmites in San Luis, Argentina.

Beyond this, only the buildup of sedimentary deposits plays a practical role. Wind and water can transport previously formed rocks and minerals from the original ("primary") site of their formation to other sites, sometimes at a great distance, where they can be found concentrated as "secondary" deposits.

Weathering as a process is also not considered a major source of gemstones. Only turquoise, chrysoprase, malachite, and azurite resulted from weathering processes.

This excursus into the history of our planet gives only a broad outline of the complicated processes that took place in the evolution of minerals and rocks. So many favorable circumstances must fortuitously concur if gemstones are to be formed that it seems a miracle, or a benevolent disposition, that these complicated chemical and physical prerequisites occurred even once. That in fact deposits can be found in several regions of the earth seems more than miraculous. But they remain rare accidents, and the rarity of gemstones is therefore the result of the enormous complexity and incredible coincidence of their formation.

Durability as a Property of Gemstones

The third characteristic a mineral must possess to qualify as a gemstone is durability. For unlike most of the beauties of nature, the gemstone is destined for eternity. A precious stone we hold in our hands today will still be displaying the full splendor of its sparkle and luster to our descendants a few thousand years hence. Gemstones owe this enviable property to their ability to withstand such physical attacks as abrasion and scratching, as well as corrosion, chemical effects, and the bleaching action of light. They are thus resistant to processes that might diminish their beauty, luster, and color.

The crucial factor of hardness is due to their strong cohesion, which in turn depends on the arrangement and nature of their atoms. But all gemstones are not equally hard.

In 1812 the German mineralogist Friedrich Mohs established a scale of hardness in which he arranged all gemstones according to what he called their "scratching power." Scratching power implies that each mineral in the scale, ranging from 1 to 10, may scratch the following ones and thus is harder than those with lower numbers. But the scale is arbitrary and does not indicate a relationship in the degree of hardness, for the differences between individual minerals are not equal.

The levels are represented by the following minerals:

Talc	1	Feldspar	6
Gypsum	2	Quartz	7
Calcite	3	Topaz	8
Fluorspar	4	Corundum	9
Apatite	5	Diamond	10

The relativity of the hardness scale becomes apparent from the fact that the difference in hardness between stages 9 and 10, corundum and diamond, is greater than that between 1 and 9, talc and corundum. For this reason intermediate values are usually indicated not by decimal places, but by such approximations as $8\frac{1}{2}$ or $5\frac{1}{4}$. A majority of the dust particles floating in the earth's atmosphere are composed of quartz, whose hardness is 7. From hardness 7 upward, therefore, every gemstone is proof against the abrasive effects of dust.

It is this resistance and durability which enables diamonds, rubies, sapphires, chrysoberyls, spinels, emeralds, topazes, and many other precious stones to retain their undiminished value beyond one human lifetime for many generations, and even, because of their scarcity, to increase that value considerably.

Diamond

Diamonds, the best-known and most popular gemstones, are composed of a single element – carbon (C). The diamond's chemical composition, then, is indistinguishable from that of graphite or coal, but diamond crystals have a considerably stronger cohesion, thus attaining a degree of hardness unequaled in the mineral kingdom. Fortunately this extreme hardness varies in different directions of the crystalline structure – it would otherwise be impossible to cut diamonds. Since the mechanical grinding process requires an even harder abrasive medium, diamonds are cut with diamonds; these are in the form of *bort* – minute diamond crystallites, some of whose hardest sides always touch the diamond on the lapidary's wheel.

The value of cut diamonds is determined by an international, extremely rigid system of evaluation known for simplicity's sake as "the Four C's": color, carat, cut, and clarity. The most highly valued are the colorless diamonds, especially those with a barely discernible bluish tinge. A subtle color scale ranges from blue-white through white and yellow to brown diamonds. In addition to these "normal colors," there are "fancy diamonds" of various strong colors, such as green, red, or blue.

The weight of diamonds is measured in carats, a standard unit of weight which corresponds to .20 gram.

A wide range of cuts are applied to diamonds. The most common, which brings out the natural "fire" most fully, is the so-called brilliant cut. Favorite fancy cuts are the elliptical marquise cut, the rodlike baguette cut, the emerald cut, and the drop form.

By international agreement, inclusions in diamonds are regarded as diminishing their value only when they are pronounced enough to be visible through a lens or loupe with a tenfold magnification. Otherwise diamonds are described as "loupe clear" or internally flawless.

Ruby

The ruby owes its color and its exceptional rarity to a trace of chromium which settled in the mineral during the crystallization of the ruby substance. As a rule chromium appears regularly, but sparsely, only in the deeper levels of the earth; only the rare occasions when chromium rose to higher levels and combined with aluminum oxide could produce this most precious red corundum known as the ruby. Its delicate color gradations in all shades of red are universally admired. Because the mining of this stone is also extraordinarily difficult, the ruby is rightly ranked among the great treasures of the mineral kingdom. The most beautiful rubies come from the almost inaccessible high Mogok valley in Burma; to this day native families, working in teams, sift the soil laboriously hacked out and dug by hand, and, when possible, sieve it through water. This is the site of the most coveted, rarest, and therefore most valuable color variant, the famous carmine red known as "pigeon's blood." Other shades of red are typical of other deposits, in Thailand, Ceylon, Cambodia, Tanzania, Afghanistan, and North Carolina in the United States. But the color alone is not sufficient to identify the source, because all the sites where rubies are found yield rare as well as more common colors.

To determine origin and authenticity, the experts prefer to rely on the pattern of inclusions rather than color. Rubies without any inclusions are extremely uncommon; almost all contain tiny crystals of foreign matter; their nature allows the gemmologist to make his deductions. So-called silk in corundum is a typical example; it is a delicate, glittering silvery web of very fine rutile needles, which may be concentrated into a star when the surface is cut in a domed shape.

Large ruby crystals are extremely rare – far rarer, for example, than large diamond crystals and also less frequent than large crystals of other varieties of corundum. The largest known star ruby, the size of a walnut, weighs 138 carats; this stone, known as the Rosser Reeves Ruby, is on display in the Smithsonian Institution in Washington, D.C. This star ruby, however, is in no way the largest extant ruby. To my knowledge that honor belongs to the stone surmounting the Russian Imperial Crown. The second-largest so-called ruby is the world-famous Timur Ruby (weight: 352.7 carats), which is in the private collection of Queen Elizabeth of England; it is, in fact, a spinel.

Sapphire

Like the ruby, the sapphire is also an aluminum oxide. Rubies and sapphires constitute the gemstone family of corundum. All colored corundums except the red – that is, the ruby – are called sapphires. Sapphires occur in a wealth of magnificent colors, but the most widespread and best known is the blue; the deep cornflower blue variety is by far the most popular, the rarest, and the most valuable.

Thus the sole difference between ruby and sapphire is in color. As chromium is the cause of the red shades in ruby, so titanium and iron are responsible for the innumerable blue variants in sapphire. Sapphire is less rare than ruby because iron and titanium occur more frequently than chromium at the higher levels of the earth. In all other ways, sapphire shares the properties of the ruby, especially by the measure of its hardness of 9, the basis of its durability, as well as its high refraction, the cause of its intense sparkle. Sapphires, again like rubies, are distinguished by their inclusions; the formation of star stones is also frequent and typical.

Sapphire deposits are found in Ceylon, Burma, Thailand, Tanzania, Cambodia, Australia, and the United States. As is true for the ruby, certain shades of blue are typical of sapphires found in particular localities. But descriptions of color as related to geographical areas, such as the Burma sapphire, are misleading, because the typical Burma color is found in other sites as well.

The ancients already collected the cherished sapphire, royal treasuries competed for their possession, and a Papal Bull went so far as to give approval to the general veneration of the blue gemstone. Pope Innocent III decreed that every bishop and every cardinal must wear a sapphire on his right hand, with which he bestowed blessings.

Emerald

The green of the emerald is incomparable in its beauty and depth. From pale leaf-green to a subdued pine-green, this most precious representative of the beryl group exists in a wide range of tones. The rarest and most valuable color is the dewy green of new spring grass. The fact is that the basic material of all beryls, a beryllium-aluminum silicate, is completely colorless in its chemically pure state. Only a trace of chromium is sufficient to give emerald its color and thereby its unique beauty and pride of place, not only in the beryl family, but in the whole realm of colored gemstones.

Emeralds are very rarely completely free of inclusions. Liquid- or gas-filled cavities and mineral inclusions combine to make that garden − known as *jardin* − of green tendrils, leaves and branches within a cut emerald which makes each stone so endlessly different. A look through the gem microscope into the interior of an emerald is therefore always an exciting spectacle, one which allows the expert to gain some knowledge about the nature and origin of the stone.

The most important sites are found in Colombia, where some of the deposits now being exploited were known to the Incas, though they were lost thereafter. Emeralds of commercial quality are also found in Rhodesia, South Africa, and Brazil.

In contrast to the diamond, the cut of an emerald is not usually designed to bring out the most intense "fire" − that is, to direct the rays of light within the stone so as to reflect the maximum amount of light. Rather, the cut should allow the observer to enjoy the intense green color and to look into the stone's interior. Consequently the common emerald cut is designed to show the "garden" of inclusions to best advantage.

Pearls

The pearl in its natural state is a treasure. Unlike a gemstone, which needs skillful cutting to bring out its brilliance and sparkle, a pearl does not need the human touch to achieve its full beauty. It is a finished jewel in its original form. Set in a ring or matched with other pearls to form a necklace, it remains as it was taken from the sea: noble, enticing, and mysterious.

The pages of human history are filled with numerous myths and legends to account for the miracle of pearls. Ancient Indian myths trace the pearls' origin back to the clouds; pearls are said to have descended from them into the depths of the sea on the far horizon, where sky and water touch. The Persian poet Saadi tells of a droplet of rain which, falling into the sea, humbly accepted its fate of being mingled with the ocean; for this it was laid by Aphrodite in a shell and there became a pearl. At the full of the moon, so says a Japanese legend, the tears of the Queen of the Night fell into the green waters of Tatoku and were changed into pearls. An old Hebrew legend speaks of pearls as the tears shed by Eve when she was turned out of Eden. On his third Atlantic crossing, while rounding the island of Trinidad toward the mouth of the Orinoco, Columbus saw half-open oysters hanging on the mangrove roots at low tide and thought the pearls were torpid dewdrops.

Science, on the other hand, sees pearls as organically developing over a period of from three to fifty years in the living body of a mollusc, hidden within the protective shell. The idea that a pearl grows around a grain of sand in the shell is contradicted by the fact that in hundreds of scientifically examined and millions of drilled pearls no grain of sand has *ever* been found.

Rather, as a result of an irritation of the shell-building skin — epithelium, a single-celled membrane that surrounds the animal's body beneath the shell — a cyst develops by intensive multiplication of cells; in this so-called pearl sack the pearl is formed by the secretion of shell-building substances (conchiolin and calcium carbonate). Spherical pearls are purely accidental. In the particular process pearls are built up in domed layers. The layers, consisting of minute platelets of mother-of-pearl (aragonite = the orthorhombic modification of calcium carbonate), are cemented together by conchiolin, a horny substance similar to that of fingernails. These platelets slightly overlap. This overlap cannot be detected either by the naked eye or the magnifying glass; it can be seen only under the microscope. But light is reflected, diffracted and refracted a thousandfold by this structure. This causes the gem to shimmer with a delicate silken sheen and to glow as if lit from within. Since a pearl oyster can live for two hundred years, the growth of a pearl may continue from twenty to fifty years; or the same process can be repeated in one and the same shell. Some pearls therefore grow to the size of a pigeon's egg, and occasionally dozens of pearls are found in a single shell.

Besides the shape, color, and size, the optical surface characteristics, – luster and orient – determine a pearl's value. Luster is the unique pearly sheen of its "bloom" (skin), while the shimmering iridescence, seemingly projected from within, is termed orient. These two features also help to distinguish the precious natural pearl from its imitation, for imitation pearls cannot attain either luster or orient in their highest form. It is these qualities, too, that have made many pearls world famous. The Pellegrina, for example, weighing 3.2 ounces, and with such a delicate shimmer as to seem almost transparent, was owned by Philip II of Spain and later by Louis XIV; acquired in 1826 by Princess Tatiana Youssoupoff, it was subsequently presented to the Zosima Museum in Moscow. A more varied history belongs to the drop-shaped pearl Peregrina, the "Incomparable," weighing 7.1 ounces, which was found in 1550 by a Negro slave on the coast of Panama; it appeared in paintings by famous artists as it adorned several Spanish queens. A few years ago the Peregrina was bought by the actor Richard Burton for his wife Elizabeth Taylor.

Pearls are not only the gift of the sea; streams and rivers offer charming fresh-water pearls whose pastel-shaded bloom is attractive on the young.

Gold

Among the precious metals – gold, silver, and platinum – that are the foundation of the jewelry trade, gold takes a predominant position. Mankind's esteem for gold reaches back to prehistory, and to tell its history would mean to write the history of mankind. The beauty of its warm, resplendent color and its "nobility" – that is, its extraordinary physical and chemical properties (it is termed a precious metal because of an exceptional inactivity, a reluctance to dissolve or to combine with other elements) – as well as the rarity of sizable concentrations in the earth's crust, brought gold very early to the status of a royal metal. Gold became the emblem of the sun, an attribute of gods and kings, and thus a symbol of wealth and might, the epitome of human longing and cupidity. Transcendent mystical importance has also been ascribed to it.

Only relatively small quantities of gold are found in the earth's rocky crust; it amounts to about 0.0002 percent of the total planet. The richest gold deposits are found in South Africa, on the Witwatersrand near Johannesburg. The precious ore is excavated in rock strata from six to thirty feet thick. These are called "reefs" and are found in mines several thousand feet deep. The gold is extracted with costly mining equipment. Other important deposits lie in Alaska, Australia, Brazil, Burma, India, California, Canada, Mexico, and Siberia. Formerly gold was mined in considerable amounts, as measured by the standards of the time, in the Near East and in Central Europe – for instance in the Fichtelgebirge, in the Harz mountains, on the Napf in Switzerland, on the Upper Rhine, in the Salzburg district, and in Silesia. European deposits are still mined in Sweden and Transylvania. Almost all rivers carry minute quantities of gold. Because the shining yellow metal was extruded relatively late – in the hydrothermal phase of ore formation – it frequently occurs in conjuction with quartz. Mountain gold fills fissures and lodes in the earth's crust. When gold crystallizes, it very rarely forms regularly-shaped crystals. Most often it is found as native gold in the form of botryoidal clumps, thin leaves, sheets like tin, or small grains. Flushed by rain out of crumbling rock and washed by water into "secondary deposits," gold is found water-worn into nuggets, as sand in river gravel, or as dust in alluvial deposits.

The oldest process for separating out gold is panning – washing the gold-bearing pebbles, gravel, and sand in water. In the course of this recovery from alluvial places, small flakes and grains of gold sink to the bottom of the pan because of their high specific gravity. The method is primitive and unproductive; yet even today in many places – such as the Uyu river in North Burma – this simple method is still employed.

Modern methods break up the ore in rock crushers and then process it in pounding machines and mills with water and mercury, so that a large part of the gold amalgamates with the quicksilver. By distillation and further precipitation, by cyanidation (or by still more advanced methods), the unalloyed gold is separated from the amalgam.

In this, its purest form, described as 24-carat gold, it is a soft metal, not suitable for objects of everyday use. It must therefore be alloyed with other metals such as silver (white gold), copper (red gold), or aluminum (blue gold), according to the desired color and purpose. The amount of alloy determines the fineness of the gold. Most countries have stringent regulations for the degrees of fineness and detailed hallmarking requirements for gold. The designation "18-carat" or "750" means that 18/24 or 750/1000 (75 percent) of the metal consists of fine gold. Similarly, 14 carats equal 585/1000 of gold. The term carat for the fineness of gold (k) thus has nothing to do with carat as the unit of weight for gemstones (ct).

So long as people of discernment exist, gemstones will be treasured. Their beauty and brilliance affect us so strongly that we do not need any explanations of their chemical and physical origins to understand their attraction. But knowledge of their nature and origin can add to their interest, and cannot rob them of their magic or diminish their radiance.

The earth. Since the beginning of time the earth's mineral-making processes have been operating and gemstones have been found in rocks of all the earth's geological periods. Precious stones not dug from mines are usually found in river gravels. As the earth's crust continues to change and weather, and rivers cut through geological strata, gem-bearing deposits may be exposed and valuable crystals may find their way into river gravels.

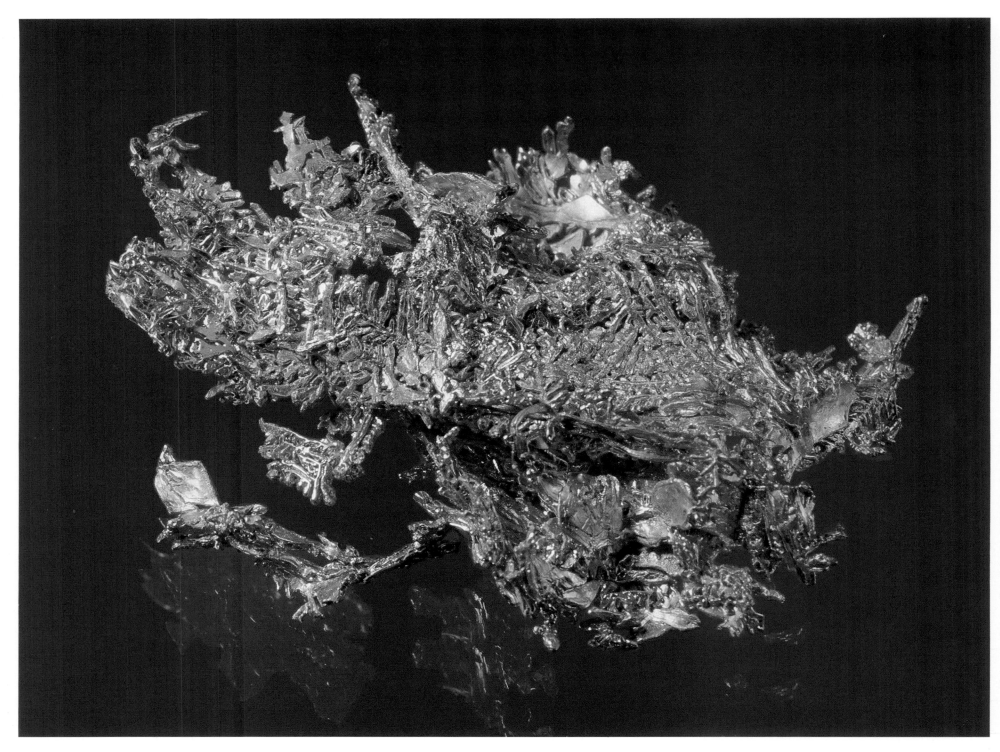

Gold—beautiful, malleable, durable—is the supreme raw material for fashioning objects of art. In ancient times gold had a mystical significance and was often associated with the sun, the giver of life, the source of all energy. Symbolic suns appear on many of the precious ornaments of ancient cultures. The nugget is from Placer County, California.

Labradorite, polished slab. This form of plagioclase feldspar (calcium sodium aluminium silicate) shows a vivid iridescent play of colors, caused by light interference by closely spaced twinning planes. The name is derived from the locality where it was first discovered.

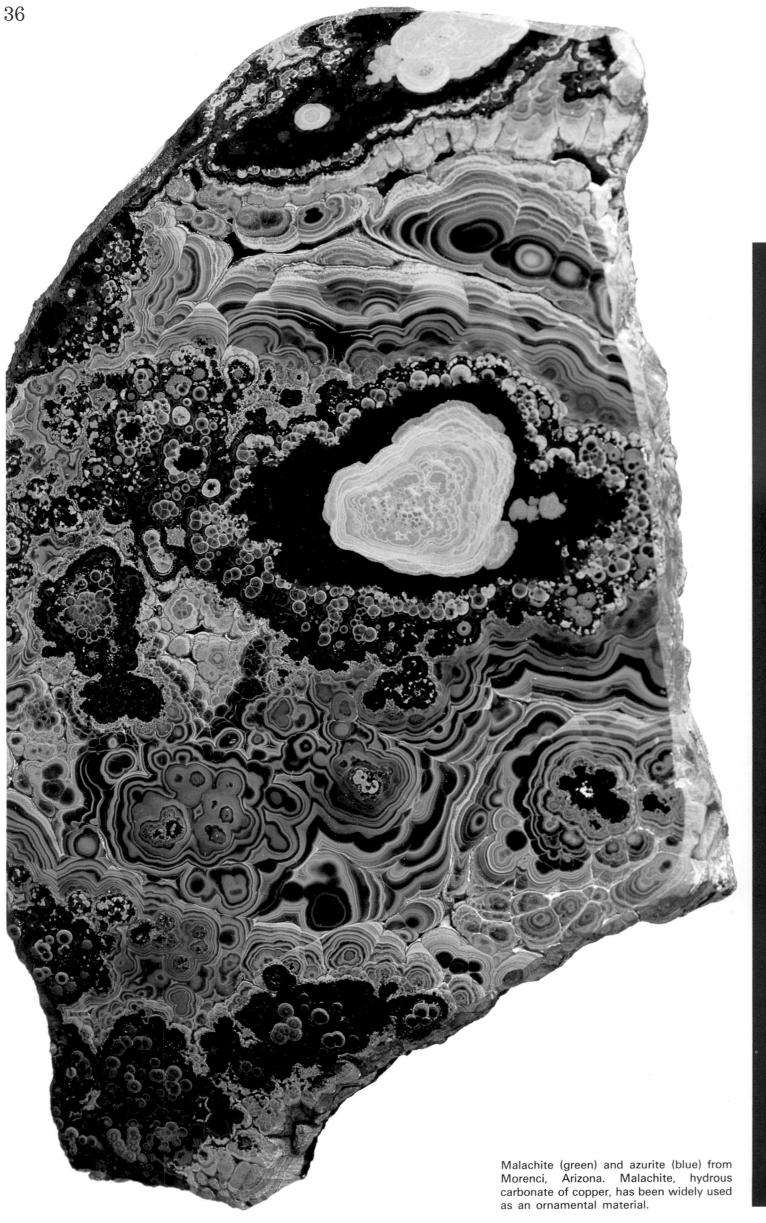

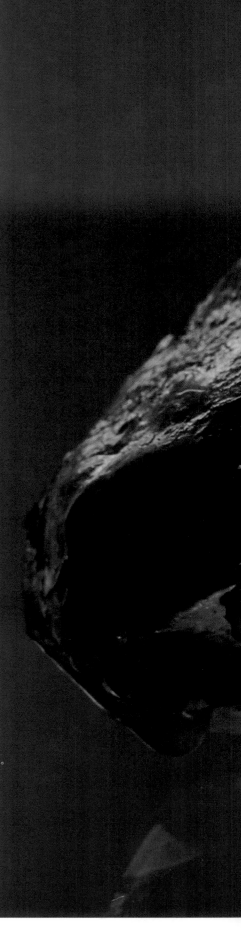

Malachite (green) and azurite (blue) from Morenci, Arizona. Malachite, hydrous carbonate of copper, has been widely used as an ornamental material.

A pearl embedded in an oyster. Unlike a gemstone, which requires skilful cutting to achieve brilliance and sparkle, a pearl in its original form is already a finished jewel. Beyond the shape, color and size, it is the optical surface characteristics, lustre and "orient," which determine the value of a pearl. (Enlarged)

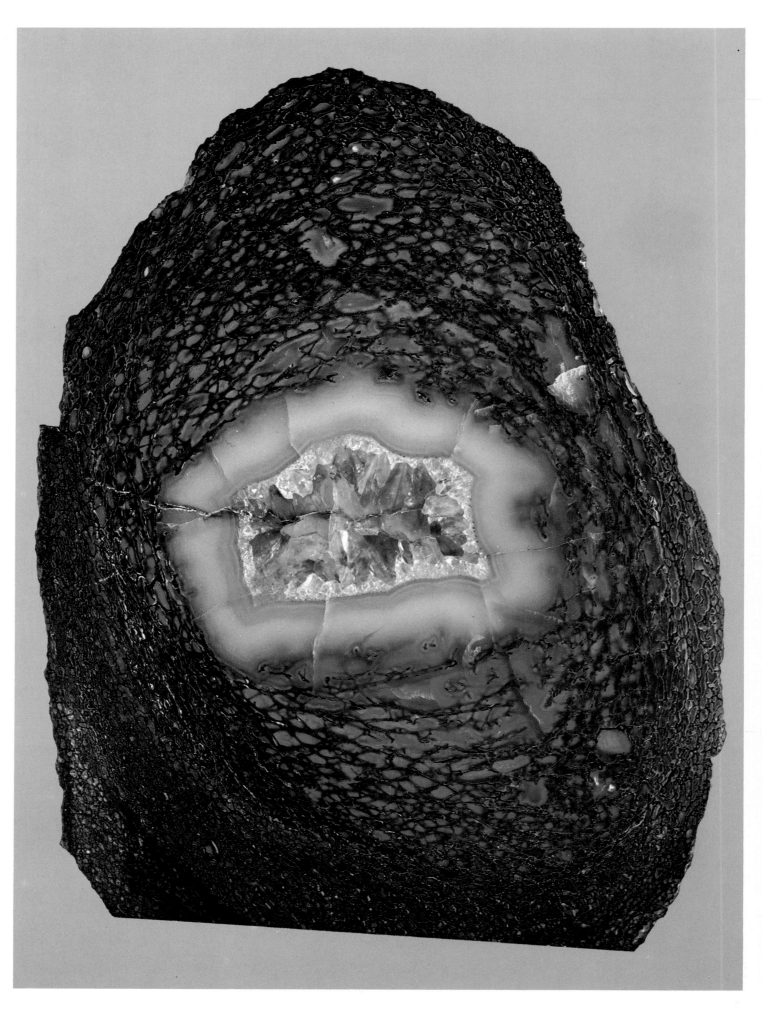

Agate with amethyst replacing dinosaur bone. In this example of petrification, the dinosaur bone has been replaced by agate and the central cavity filled with amethyst.

"Bull's eye" agate from Uruguay. This form of agate is said to be so named because of the resemblance to a target or "bull's eye" shown by the stone.

The world's largest uncut emerald crystal, weighing 16,020 carats, found in Muzo, Colombia. Emerald mines today are scattered about the world, in India, Russia, Austria, America (North Carolina), Brazil and other places, but the finest stones come from Colombia. An "outsize" emerald of fine quality such as the specimen shown here is so rare that its commercial value amounts to a gigantic figure.

Chrysocolla and quartz. Quartz, oxide of silicon dioxide, is normally colorless, but this specimen has been rendered a rich blue by intermixture with chrysocolla, a copper silicate mineral.

Amethyst crystal. The amethyst of gem quality is transparent quartz ranging in color from pale violet to deep purple. This specimen was found in Guerrero, Mexico. Ht. 5.8 cm.

Beryl. Emerald crystal in matrix from Muzo,
Colombia. The basic material of all beryls
is a beryllium-aluminium silicate which
in its chemically pure state is completely
colorless. Only a trace of chromic acid is
sufficient to give emerald its color, ranging
from pale leafgreen to a firtree green.

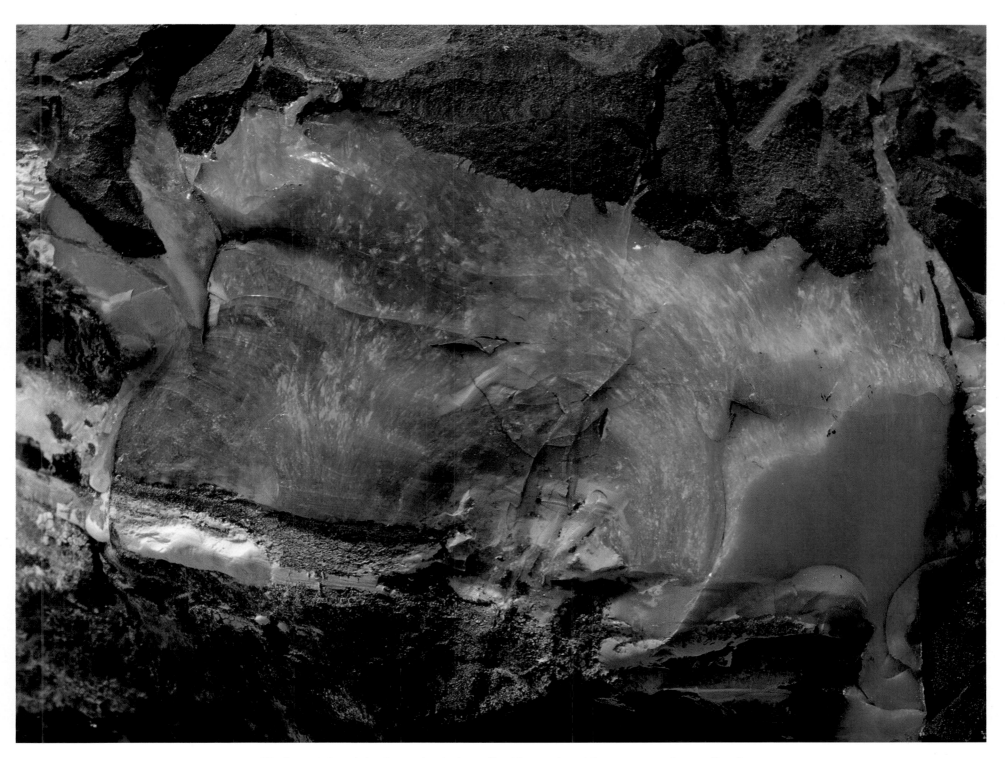

Black opal found in Queensland, Australia. The opal, semi-transparent, is usually of shimmering rainbow-like colorations. More rarely, it may be colored red, green, blue, yellow and black. In addition to Australia, it is found in many other countries.

Collection of unassorted rough diamonds as they come from the mines. The earliest diamonds most likely came from the river gravels of India. The diamond is composed of pure carbon, but its great hardness, brilliance, and "fire" are unsurpassed by any other substance.

The Star of Asia. This extraordinary 330-carat cabochon-cut star sapphire is one of the finest in the world. It is unusually large and has an excellent combination of strong, sharply defined rays on a deep, intense blue background.

The Rosser Reeves Ruby, 138.7 carats. Remarkable for its translucence and color, this gem (probably from Ceylon) is the world's largest and finest star ruby. Unseen slivers of rutile—a common mineral—reflect light in a vibrant six-point design.

The Maharani, Cat's-Eye chrysoberyl, of 58.2 carats. Thousands of very slender microscopic channels in parallel arrangement reflect a band of light from these gemstones. The sharpness and brilliance of the band depends on the number and size of the channels.

Polishing a diamond. The stone is held against a revolving iron disc coated with a mixture of oils and diamond dust to produce the diamond's flat surfaces or facets. Most diamonds have 58 facets, and the angle between adjacent facets must be formed with minute accuracy; the slightest variations can reduce the brilliance of the finished diamond.

A wide range of cutting styles are used for diamonds. The most common, in which the natural "fire" is brought out to its maximum extent, is the so-called brilliant cut. Favorite fancy cuts are the ship-shaped marquise cut, the rod-like baguette cut, the emerald cut, and the drop form. Before the Second World War, cutters and traders made Amsterdam and Antwerp world diamond capitals. Today Israel is also important.

1 Round brilliant cut (crown). This is the most common cut. The standard round brilliant consists of 58 facets: 1 table, 8 bezel facets, 8 star facets, and 16 upper girdle facets on the crown, plus 8 pavilion facets, 16 lower girdle facets and usually a culet on the pavilion or base. Ideally, the brilliant cut achieves total reflection.

2 Round brilliant cut (pavilion).

3 Elongated cushion, or Indian cut.

4 Scissors cut. The facets resemble scissors in an open position.

5 Emerald cut. A form of step cutting, rectangular in shape, but with corner facets. The number of rows of step cuts may vary, but there are usually three steps on the crown and three on the pavilion, or base.

6 Rectangular step cut. The step cut and brilliant cut are the two basic classifications of cutting. In step cuts, all facets are four sided and in steps or rows, both above and below the girdle. Although the number of rows may vary, the usual number is three on the crown and three on the pavilion. Outlines vary, but all steps are parallel to the girdle.

7 Square emerald cut. A form of step cutting with a square girdle outline modified by corner facets.

8 Marquise cut. A style in which the girdle outline is ship-shaped. The faceting is a modification of the brilliant cut.

9 Lozenge cut. A four-sided usually step-cut method of cutting a diamond.

10 Oval shape, a style based on the brilliant.

11 Heart shape. A modified brilliant cut in the shape of a heart. The faceting is standard.

12 Pear shape. The pear or so-called "drop-of-water" shape has 58 facets and is cut in a manner similar to the brilliant.

The Jubilee Diamond, a 245.35-carat pure white cushion-shaped brilliant, which many gem experts believe to be the most perfectly cut of all the large world-famous diamonds. Its facets are so exact that it can be balanced on the culet point, which is less than two millimeters across. It is the fourth largest cut diamond known. The Jubilee (originally called the Reitz Diamond) found in the Jagersfontein Mine, South Africa, in 1895, weighed 650.80 carats in the rough. After being cut in 1897 to 245.35 carats, it was renamed the Jubilee in honor of Queen Victoria's Diamond Jubilee.

WHY DOES MAN ADORN HIMSELF?

ERIKA BILLETER CURATOR, MUSEUM BELLERIVE, ZURICH

"The enjoyment of beauty produces a particular, mildly intoxicating kind of sensation. There is no very evident use in beauty: the necessity of it for cultural purposes is not apparent, and yet civilization could not do without it. The science of aesthetics investigates the conditions in which things are regarded as beautiful; it can give no explanation of the nature or origin of beauty; as usual, its lack of results is concealed under a flood of resounding and meaningless words. Unfortunately, psychoanalysis, too, has less to say about beauty than about most things. Its derivation from the realms of sexual sensation is all that seems certain; love of beauty is a perfect example of a feeling with an inhibited aim. Beauty and attraction are first of all the attributes of a sexual object."

That is what Sigmund Freud wrote in his essay "Civilization and Its Discontents." And his words serve very well as an introduction to the question as to why we wear jewels. In fact, beauty and sexual attraction are two of the attributes man seeks to attain by self-adornment.

But if jewelry is worn primarily for the sake of beauty and sexual attraction, we shall see in the course of our investigation that there are other factors in our relationship with jewelry. In fact, jewelry must always be considered as closely related to the wearer; like clothing, it is only that relationship that brings it to life. In nature, beauty and the sexual instinct go hand in hand as a matter of course; in human society jewelry is their point of coincidence. Jewelry is the artistic sublimation of a natural human urge. This concept is amply confirmed by examples provided by the history of civilization, literature, and tradition.

These are the terms in which Solomon sang the praises of the Shula-mite in the Song of Songs: "Thy cheeks are comely with rows of jewels, thy neck with chains of gold. We will make thee borders of gold with studs of silver." And when after fasting for three days Esther entered the presence of Ahasuerus, she was bejeweled like a queen, *ornata virtutibus,* and glittering in royal robes like the bride who sees the bridegroom.

In every culture and in all ages jewelry was employed as a means to make a bride seductive. Even today brides are still decked out with special care for their wedding day. Rich and poor are alike on this point. Painters have left us innumerable portraits showing brides sparkling with jewels. In spite of the fact that right up to the eighteenth century commoners were forbidden as a matter of principle to wear jewelry – it was not until the French Revolution that the royal injunction was abrogated – the daughters of bourgeois families wore rings.

Historians have penned magnificent descriptions of marriage feasts, telling how radiant the bride looked in her gorgeous jewels. From Alexander the Great's marriage to Roxana, daughter of a Bactrian noble-man, to Catherine de Medici, who wore "not only a quantity of precious stones but the finest and largest pearls that had ever been seen" when she married the Duke of Orléans, later King Henry II of France, descriptions of those jewels still thrill us today. At the wedding of Mary, Queen of Scots, to the Dauphin the bride's pearls and precious stones surpassed anything the Court had ever seen.

No reports of this sort about middle-class weddings have come down to us, for only valuable jewels had the honor of being recorded by history. But we know that in Scandinavia poor bourgeois girls could borrow jewels from the State so that at least on their wedding day they could be more attractive than their peers. Among primitive peoples too it was customary to deck out the bride in a special way for that occasion. Elsy Leuzinger, in her study on the nature and form of jewelry among African tribes ("Wesen und Form des Schmucks afrikanischer Völker"), says that in Togo brides belonging to various tribes were dressed in silk and satin and exhibited to the villagers wearing all the family jewels, with gold chains and brooches and ropes of glass beads.

Women know that their erotic aura is intensified by jewelry and feel a basic urge to make the most of it. Men are aware of that too and are very glad to use jewelry as a means to win women. Goethe raised a unique monument to women's weakness for jewelry. His Mephistopheles smuggled a jewel case into Gretchen's bed chamber in the hopes that it would make her well disposed toward Faust.

> *Was ist das? Gott im Himmel! Schau*
> *so was hab ich mein Tag nicht gesehen!*
> *Ein Schmuck! Mit dem könnt eine Edelfrau*
> *Am höchsten Feiertage gehn.*
> *Wie sollte mir die Kette stehn?*
> *Wem mag die Herrlichkeit gehören?*
> *Wenn nur die Ohrring' meine wären!*
> *Man sieht doch gleich ganz anders drein.*
> *Was hilft euch Schönheit, junges Blut?*
> *Das ist wohl alles schön und gut;*
> *allein man lässt's auch alles sein;*
> *Nach Golde drängt*
> *Am Golde hängt*
> *doch alles! Ach, wir Armen!*

> (What's that? God in Heaven! Look,
> I've never seen anything like it in all my born days!
> A jewel! A noblewoman could wear
> it on the greatest feast days.
> How would the chain suit me?
> Whom do all the lovely things belong to?

If only the earrings were mine!
They make one look quite different.
What's the use of beauty, girls?
It's all very fine;
but where does it get you?
It's gold people want,
so gold is all! Oh, poor us!)

Gretchen's rapturous outburst on discovering the jewelry gives us an inkling of its emotional value. Beautiful jewels show a person to the best advantage; they have a fascination all their own. Since they enhance a woman's social standing they become status symbols in the eyes of many men as well. The urge to appear more beautiful is linked with the idea of wealth and honor in the material sense too. And these two concepts are contained in another interpretation of Goethe's text. Faust's jewel case prefigures the wedding gift. The custom that required the groom to make a present to his bride on their wedding day or the morning after is observed by a gift of jewelry. A nobleman presented his bride with the most costly pearls and precious stones.

Many examples of this have been handed down by historians. One might recall, for instance, the famous pearl known as "Peregrina" that King Philip of Spain sent Mary Tudor of England as a wedding present. Emperor Maximilian I sent a diamond to the daughter of Charles the Bold of Burgundy when they were affianced. Shah Jahan, who built the most beautiful tomb in the world, the Taj Mahal, for his wife Mumtaz, presented her with the Pearl of Asia, which measures over three inches in length and five across. Even today the price paid for a wife among some African populations, though consisting mostly of household goods, always includes jewelry. In most African tribes pearls, silver rings, brooches, and earrings have usually formed part of that price.

Even among primitive peoples wearing jewelry suggests personal advancement on two counts. Jewelry satisfies pride of possession even if it is also employed for aesthetic purposes. This may well be a phenomenon produced by civilization. For in the earliest times, when a man painted his body and wore chains made of grass, shells, and flowers, he was probably prompted to do so chiefly by the urge to beautify his person. But he was always conscious, too, that it enhanced his personality and his power to so adorn himself. Priests and shamans, who led the tribes, wore jewels as emblems of their authority. And there is one piece of jewelry that has always and everywhere been the embodiment of that authority, namely, the head ornament. It offers a man the most clearly visible means to assert his rank and dignity. Phoenicians, Assyrians, and Egyptians wore head ornaments in the shape of frontlets, circlets, and diadems. The Indian idols in the Pre-Columbian cultures were crowned with feathers. In the prehistoric rock paintings of the Sahara, the Bronze Age sculptures of Benin, and the idols depicted on the cliffs at Ajanta, headdresses served to indicate social position. The tiara is still the outward sign of the Pope's spiritual authority, just as the crown symbolizes the power and the majesty of secular rulers.

In the Kremlin, the Hofburg in Vienna, the Tower of London, and the Crown Treasure of Sweden are preserved the magnificent crowns that emperors and kings had made for their coronations. The history of those monarchs' uncontested authority is exemplified by the crown of the Roman Empire that Otto I wore when he was crowned in Rome in 962. It was used at the coronation of each of his successors and such was the veneration with which it was regarded that none dared to wear it unless he had previously fasted for three days. What the crown symbolized for a king, the gemmed cap symbolized for a burgher. True, in the twentieth century the ultimate vestige of the precious head ornament was the fashionably extravagant hat, but that too was a status symbol. The disappearance of the hat in the last decade or so affords us an interesting insight into the development of the personality at the present day.

In the final analysis the link between precious ornaments and personal prestige in both the sacred and the profane fields is now reflected exclusively in official robes, military uniforms, and ecclesiastical vestments. They serve as outward signs of the wearer's rank and dignity and raise him unmistakably above his fellow men. Medals and orders perform the same function. Thus there is no doubt that ornamentation is linked with a strong urge to display; and this too seems to have always been one of its inherent characteristics. Among some tribes of Black Africa it is customary for ornaments to be reserved to the chiefs. Priests and medicine men wear jewels as insignia. They can serve to display a man's wealth and social position before the eyes of the other members of the tribe.

The urge to adorn oneself dates back to the dawn of mankind. Burials have yielded skeletons surrounded by pieces of jewelry that have survived the dead for thousands of years. Their imperishable materials announce a claim to eternity. Is that not enough to give jewels an aura of mystery? Man's first attempt at artistic achievement was to adorn his own person. This impulse is still alive today. There is not a woman who does not desire jewelry as a means to enhance her beauty. Even nuns wear a gold ring as a sign of their betrothal to Christ.

We have already seen that jewelry serves to express a wide range of concepts. In the shape of a ring, notably the plain gold wedding ring, it is a symbol of a close relationship. That is still the piece of jewelry that many women desire most ardently, for even today it symbolizes betrothal and the marriage tie. It stands for plighted troth and serves as a token of love. The exchange of rings at the wedding is a symbolic act and still forms the climax of the ceremony. "With this ring I thee wed." In the Middle Ages the ring was a pledge of love and friendship and it has remained so to the present time. "Myt wyllen dyn eygen" was the motto Count Frangipani had engraved in the ring he gave his wife, and it could still be inscribed in a wedding ring today. The ring as symbol of matrimony is one of the few attributes that have survived the passing of the years. It is one of the few links with tradition still recognized and accepted by the younger generation. Its formal perfection has often provided scope for speculative fancies and offered welcome opportunities for superstitious practices. In myths and legends it is credited with prodigious magical powers. It was to a ring that Gyges owed his ability to make himself invisible; Polycrates had a ring that brought him luck.

"Heed the secret significance of my gift rather than the gift itself. The circular shape of the gold rings set with precious stones refers to eternity, their number to *constantia mentis,* constancy of spirit, the gold to *sapientia,* wisdom," Pope Innocent III wrote to Richard the Lion-Hearted when he sent him a present of four rings in 1198. We may be sure that Richard did not view the rings merely as ornaments but also pondered on the message they conveyed. Rings have always been worn as talismans. This word brings us to the magic properties attributed to gems, which were a decisive factor in man's relationship to them, at least in the distant past.

Literary sources, from Herodotus, Pliny, and the ancient gemmologies to the medieval treatises, lead us to infer that there was a time when even the least important gem was a talisman and every pendant was regarded as an amulet. Both words come from the Arabic. Talisman means magic charm; amulet is the English equivalent of the Arabic word *hamalet.* What is and what is not a talisman or amulet is a purely personal matter. For some people anything can become an amulet; others feel no need at all for magic. But Goethe is a reliable authority when he says that "superstition is an essential part of human nature" and constitutes the "poetry of life." Faith in amulets derives from man's belief in his capacity to acquire magic powers that are not given him by nature. He alone can recognize those powers, and he invokes them in the shape of certain objects. Thus a piece of jewelry, a precious stone, or a plain gold chain can become a magic charm with which a person endeavors to shield himself from evil. This attitude springs from the unconscious depths of a primal anxiety that urges him to seek protection in the magic of talismans and amulets against the unknown forces that seem to rule his life. And even if he does not believe in supernatural forces and the dark powers of fate, there still remains the real threat of sickness and death to be warded off.

Thanks to the cults of primitive peoples, jewelry has maintained its dual nature up to our own times. Pieces of jewelry are referred to with incantatory expressions in order to endow them with magic powers. "Old family jewels," writes Elsy Leuzinger, "are credited with possessing the qualities of their previous owner. Through close contact with his person they have absorbed his life force." It is often hard to decide whether primitive populations consider a jewel as an ornament or an object of worship. As a rule it is expected to perform both functions. In India the wearing of amulets is still very widespread. To Indian eyes they possess a sacred quality. On certain days they are taken off and worshipped, for they are imbued with the powers of the gods in whose image they are made. One of the many proverbs linked with the belief in amulets says: "Even the Lord of the World can do nothing to a man who wears an amulet with the number 20." For one person the amulet is a temple, for another a mother. Its purpose is to conjure up good spirits and ward off the Evil One. Some Indians wear as many as ten amulets at a time. They are made of gold or silver and their beautiful shapes are very decorative. This is a striking example of their dual function as jewels and magic charms.

"An amulet is anything worn round the neck or on any other part of the body or attached to the person in any way in order to drive away sickness and fortify the physical constitution," said Blumler in the book on amulets he published in 1710. Precious stones were considered particularly apt to satisfy that need for protection and innumerable tales of their magical and miraculous action have been told in the course of the millennia. Each gem possessed its peculiar miraculous powers and embodied its peculiar forms of protection. And the wearer of a gem formed a personal relationship with what he viewed not only as a jewel but also as a talisman. But it is always the personal attitude of the wearer that determines the function of the gem. So we can never establish with any certainty whether the noblemen depicted in the Renaissance portraits arrayed in splendid jewels wore their precious stones out of an exaggerated love of adornment, to show off their wealth, or perhaps also as magic charms and "secret weapons."

Stones were revered as sacred objects from the very start. This is confirmed by the sanctuaries dedicated to them in early times and also by the great consideration with which stones in general and precious stones in particular were regarded. Gems have been found as votive offerings in the tombs of the Pharaohs. They sparkle in the Pope's tiara and adorn the crowns of kings and emperors. In the ancient Oriental representations of the gods precious stones are seen as divine attributes. During the Middle Ages craftsmen lavished valuable gems on images of the saints, reliquaries, and altar vessels. It was only gradually that they came to be used for ornamental purposes in the realm of fashion. The Bible has a warning against wearing precious stones for love of display. Stone amulets, either cut or left in their natural shape and set in gold or silver, have come down to us from many different epochs. They did not all have to be made of costly gems.

Amber, rock crystal, coral, and serpentine were often made into pendant amulets. Amber amulets of this sort have been found in Mycenaean, Etruscan, and Phoenician graves. Homer tells us that Penelope wore northern gold round her neck. Coral too afforded opportunities for mystic speculation. According to Greek mythology it was congealed spurts of blood that had gushed from Medusa's head when it was cut off by Perseus. As such it was endowed with magical powers and therefore employed in amulets. Coral was also placed in tombs to protect the dead against spirits. The ancients believed in its sacred character and therefore, as Solinus says, used it as a jewel. Paracelsus valued coral as protection against magic spells. Superstition fed and thrived on legends of that sort, as proved by the fact that King Ferdinand I of Naples is said to have always worn a coral horn to ward off the evil eye.

Some pieces of jewelry were worn as amulets even though their shape gave no hint that they served that purpose; others could be recognized at a glance as amulets by their outward appearance. Pendants in the shape of hearts or crosses were popular charms and women were fond of wearing rock crystal balls on their girdles. But amulets were made in such a multitude of shapes that we may well believe Blumler when he says that anything a man or woman wore as a pendant was an amulet. Nowadays young goldsmiths take pleasure in reverting to the shapes of amulets and other magic jewels. Do they realize that when they include hearts, hands, and even eyes in their designs they are adopting primeval forms used long ago for amulets?

The heart as the center of life and the seat of the soul had a place of its own among talismans and amulets. It was, and still is, the symbol of love and friendship. Eye-shaped amulets can also claim an equally long past. From the apotropaic representations of eyes made in Greece and Egypt to the eye-shaped amulets still worn by populations of the Mediterranean lands, the eye form has always performed a magic function in the history of jewelry, always affording protection against the evil eye. Amulets in the shape of hands are still worn by Muslims. That symbol too dates back to the earliest times. We find it in prehistoric rock paintings as a defense against disaster. But we should not forget that, over and above their magic powers, amulets are delightful ornaments.

In Hansmann and Kriss-Rettenbeck's study entitled *Amulet and Talisman* there is the reproduction of a portrait of a boy of the Habsburg family painted by Hans Meilich. On his brocade and lace doublet he wears splendid jewelry, whose details show it to be "magic armor." In fact, each piece serves to shield him from harm. The pendant on his breast is shaped like a reliquary and bears the monogram of the Virgin Mary; the nine amulets hanging from his belt include a claw set in precious stones, a pomander, and little apotropaic bells. A portrait of this kind should call our attention to the dual nature of jewelry and the protective function entrusted to it side by side with its purely ornamental purpose. In Black Africa it still performs that function today.

Pearls too are worn not only for their aesthetic value but for social prestige. Those unblemished spheres have always held a particular fascination, which led to their being given a symbolic value in the days of myths and sagas. For Christians the pearl became the emblem of the Mother of God because Mary gave birth to "a precious pearl." In ancient Chinese poems the pearl is revered as the symbol of wealth, honor, and longevity. The Indians believe that it sprang from the tears of a goddess or the dewdrops of the mangrove, which fell into the water under the first rays of the rising sun and turned into pearls. In popular language pearls still stand for tears. Here too classical literature provides us with a striking example. Lessing's Emilia Gallotti dreamt that her bridal jewelry was changed into pearls. "And pearls mean tears, Mother," she said. Indeed pearls meant tears to many queens. The prettiest story of a queen's attachment to her pearls is told of Queen Louise of Prussia, who was forced by lack of money to sell her jewelry but could not bring herself to let her pearls go with the rest. "I love them so," she said, "and kept them when I had to choose between them and my diamonds. They suit me better for they mean tears, and I have wept so much." This confession is a most poignant expression of the close personal relationship that can arise between a woman and her jewels.

These mystic interpretations of gems, pearls, and certain forms of jewelry lead us to the very heart of superstition. They represent one of the last links with the shamanism and animism that lived on in primitive cultures well into the present century. Which of us has no special relationship with a piece of jewelry we inherited? Even today we feel a special fondness for a jewel that belonged to a person now dead and are unhappy if we lose it. That emotive relationship to a jewel is the last vestige of the attitude of primitive peoples who boggle at the mere idea of taking off a plain iron ring because they fear it would amount to being abandoned by their talisman. And what should we think of the Wendish woman who, on her husband's death, removes the copper-wire ring she received from him and wore all through her married life, cuts it into pieces and places them on his grave? The two primary functions of jewels, to enhance the wearer's beauty and display his wealth, are turned inward, so to speak, by their quality as amulets. In fact, those who are aware that their jewelry possesses that quality feel stronger and superior in the knowledge of the protection it gives them. The visible, outward distinction conveyed by a jewel is transformed in the amulet into an inward distinction known to the wearer alone. One never exists without the other. And every amulet serves also as an ornament. Its function is to emphasize a person's strong points. For that reason in every culture the images of gods and ancestors are adorned with jewels. Reliquaries, monstrances, and other church ornaments were formerly embellished with gems and in both pagan antiquity and the Christian era the basic material for temples, statues of the gods, and sacred vessels was gold, which has always held a strong fascination for mankind.

The great early civilizations saw in gold the sun's reflected splendor and credited it with divine powers. Gold gave a hint of the magnificence of paradise and held the promise of immortality. How could gold, even in our own secularized times, fail to provide a most coveted material for our adornment? All through the Middle Ages the goldsmiths' guild was one of the most highly respected and considered itself above the rest. When its patron saint, Eligius, slipped the gold wedding rings on the fingers of the bride and groom, he gave them his blessing at the same time. Nowadays we may have lost faith in that blessing, but the ring at least has kept its symbolic significance.

The same may be said of jewels in general. We are no longer conscious of their sacred character or of their closeness to magic spells and imaginary powers. But the urge to wear jewels is as strong as ever. If they have lost much of their symbolic significance, the primitive notion of how they originated has survived. The display of the animal has been transformed by man into self-adornment. As I said at the beginning of this essay, man's need to wear jewels is a natural drive that was sublimated in art. It is linked with magic concepts connected with both their material and their form. A jewel is, and always has been, a symbol even if its symbolic significance now subsists only in the profane sphere. Whatever else it may be, a jewel is still a fascinating object, whether that fascination derives from mysterious magic formulas or from its visual beauty and intrinsic value.

Tishbuk Lulu from San'a, capital of Yemen, adorned for her wedding day. Peasant jewelry is timeless. Such Hebrew bridal costumes are still worn occasionally by Jewish brides.

King (*lukengo*) Bope Mabiinc, the late king of the Kuba, an important tribe in central Kasai, Zaire. Bope is seen here in his sumptuous state dress.

Bronze spiral breast ornament typical of the Bronze Age. From Wixhausen, near Darmstadt, Germany, c. 1500-1200 B. C. W. 15.2 cm.

The "Stag" Circlet. This head ornament is said to come from Es Salhiya, on the eastern edge of the Nile Delta, near Avaris, the capital of the Hyksos. It almost certainly dates from the period when these Asiatics ruled Egypt. Five animal heads —a stag and four gazelles—are mounted on a band, all made of electrum. The gazelle motif is native to Egypt. The stag is more unusual; it probably shows Asiatic influence, as do the style and workmanship. Egyptian, 17th–18th Dynasty, c. 1650 B. C. Ht. of stag's head 8.5 cm.

Glass beads: grotesque faces (fused to surface) in yellow; dark blue; yellow with eyes of white and blue; and blue, white, and yellow. In ancient Egypt almost everyone wore beads. The Egyptian for bead was "sha-sha," and the syllable "sha" was the word for luck. Egyptian, Roman Period. Hts. 1.7 to 2.3 cm.

Heart scarab with pendant chain. The scarab, carved in green stone, is from the body of Hatnufer and is inscribed on the underside with Chapter XXX B of the *Book of the Dead*. The mounting and the chain are of gold. The Egyptian name given to the sacred beetle was Kheper, "to come into being." It was the emblem of the deity Kheperi, who symbolizes the rising sun born anew each morning. Egyptian, 18th Dynasty. From Thebes, Tomb of Ramose and Hatnufer. Ht. 6.6 cm.

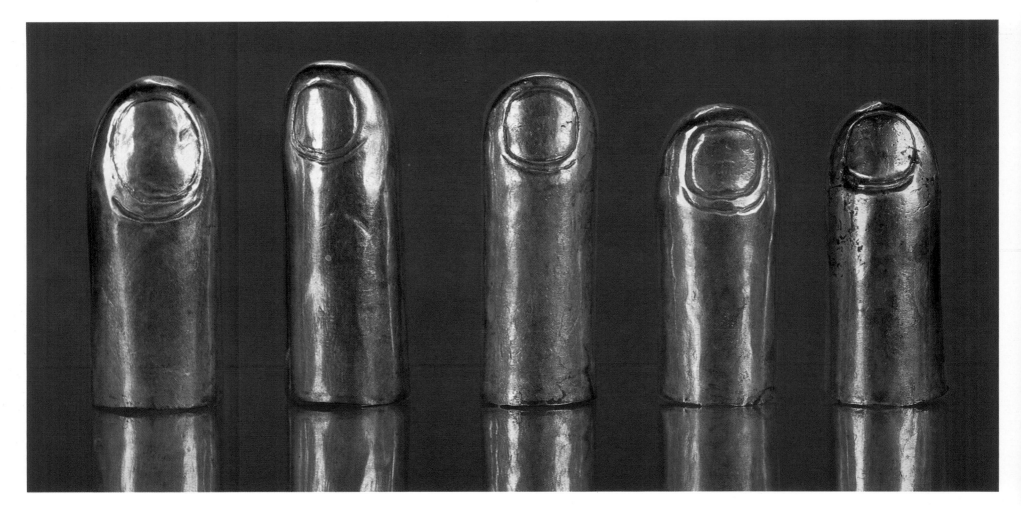

Finger and toe stalls of sheet gold. Each stall was made in two pieces—a cap beaten out for the tip, and a tube made of sheet metal. The tube was soldered down the seam and soldered to the tip. Such stalls were used to protect the fingers and toes of the mummies. Egyptian, 18th Dynasty, reign of Tuthmosis III. From Wadi Gabbanat el Qirud, Thebes. L. 3.6–5.5 cm.

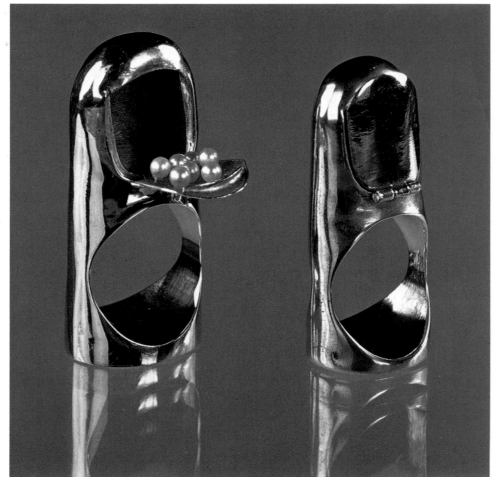

These modern gold finger rings (the one at right beaten after the artist's own thumb) by Barbara Gash, Darmstadt, Germany, bear a striking resemblance to the ancient Egyptian finger guards of gold featured above. Made in 1972. Ht. finger ring, right, 4.5 cm. Collection of the artist.

Detail of a gold necklace decorated with fine granulation. It has nine anchors and a circular pendant with an inverted crescent over the boss, a Phoenician motif indicating the sun and the moon in association. Etruscan, 7th century B.C. from Vulci. Diam. of circular pendant 2.8 cm.

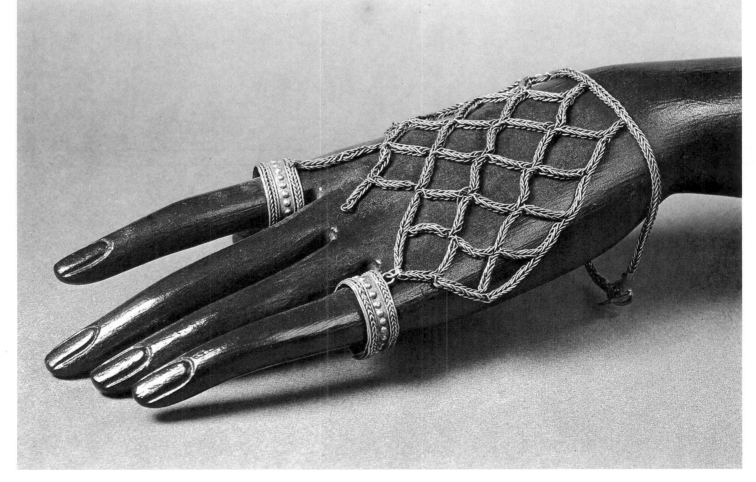

A glove of gold made of diamond-shaped net, with a double chain covering the palm, and the back held at the wrist by a chain circlet, and clasped over the fingers by five rings (three are missing). Persian, c. 1000 B.C. From the Ziwiye Treasury. The Ziwiye Treasury shows the stylistic modifications that took place when some of the Scythians came in contact with the Trans-Caucasian civilizations and absorbed their way of life. After a landslide between Kurdistan and Azerbaijan, an Assyrian bronze sarcophagus was found which contained this unusual golden glove and other treasures, probably made in the royal workshop by skilled metalworkers of various origins.

Crown of gold, pearls, and precious stones. The Chinese developed extraordinary dexterity and inventiveness in their use of precious metals. Here the five *feng-huang* (phoenixes) circling the brow are braided gold wire, the wings and tails of plain and filigree goldwork. Emblems of the empress, the *feng-huang* also symbolize peace and prosperity. Flowers, leaves, and butterflies hover on twisted stems of gold, trembling at the slightest movement of the crown. Uncut rubies, pearls, and "cat's-eyes" further enhance the sumptuous effect. Chinese, Sung Dynasty (960-1279). Ht. approx. 18.4 cm; W. approx. 20.3 cm.

Hairpin of gold and precious stones decorated with crabs, insects, and flowers, the traditional Chinese symbols of good luck. Chinese, Ching Dynasty (1644-1912).

Pendant in the form of a trophy of arms. Three 60 carat baroque pearls compose the body of an armor-clad figure. German (Augsburg?) c. 1680. Ht. 11 cm.

Miniature replica brooch of the Russian Imperial Crown, exquisitely manufactured of gold with diamonds. Russian, c. 1800-1810. Overall Ht. 3.5 cm.

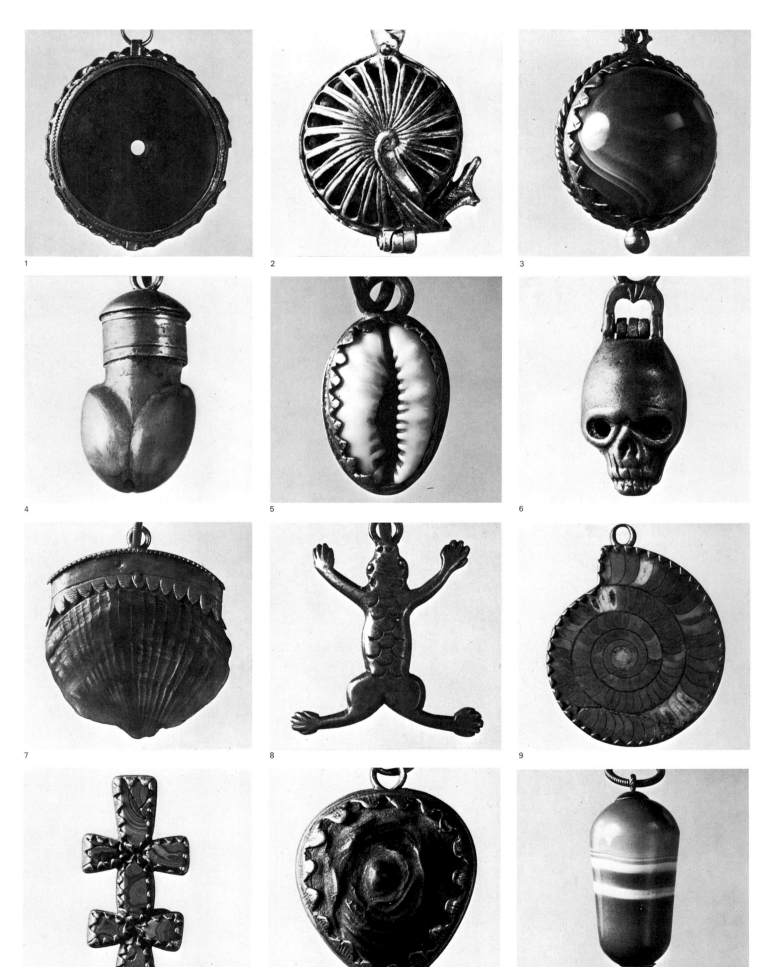

In earlier times magic and the power to heal the sick were closely interwoven and the making of amulets and talismans formed an important part of the jeweler's work. Beads bearing magic inscriptions were transformed into amulets and gem-stones were vested with curative powers.

1 Carnelian stone mounted in gold-plated silver. Carnelian was thought to stop bleeding and to reduce fever. 16-17th century. Diam. 5.4 cm.

2 Silver bisam-apple in the form of a snail. Such amulets were filled with strongly aromatic ingredients that were said to have therapeutic and protective powers. 18th century. Ht. 2.7 cm.

3 Agate ball. A so-called gout ball, mounted in silver. Reputed to ease rheumatism, gout, cramps, and to protect against poisonous snakebites. 17th century. Diam. 3 cm.

4 "Penis" made of horn and mounted in silver. Believed to increase male potency. 16th century. Ht. 4.2 cm.

5 Cowrie shell in silver mounting with sexual symbolism. 18-19th century. Ht. 2.2 cm.

6 Silver crab's-eye box in the form of a "death's head." Worn as a protection against illness. 17th century. Ht. 1.8 cm.

7 "Asp's tongue" made from the scale of an African anteater, used as a defense against demons and as a sexual stimulant. 17th century. Ht. 3.6 cm.

8 Amulet in the shape of a frog, a symbol of fertility. 18-19th century. Ht. c. 2.3 cm.

9 Disc of petrified snail, mounted in silver. Used as a guardian against lightning and as a good-luck charm. 18th century. Ht. 4.6 cm.

10 Double-beam cross set with seven malachite stones in a silver mounting. Worn for protection during pregnancy. 18th century. Ht. 4.4 cm.

11 Ibex-horn pendant, mounted in silver (so-called eagle or rattle stone). Worn for protection during pregnancy. 17th century. Ht. 2.8 cm.

12 Pendant of banded agate. The ancient Egyptians recognized the power of agate to protect against spider bites and thunderstorms. Through the ages the stone was used to guard against disease and misfortune. 18th century. Ht. 3.8 cm.

Gold earring representing the sun-god Helios. Greek, 3rd century B. C. Diam. 4 cm.

A young woman from Chad, Central Africa, adorned for market day. She not only values her amulets as ornaments but like her ancestors, she has faith in their magical powers to protect her.

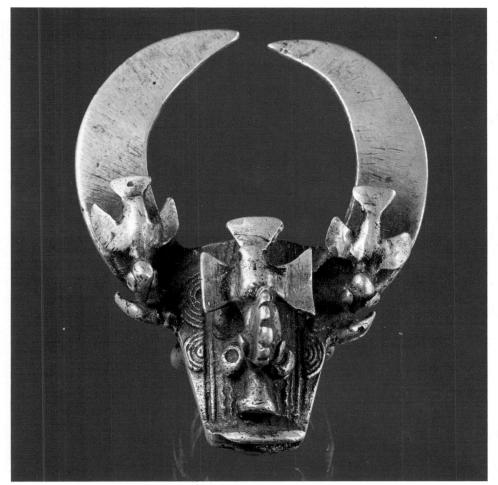

Cult finger ring of yellow bronze, worn only by male members of the cult on special occasions. The birds symbolize immortality. Senufou, Ivory Coast, Africa. Ht. 8.2 cm.

Gold earring, typical Ashanti style, thought to have belonged to the queen mothers of Ashanti, a tribe living in Ghana. 18th-19th centuries. Diam. 6.2 cm.

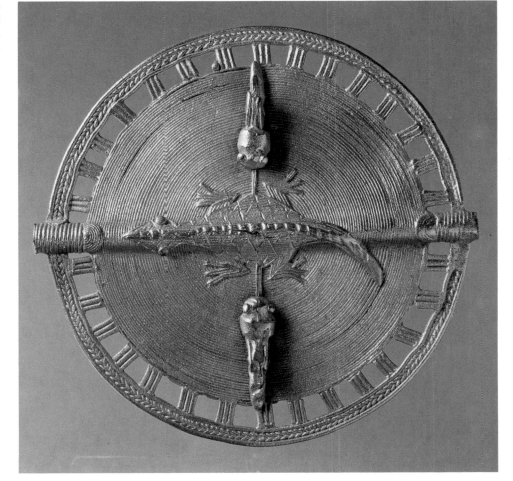

Gold pendant with crocodile motif, worn by women of the Baule Tribe on festive occasions. According to the Baule legends, the crocodile is regarded as sacred. Ivory Coast, Africa. Diam. 7.8 cm.

Leather belt decorated with agates, colored stones, and small tin nails, produced by Serbian artisans and of a type worn by men of the wealthier class in the 17th century. The beautiful color effect was obtained by arranging stones of brighter and darker tones. According to Serbian legend, agate was used extensively in jewelry for protection against disease. Serbian, 17th century. L. 83 cm.

Silver necklace set with agate stones. Such necklaces, worn in Serbia in the 16th and 17th centuries, were a survival of the torques worn by Roman soldiers as a special decoration. By the 12th and 13th centuries, necklaces in the form of torques were quite often used as female jewelry. In the 17th century, especially in eastern Serbia, they were decorated with agates, believed to bring luck. Serbian, 17th century.

Pair of ivory armlets with a design of dance swords and Portuguese heads. From Benin, Western Nigeria, a city which is equally famous for its bronzes and for its ivories. The swords can be understood as a symbol of authority; they are carried by or in front of chiefs and the king on ceremonial occasions. The Portuguese heads have a simi ar significance, related to the strict control and monopoly over trade with Europeans maintained by the kings of Benin. These armlets were worn by the king during certain important ceremonies. They were probably made in the 16th century. Ht. 12.5 cm.

1 Gold finger ring from Thebes inscribed with prenomen of Tuthmosis III. Blue glazed steatite scarab on reverse side. Egyptian, 18th Dynasty. Diam. 3 cm.

2 Roman key ring of bronze. It has been suggested that during the time of the Roman Empire such rings were keys to caskets containing jewels or other valuables, and that they were worn by the owner of the casket or by a trusted servant. Roman, A.D 1st-4th century. Ht. 3.4 cm.

3 Gold signet ring with flexible plate. Border inscription in Latin: ELENACANA. Late Merovingian. First half of the 8th century. Ht. 2.5 cm.

4 Mourning ring for the English Princess Amelia. Flat hoop widening at the shoulders; enameled in white with gold inscription: "PSS. AMELIA DIED 2 NOV. 1810 AGED 27" English, 1810. Diam. 2.1 cm.

5 Jewish wedding ring of gold and enamel. The bezel is flexible and the gold plate bears a Hebrew inscription, "Mazal Tov", meaning "Good Luck." Venice, 16th century. Ht. 2.1 cm.

6 Gold finger ring decorated with four birds (symbols of the immortality of the soul). Ivory Coast, Africa. Ht. 4 cm.

7 Gold finger ring with idealized portrait of Germanicus Caesar (presumably the Roman general) cut from an agate cameo in three zones of color. Italian, by Morelli, early 19th century. Ht. 4.3 cm.

8 Finger ring of apple green jade, heart-shaped, with cabochon sapphires, and small diamonds in a setting of 18–carat gold by New York jeweler David Webb. Made in 1970. Total Ht. 3.5 cm.

9 Diamond and enamel finger ring. The bezel opens to reveal a heart. Italian, 16th century. Diam. 1.7 cm.

10 Silver finger ring, a so-called punch ring, worn by the men and women of Mali, West Africa. Ht. 3.2 cm.

11 Thumb ring of white jade inlaid with emeralds. This beautiful ring was designed for shooting arrows, protecting the thumb from the bowstring, and was used by the Sultans of Turkey. Turkish, 17th century. Ht. 4 cm.

12 Gold finger ring delicately ornamented with enamel and pearls. The bezel opens and its reverse side is also embellished with gold. Italian, 16th century. Total Ht. 2.6 cm.

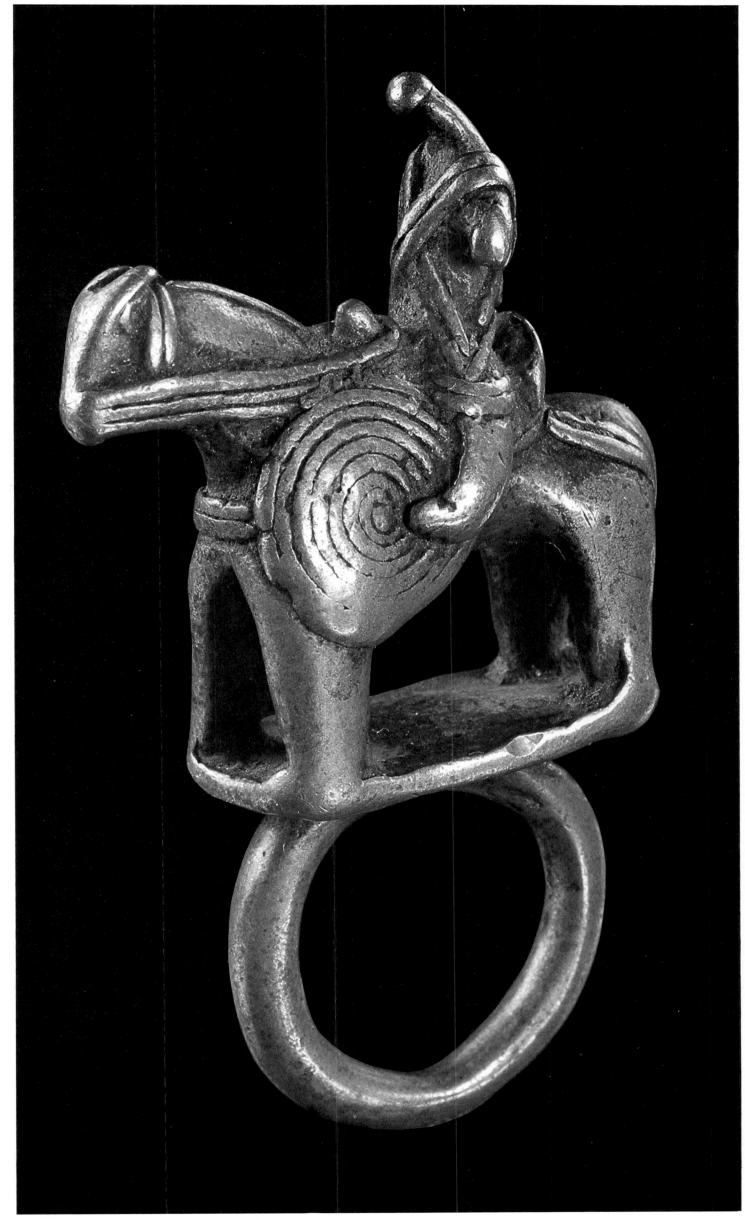

Bronze finger ring with horse and rider, cast in the lost-wax technique. The ring is worn by the high chiefs of Mali as a symbol of power and dignity. Dogon, Mali, West Africa. Total Ht. 6 cm.

Necklace and earrings of subtle beauty made of gold and pearls with miniature landscapes in stone mosaic. Italian, early 19th century. (Slightly enlarged.) Originally in the Royal Bohemian Collection, Konopiste Castle, near Prague.

Engagement-wedding ring, the so-called twin ring, consisting of two gold bands, the ends of which bear the symbolical device of clasped hands. The inside band is engraved in antique-style letters: WGZSFH bzw. DSDMNS, a variation of the inscription which usually appears on such rings: "What God has joined together, let no man cut asunder." The ring as a symbol of marriage traces back to early days. It is said that the ancient Egyptian placed one on the finger of his bride to signify his confidence in her as the custodian of his house. This apparently was the origin of the wedding ring adopted by Christians in the Middle Ages. German, 1586. Diam. 2.6 cm.

The watch of Peter the Great, Tsar of Russia (1682-1725) with a miniature of his wife, Tsarina Catherine I. She ruled from 1725 to 1727. The enameled portrait is inscribed at the right edge with the initials G and M and the date 1725. These stand for Grigori Semenovich Musikiski, the well-known Russian miniaturist who worked in enamels. The works of the watch, and no doubt the case, were made in London by the watchmaker Abraham Heydrich. Presumably Peter the Great bought the watch and case in London and the miniature of his wife was inserted later. English, early 18th century. Total Ht. 7.6 cm.

Hat clasp (part of an Order of the Knights of St George Garniture) with brilliants and rubies, silver gilt, made for the Bavarian Elector Maximilian III Joseph in 1760. Ht. 9.5 cm.

Bow-shaped hatpin of brilliants encircling rose-cut brilliants, silver gilt, made for Maximilian III Joseph in 1765 by the Munich jeweler, Johann Staff. Ht. 11.8 cm.

Diamond necklace given in 1811 by Napoleon I of France to his second wife, Marie Louise, on the birth of their son, the ill-fated king of Rome. After the death of Marie Louise, the necklace passed to successive members of her family, the Habsburgs of Austria. The most recent royal owner was Prince Francis Joseph II of Lichtenstein, who sold it in 1948. Total wt. of diamonds 275 carats.

Crown of Her Imperial Majesty, Empress Farah of Iran, made for her coronation in 1967. It is set with 36 emeralds, 34 rubies, 2 spinels, 105 pearls, and 1,469 diamonds, all selected from the Gem Treasury of Iran. The entire weight of the crown is 1,480.9 grams. It is the latest addition to the crown jewels of Iran, perhaps the richest and most dazzling single collection of jewels in the world. Once the personal property of the shahs, the gems constitute a priceless national asset which backs up the Iranian currency. Made by Van Cleef & Arpels, Paris, 1967. Diam. 21 cm.

Aigrette for the sultan's turban made of feathers and a 5-cm.-long emerald. Turkish, 16th-18th century.

Sultan's dagger. The handle is of white jade inlaid with rubies. Turkish, 18th century. Total L. 40 cm.

The so-called Pearl Diadem which belonged to King Otto of Greece and was worn by his consort. It consists of a row of pearls with a lavishly ornamented frame of brilliants containing 16 large pear-shaped pendant pearls and 16 large pear-shaped pearls above. Munich, c. 1825, perhaps by Kasper Rieländer. W. 18 cm.

Star of the Order of St George with emeralds, brilliants and rubies set in silver. It was made for Ludwig I, King of Bavaria (ruled 1825-48). In 1729 the Elector Charles Albert reinstituted the Order of St George which had been first founded in the 12th century as a crusading order. Munich, c. 1830. Diam. 12.4 cm.

The Persian Order of the Sun and Lion, set with brilliants. Presumably Sultan Abdul Hamid II of Turkey received this order as a gift from Nasr-ed-Din, Shah of Persia. In itself, the order comprises a collection of brilliants. Persian, 19th century. W. 9 cm.

Ras Tafari, known as Haile Selassie, in court dress on his festival day, November 2, 1970, in Addis Ababa, celebrating the fortieth jubilee of his reign as emperor His gold-bedecked uniform took ten outstanding Savile Row tailors three months to complete.

These modern finger rings by E. R. Nele of Frankfurt call to mind the statement of the Roman philosopher Seneca on the extremes of fashion: "We adorn our fingers with rings, and a jewel is displayed on every joint." Sculptress, graphic artist, and jeweler, Nele produces a variety of objects often bold and witty in form, highlighted by the use of beautiful gems.

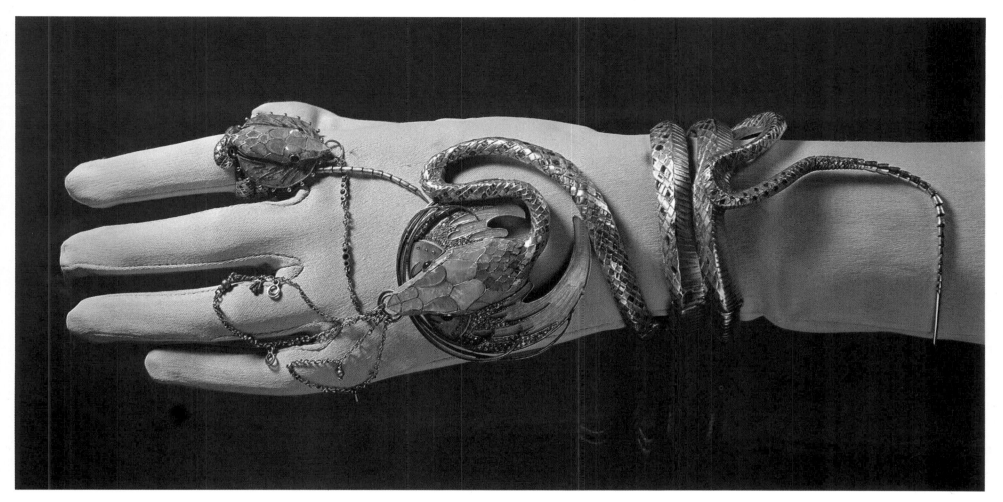

An Art Nouveau-style hand ornament designed for Sarah Bernhardt (a great lover of jewelry), so rich and decorative that it has an almost Oriental feeling of opulence. It was worn by her in the role of Cleopatra. The curly tail of a snake in champlevé enamel encircles the wrist; the head—which is of carved opal, enamel, and gold, with flashing ruby eyes—rests on the back of the hand; holding it in position are delicate chains that join it to another snake's head on the forefinger. Designed by Alphonse Mucha, c. 1906, and executed by Fouquet.

Gold chain carrying an Art Nouveau pendant in the shape of a peacock made of gold, enamel, brilliants, and moonstones. Jewelry was perhaps the most effective of all the Art Nouveau creations. In a reaction to the culturally static, industrialized age, artist-jewelers created new and sinuous forms, inspired by nature. Art Nouveau jewelry was mainly concerned with symbolic and decorative ideas. The chief subjects were flowers, butterflies, serpents, insects, and women. L. Gautriat, Paris, c. 1900. W. 6 cm.

Necklace by René Lalique—made for the Paris Exposition of 1900— which shows Lalique's great craftsmanship and sensitivity for color. Nine perfectly matched Australian opals of 16 carats each alternate with nine plaquettes, each containing a sculptured Art Nouveau figure of gold in *plique à jour* background. Black enamel swans are superimposed on each side of the figure. Siberian amethysts are at the base of figure as well as in the chain with the opal drops. Decorative elements are used functionally: The locks of hair, in black enamel, hold the plaquettes with the opals. René Lalique, Paris, 1900.

PRECIOUS ORNAMENTS IN ANCIENT CIVILIZATIONS

GUIDO GREGORIETTI CURATOR, MUSEO POLDI PEZZOLI, MILAN

It is only comparatively recently that scientists have sought to determine the origin and evolution of primitive cultures. Although great progress has already been made in this direction, they are still obliged to rely on very fragmentary information, provided mostly by the artifacts found on archaeological sites, which are made of unalterable materials that have resisted the passage of time. These include pottery, stone, bronze (when not too greatly damaged by oxidation), horn, ivory, silver (found on protected sites), and above all gold, the incorruptible material *par excellence.* The most ancient pieces of gold jewelry found thus far date back to the beginning of the third millennium B.C. They are still in a perfect state of preservation after 5,000 years. All other artifacts, made of such perishable materials as wood (except in Egypt, where wood survived due to favorable climatic conditions), vegetable fibers, woven fabrics, metals other than those mentioned above, and leather, are completely lacking and leave a huge gap in our knowledge of ancient cultures.

This gap has been filled in part by the inferences and intuitions of scholars, who have reconstructed the characteristics of certain cultures and the course of their evolution by examining the available material and the sites where it was found.

The problems that remain to be solved are why the earliest civilizations sprang up on one continent rather than another, and how it is that there are still today tribes living in the neolithic mode when the art of writing had already been invented in Mesopotamia in the third millennium B.C. There is no doubt that the inhabitants of that region were influenced by factors that exerted a decisive effect on the early development of their intelligence and consequently on their social evolution.

There is reason to attribute that precocious development first of all to the favorable climatic and geographic conditions and secondly to the development and exploitation of livestock breeding, which provided an indispensable source of food. Livestock breeding entailed the need to discover land for grazing and therefore obliged those ancient people to lead a nomadic life, which brought them into contact with other cultures. This in turn permitted them to exchange experiences and to develop new knowledge and skills. The scope for all this was expanded by the capture and training of the horse, the major means of locomotion. The invention of the wheel by the inhabitants of Mesopotamia (in an age when it was still unknown to the Egyptians), together with the discovery of metals (first and foremost gold) and the processes of smelting and alloying them, provided them with new weapons and utensils. They were now in a position to attain still more ambitious goals and to organize their social life on a sedentary basis, settling preferably near the banks of the great rivers, whose waters were essential to the development of agriculture. Another of the major factors in this evolution was the horse. Scythian chieftains, in accordance with an extremely ancient tradition, had their horses buried with them; the higher their rank, the larger the number of horses sacrificed near their burial mounds. This shows how highly the animal was esteemed – confirmed by the splendid gold trappings with which it was frequently adorned, as if to acknowledge and consecrate its eminence.

Some of the most important recent archaeological discoveries concern the southeastern region of Mesopotamia (Iraq) near the mouth of the Tigris and Euphrates. They have demonstrated the existence of a Sumerian civilization that was so highly developed at the end of the fourth millennium B.C. as to challenge the chronological seniority of ancient Egyptian civilization. As has already been mentioned, the Sumerian nation knew the wheel, the horse, and the engraved seal long before the Egyptians.

Nevertheless, those signs of their advanced evolution – and they also include, of course, writing – are not the only ones. The Sumerian population was the first to establish a political and social order and to engage in fervent religious practices, thus laying the foundations of a unitary civilization that produced splendid achievements in the artistic sphere as well. At a time when most tribal peoples of the Eurasian continent still lived in natural shelters and fed on the products of fishing or hunting, or at the most – and that was a rare exception – bred sheep and cattle, the inhabitants of the royal palace of the city-state of Ur, (a palace built in masonry consistent with the most advanced rules of architecture) dressed in splendid clothes, adorned themselves with precious jewels, and listened to music produced by harps and other instruments. Beyond the city walls the land was cultivated intensively and a system of canals brought water from the Euphrates many miles away to irrigate the fields.

Gradually, the climate became less favorable and, aided by the vagaries of war, produced a situation in which for centuries the region was virtually uninhabited. Generations of robbers took advantage of the situation to carry out clandestine diggings and make off with everything of value. First, needless to say, they took jewelry and goldwork.

The Chaldean ruins of the biblical city of Ur, situated in present-day Al-Mugayyar, were visited in 1626 by the Roman orientalist Pietro della Valle. In 1840 the site was studied by W.K. Loftus who, like his predecessor, brought back some inscribed bricks and seals that enabled the city to be identified. The first diggings at Ur were undertaken on behalf of the British Museum by the English Consul at Bassora five years later. Other diggings were made in 1919 by H.R. Hall, and in 1922 an expedition sponsored jointly by the British Museum and the University of Pennsylvania under the leadership of the English archaeologist Sir Leonard Woolley systematically excavated Ur for twelve successive seasons. Their finds included the tombs of King Meskalamshaz and Queen Pu-abi (whose name in inscriptions was formerly read "Shub-ad") (1st Dynasty). The wealth of fine jewelry and goldwork they contained made an important contribution to our knowledge of Sumerian civilization at the beginning of the third millennium B.C.

The jewelry in Queen Pu-abi's tomb caused the greatest excitement. She had been laid to rest in a large crypt, and the upper part of her body covered with a sort of mantle made of beads in gold, silver, lapis lazuli, carnelian, agate, and chalcedony bordered at the hem with a fringe of small tubes of carnelian and lapis lazuli set side by side. Beside the Queen's right arm were three long gold pins with heads of lapis lazuli, three fish-shaped amulets, of which two were in gold and one in lapis lazuli, and a fourth in gold with two seated gazelles. Her thickly padded wig was encircled by a broad gold ribbon that supported three flexible gold wreaths of diminishing diameter placed one above the other. The first, which covered the forehead, was made of large overlapping rings; the second of naturalistically modeled ivy leaves; the third of long willow leaves in groups of three, topped by flowers whose petals were adorned with blue and white incrustations. Fixed into the back of the wig was a Spanish-type comb whose five teeth were decorated with gold flowers at the points. Heavy earrings of the same metal in the shape of twinned semi-tubular hoops tapering toward the lobes completed the headdress. Round her neck the Queen wore necklaces of semi-precious stones and on her fingers were several rings.

In refinement of execution these jewels match the gold plate, the ornamentation of the chariots, the symbolic animals, and the musical instruments found in the vast burial crypt, all of which involved the use of great quantities of gold and semi-precious stones. The quality of the goldwork leads us to believe that it must have been the highly developed outcome of a culture and a tradition that had ripened gradually through the centuries. The royal tombs at Ur also contained the remains of household servants, animals (including horses and asses that had drawn the funeral cart), soldiers of the guard, and two long rows of dignitaries of both sexes who had sacrificed their lives – apparently by poison – and followed their sovereign into the other world. Ceremonial costumes in gold brocade, the most valuable ornaments, and elaborate headdresses were compulsory for so glorious an end. The forms invented by the Sumerian jewelers met all, or nearly all, the demands for ornamentation that arose during the centuries of history that have elapsed since their times, and were undoubtedly more numerous and varied than those in fashion today. Men wore bangles on their wrists and arms, rings on their fingers and ears, gold pectorals and rigid neckpieces.

As we have seen from Queen Pu-abi's sumptuous attire, women of the highest rank often wore padded wigs. Even those of lesser degree bound their hair with a ribbon woven with gold thread. Tubular forms were much used for necklaces, bracelets and earrings. As a rule five bangles were worn on the same wrist. Circles and discs were common ornamental forms used in the composition of jewelry, which often included a quantity of minute tubular elements set close together.

The many-petaled stylized flower became a favorite motif at a later date. It was so common that for centuries it was the typical feature of Mesopotamian ornamentation, just as the lotus flower was in Egypt and the palmette in Greece. The royal tombs at Ur prove that the trend in decorative forms at the beginning of the third millennium B.C. was toward a highly developed naturalism. Animal figures were widely used together with floral motifs and grew to be fundamental elements in Mesopotamian decoration; at the outset they were undoubtedly endowed with a magical-religious significance. During an initial period symmetrical geometric patterns executed with extraordinary precision were employed – in Queen Pu-abi's rings, for example. This was followed by an evolutionary phase that spread, with slight variations and a few characteristics of local origin (or developed under Egyptian influence), to Assyria and Babylonia and later to the Hittites until the first millennium B.C.

Simultaneously with the development of the Sumerian, Assyrian, and Babylonian civilizations, in the Nile Valley there took place the development of the most enduring culture in all of ancient history. The architectural forms, still so impressive both for their spectacularly large sizes and for their severe geometric shapes, were only one of the many refined forms of expression developed by the Egyptians. Sculpture, painting and all branches of the minor decorative arts were also practiced with a remarkably high degree of craftsmanship.

The history and features of Egyptian jewelry are well known, thanks to a great number of objects that have come to light during the excavations of the tombs of the Pharaohs or those of other important persons. Those who were privileged to wear jewels or precious ornaments were few: the Pharaoh, the members of his family, and the highest dignitaries of the court. However, jewels of much less importance, such as strings of colored beads, were in fairly common use by the middle class.

In spite of the cleverness of the architects who built the tombs, the custom of adorning the dead with jewelry encouraged the plundering of the tombs. Even though the tombs had been built at an immense cost and afforded maximum protection, thieves discovered the secret passages into the pyramids or the cave-tombs of the Valley of the Kings and robbed the royal mummies of their jewels. Hardly a single tomb exists to which the thieves had not gained access before the arrival of the archaeologists.

Apart from Montet's discovery in Tanis in 1940, only the tomb of Tutankhamen (18th Dynasty) – found in the Valley of the Kings at Luxor in 1922 – was undamaged. It had been violated by thieves but they must have been surprised by the guards of the necropolis, for although they left the tomb in disorder, they removed only a few small articles made of valuable metals and a quantity of precious ointments. The abundance of jewels and other objects found in the tomb of this romantic but inconspicuous young king provide us with a mere glimpse of the splendor in which the great monarchs lived.

Three thousand years of Egyptian history (from the fourth to the first millennium B.C.) brought about little change in the decorative patterns of jewelry. Fundamentally, Egyptian jewelry is concerned with planes and color, although variations are to be found. The technical methods used were quite sophisticated: besides the goldsmith's work that developed from very early times, precious stones (the favorites were carnelian, turquoise, and lapis lazuli) were carved and polished and were very much in demand for jewelry. Other stones such as rock crystal, green feldspar, garnets, and amethysts were also employed, enriched with vitreous pastes, enamels and faïence. The most important substitute material was faïence, which was manufactured from predynastic times.

The ancient jewels that have been found reveal that personal ornaments often had a symbolic significance. The scarab, vulture, falcon, the eye of Horus, the royal uraeus (sacred asp), the lotus flower, and the sun disc were among the most popular motifs.

A bracelet found at Abydos is composed of plaques (alternating gold and turquoise) in the form of the *serekh*, the façade of the royal palace, and each of the twenty-nine plaques is surmounted by a figure of the falcon of Horus. This remarkable piece of jewelry was found on the mummified arm of a Thinite princess.

Pectorals occupied a special place in the development of Egyptian jewelry. The pectoral of Se'n-Wosret II (12th Dynasty c. 1880 B.C.) in the Metropolitan Museum of Art in New York is a famous example of a pectoral made when excellence of workmanship and purity of design were valued as at no other time in the course of Egyptian history.

On either side of the pectoral the falcon of Horus supports the cartouche of the King, and the entire group of hieroglyphs may be read as: "[May the god] Horus give millions and hundreds of thousands of years to [the king] Khai-kheper-Re [Sesostris II]." The pectoral is of gold, inlaid with lapis lazuli, carnelian, and turquoise. It was found by Petrie in 1914 in the tomb of Princess Sit Hat-Hor-Yunet.

Of the jewelry worn by the princesses or wives of the Pharaohs, and buried with them for use in the next world, the fillets (diadems) are the most important. The most perfect examples are the diadem of Princess Sit Hat-Hor-Yunet (12th Dynasty), found at el-Lahun, and two belonging to Princess Khnumet (12th Dynasty), found at Dashür. All three are now in the Cairo Museum.

The fillet of Princess Sit Hat-Hor-Yunet is a simple band of gold, decorated with fifteen rosettes, inlaid with carnelian, lapis lazuli, and green feldspar. The central motif is a uraeus with a head carved from lapis lazuli, and an openwork body set with lapis lazuli and carnelian.

One of the fillets of Princess Khnumet, of openwork and cloisonné incrustation, is composed of rosettes linking lyre-shaped calyces. Over the center of the fillet is a golden vulture with outspread wings. The other fillet of Princess Khnumet, which is remarkable for its delicate work, consists of six rosette-shaped clasps holding a mesh of gold wire to which flowers and beads are fixed.

The head ornaments ranged from fillets to the unusual jeweled headdresses covering practically all the hair. An example of the latter is the magnificent gold headdress of a lady of the court of Tuthmosis III (c. 1450 B.C.), which can be seen in the Metropolitan Museum of Art in New York. The top of the head is covered with a plate in the form of a palmette, once inlaid with carnelian, turquoise and paste to match the rosettes (some 850 of them) of which the body of the headdress is composed.

Necklaces were widely used. Their most typical form was the broad collar necklace, made up of many rows of beads, usually of gold inlaid with carnelian, green feldspar, and turquoise. The handsome reconstructed example from Thebes (18th Dynasty) in the Metropolitan Museum of Art has falcon terminals to which cords were attached. Collars of this type were worn from the Old Kingdom onward, but the terminals originally had semi-circular ends. In the case of this necklace the terminals are inscribed on the reverse side with the name of Tuthmosis III. A unique broad collar necklace, found in the tomb of Tutankhamen (now in the Cairo Museum) is in the form of the vulture goddess Nekhbet and is made up of many rows of plaques shaped like stylized feathers.

Earrings are not characteristic of Egyptian jewelry and with few exceptions lack the elegance of the other forms of adornment. Most often they appear overdecorated and heavy.

Bracelets or armlets were in use since the earliest dynasties; some are of the supple type made of a fabric of little drops of glazed paste and gold; others are rigid, in a single cylindrical piece or two semi-cylindrical gold plates. They are made in a rather elaborate repoussé style — that is, hammered with a relief design from the reverse side — with scenes of animals or figures inlaid with enamels. A pair of gold bracelets that belonged to Nemareth, son of Sheshonq I (the founder of the 22nd Dynasty), is now in the British Museum. The bracelets have a representation of the infant sun-god seated on a lotus, and are inlaid with lapis lazuli.

Other beautiful examples of bracelets can be found in the treasure of Tutankhamen and in that of Tell Basta (Cairo Museum), where a solid gold bracelet in two parts is decorated with two-headed geese whose bodies are in lapis lazuli, and is surrounded by a filigree and a granulated design. The aesthetic rigor and artistic value of these bracelets can be considered equal to that of Hellenistic or Italian Renaissance masterpieces.

The imagination of the jewelers can be seen in the finger rings, some of them in faïence or in hard stone finely decorated with symbols (very often the scarab) or ritual scenes carved on the bezel; others are of gold with a gemstone in the bezel, and intricate pieces involving many symbols in one design, such as those found in the tomb of Tutankhamen. The compositional designs show the same symbols that are represented in other jewels, but in the smallest dimensions.

The end of the New Empire (c. 1085 B.C.) marks the beginning of the decline of belief in the divine origin of the Pharaohs, which had been one of the sources of inspiration and patronage to which we owe the splendid works of ancient Egypt. During the Greco-Roman period, the originality of Egyptian art and jewelry degenerated and became devoid of any significance, imitating foreign patterns slavishly and bringing to an end one of the longest and most glorious chapters in the history of art.

Meanwhile, in the course of the first millennium B.C., a new type of stylistic expression developed, spreading to Iran and providing the dominant keynote of Persian jewelry. European goldsmiths too were influenced by some of its forms, which are reflected in what is known today as the so-called animal style of the steppe cultures.

The basic forms of the new style were diffused by the Scythians. These nomadic and semi-nomadic tribes inhabited the immense expanses of steppe along the borders of present-day Russia and in the course of centuries spread in a westerly direction as far as the Danube and even beyond. The Scythians displayed outstanding ability chiefly in horse breeding and in working metal.

The gold ornaments that have been found are attributed to the period between the first century B.C. and the first century A.D., and afford evidence of a much older goldwork tradition. There is no mistaking the peculiar characteristics of the Scythian style, which is distinguished by a crude power of expression, extreme stylization, and expressionistic deformation. As for the choice of subject matter, animal themes are predominant among these ornaments.

Clasps, plaques and the gold decorations on weapons and helmets offered ample opportunity for representation of animals and animal motifs. The commonest examples found consist of members of the cat and goat families, and the basic forms are embellished with fantastic non-geometrical and asymmetrical designs in which meandering curves and tracery reign supreme. Scythian craftsmen, first using gold alone and later inserting a few colored stones, had a preference for scenes of fighting animals, many of them with decoratively outspread horns; sometimes their bodies were adorned with figures of other animals or grouped in contracted postures with highly stylized human figures. The designs were heightened with fretwork, which also served to provide eyelets for suspending the ornaments or attaching them to garments. The Hermitage Museum in Leningrad has a rich collection of precious Scythian ornaments found in various localities from Siberia to southern Russia.

Archaeological finds indicate that the events leading to the development of European civilizations were largely due to the westward migrations of various Asiatic tribes who brought with them elements of Egyptian and Sumerian culture. The first territory to receive them was the one closest to their point of departure, namely the Mediterranean basin, which was the seat of Cretan-Mycenaean culture from the eighteenth century B.C.

The island of Crete – thanks to its peculiar geographical situation and climatic conditions, its proximity to the coasts of Asia and Africa (where civilization had developed and thrived from the earliest times), and its focal position along the Mediterranean trade routes – enjoyed increasing economic prosperity. This allowed its inhabitants to profit greatly from their contacts with other peoples, which provided them with the technical knowledge necessary to evolve a splendid artistic civilization that spread through the islands of the Aegean as far as mainland Greece.

It was in the fields of jewelry and goldwork, in which the ornamental character of those arts was exploited fully, that Cretan culture produced some of its noblest achievements. Like the Egyptians, the Cretans covered the faces of their illustrious dead with gold masks; like the Mesopotamians, they made extensive use of animal figures and rosettes in their jewelry, and of mythical scenes with human figures in their seals. The stylistic influence of Egypt was, however, almost negligible compared with that assimilated from the East.

The amazing wealth of ornamental motifs utilized in jewelry bears witness to the incredibly active imagination of the Cretan goldsmiths. Their search for novel variations on a theme led to the invention of new solutions, many of them inspired by the sinuous motions of marine fauna, particularly octopi. At the same time, they showed a fine feeling for balance in the numerous ornamental types they created that were to be drawn upon by Greek artists a thousand years later – moldings with volutes, palmettes, rosettes, ovoli framed by flutings, and so on. The robes of dignitaries and court ladies were embellished with dozens of embossed gold discs. In the many centers where the goldsmith's art was highly developed, personal ornaments included bosses, rings, neckpieces, pendants, diadems, earrings, bracelets, gold fillets, brooches and belts.

In the execution of their designs, jewelers and goldsmiths employed such techniques as granulation and damascening, as well as the insertion of glass plaques and colored stones. Among the great works of the Middle Minoan period (seventeenth century B.C.) is an extremely handsome pendant from Malia with two heraldic bees facing each other, their bodies bent in a half-circle and touching at head and tail. Four discs (three hanging and one placed between the insects' feet) plus two spheres (one between their heads, the other in a spherical cage above them) lead us to believe that this solar motif, also found in many other pieces of jewelry, may have had a symbolic religious significance.

Minoan jewels display an enormous variety of figured designs. They include not only floral elements, as a rule extremely complicated and accompanied by spirals, but also a wide range of animals – lions, gazelles, stags, bulls, horses, members of the cat family – in addition to insects (such as butterflies), birds, chimeras, and griffins. Dancing girls, warriors in combat, hunts, and mythical religious scenes are executed in relief on the large bezels of heavy rings and embossed on pendants. It was during the same period that the typical motif of the figure-eight shield was evolved for various purposes.

In the sixteenth century B.C. Mycenae became the chief center of the goldsmith's art. Though it assimilated the Minoan style from Crete, its works never attained the same quality as their island models.

The profusion of jewels produced at Mycenae during the period of the city's greatest prosperity is enormous. An exceptional piece from Tomb III is a silver pin with openwork decorations in gold foil. Enclosed by a broad, festooned horseshoe-shaped frame ending in, and topped by, lotus flowers, a female figure with bared bosom and bell-shaped skirt holds a garland in her outstretched arms. She is linked to the festooned frame by two pairs of volutes that spring from her headdress and hands. What strikes us in creations of this kind, after the originality of the composition and stylistic conception, is the high level of artistic evolution that had never before been attained in goldwork. The execution of these pieces was not entrusted to craftsmen; they were the direct products of the vivid imagination and clever hands of an artist, whose personality they reflect.

The islands of the Aegean and the Greek mainland received from Crete and Mycenae not only a highly developed civilization but also a taste for jewelry that spread in forms faithful to the original style, apart from a few local variations. When those two centers declined, the forms originated there gradually degenerated. The last feeble vestiges of Minoan-Mycenaean art, greatly influenced by Egyptian and Eastern motifs, can be seen in the jewelry found in the Treasury of Aegina, now in the British Museum, which dates from the beginning of the first millennium B.C.

As far as style is concerned, that group of precious ornaments is lacking in originality because the forms and decorative elements were borrowed from different sources. There is no mistaking the influence of Egypt in the representation of sphinx heads, kilted human figures, and animal forms copied from the banks of the Nile. Stylistic accents of a similar type occur in the later Phoenician jewelry of Rhodes and Tharros, Sardinia, which seems to have a close kinship with the Treasury of Aegina. Mycenaean reminiscences are less evident; instead, those of the geometric style, evolved under Eastern influence, are visible both in the polychrome of necklaces and in the shapes of some pendants that obviously had a symbolic or magic function.

Another cultural current that gave rise to a wealth of avant-garde experiments in metalwork invaded Central Europe by a route that followed the course of the Danube, continued to the foot of the Alps, skirted them on the North, spread through southern Germany, penetrated into France, and later reached the Iberian Peninsula, England, and Scandinavia. That intermittent current brought new techniques and forms to the backward indigenous populations of those regions at the end of the second millennium and all through the first millennium B.C. However, during the migrations and invasions that took place in the first millennium A.D., it exerted a somewhat regressive action in a Europe that had already mostly been civilized by the expansive power of Rome.

The earliest contacts are revealed by various products of the Hallstatt culture, which took its name from an area in Upper Austria famous for its extremely ancient salt mines, which are situated on the shore of a lake of glacial origin. That culture – which began in the ninth century B.C. and spread from eastern France to Croatia – covers the cultural aspects of the first Iron Age in Central Europe. Archaeological finds that can be referred to it have proved that during its second phase there were also contacts with the more advanced Mediterranean cultures. The few ornaments discovered thus far display forms based on geometric elements, which led to the development of many stylized representations of animals revealing traces of the far older Eurasian repertories of decorative patterns. The few pieces of jewelry from that period include bronze objects and some made of Baltic amber. Various features seem to afford evidence of the strong influence exerted by the forms of ancient Oriental jewelry and thus point to the existence of contacts with those Eastern cultures. This influence is also present in the Celtic artistic culture whose origin has been established by the archaeological site at La Tène in Switzerland. This culture first appeared in connection with the decline of the Hallstatt culture, and its development is linked with probable contacts between the Celts (ethnically a European people) and the Scythians. In fact, jewelry constituted the Celts' major artistic activity, and the decorative motifs – comprising a quantity of curves, spirals, and intricate tracery – reveal a remote Asiatic origin in strong contrast to, and very distant from, the manifestations of Mediterranean art during the same period.

The Celts never formed a nation in the proper sense of the word and their early expansion was limited to the area covered today by southern Germany, northern France, Spain, and the north of Italy. Sweeping through the Italian peninsula, they carried out raids into Greece and even as far afield as Anatolia, where they gave their name to the region of Galatia. However, vestiges of their culture have been found only in the countries bordering on the Rhine and Danube, in France north of the Garonne, in the western portion of the Iberian Peninsula, and especially in Great Britain and Ireland.

The stylistic tradition of the Celts persisted stubbornly – though it languished during the Roman period – well beyond the limits of Antiquity. During the early Middle Ages it grew wherever individual communities could develop and their culture could flourish. This was the case in the British Isles, notably in Ireland, which was out of reach of the Roman invasion.

The dominant feature of Celtic goldwork was always a negation of organic structures. This caused craftsmen to avoid the interplay of architectural forces and to find expression in abstract ornaments unrelated to the real world, reducing the forms of human beings, animals, and plants to an assemblage of modulated spirals. It could indeed be said that the forms in which they found artistic expression denote a veritable fear of reality. The ornaments most commonly found in the territories occupied by the Celts are rigid neckpieces and armlets made entirely of gold. Their origin has been traced back to Asian sources: in fact, they occur frequently in Sumerian and Assyrian sculpture. During the Roman period those neckpieces were termed torques (Latin *torquere,* "to twist"). The open tubular circlet can be either smooth or composed of intertwined bands; the points are always adorned with an identical symmetrical pattern in which anthropomorphic and zoomorphic motifs are combined with spherical shapes embossed with abstract decorations.

Two gold neckpieces dating from the sixth century B.C., though generally classified under the broad heading of barbarian art, belong to the stylistic sphere of the Celts. Found in Sweden – one at Alleborg, the other at

Farjestaden — and preserved in the National Museum of Antiquities at Stockholm, they display a masterly technical skill allied with an extreme formal complexity. The ornamentation in granulation and filigree work recalls the masterpieces of the Orientalizing period of Etruscan jewelry, to which they are perhaps related. But these outsize torques were conceived in a totally different spirit, as proved by the insertion in the more important of the two (that found at Farjestaden) of animal forms and human heads and figures between each of the seven circles made of lathe-turned tubular sections set one above the other.

There are several interesting specimens of this widely disseminated ornament. In Berlin, the Museum für Vor- und Frühgeschichte has a gold torque from Besseringen (fifth-fourth century B.C.) with a very refined central motif comprising five juxtaposed fusiform elements from whose sides spring two rows of discs that join the circlet of the torque; the empty space between the top of the row of discs and the torque proper contains two birds arranged symmetrically with the head turned in the opposite direction from the body. The execution is highly finished and shows that great care was bestowed on the most minute details.

The Montefortino torque (third century B.C.) in the Ancona Museum, also of solid gold, has two semi-circles of twisted strands. The hook at the back is made of two twisted snakes' heads, the one in front of two capitals whose corners are embellished with heads of wild beasts. If the decoration of this torque reveals a slight Classical influence, the leaves and branches that adorn the heavy tube of the torque in Dublin (National Museum of Ireland) are obviously derived from Roman art. The figure of the man with bent legs embossed on the cup from Gundestrup (Copenhagen, National Museum) gives us an idea of the ornamental and magical significance of the torque in Celtic society. Besides wearing one around his neck, he holds another in his right hand and a snake in his left. The Celts followed the same compositional elements on their armlets that we have seen on their torques. And another precious ornament much worn by the Celts was the ring. Its typical feature is the absence of the bezel. The hoop, generally wider in front, is either entirely covered with spiral decoration in bold relief or scattered with granulation tracery.

Ornaments intended for sewing on garments included embossed discs and plaques with anthropomorphic designs, spiraling floral tracery, and interlaced ribbons. They were often embellished with coral inserts.

The stylistic tradition of the Celts put down such deep roots that it survived the Roman invasion and in some regions persisted until the seventh century A.D. and even later. With the barbarian invasions it became integrated in the mainstream of barbarian art, which also originated in the East and found its predominant expression in metalwork.

Enameling was a technique highly developed among the Celts, particularly in England and Ireland, where, as we have seen, their art persisted longer than elsewhere. The treasure from the ship-burial at Sutton Hoo (now in the British Museum) bears witness to the technical perfection and stylistic rigor that art in the Celtic tradition attained during that period. Precious objects embellished with multi-colored enamel were not the only finds made at Sutton Hoo in 1939: there were also some made of gold alone, like the fibula decorated with three plain semi-circles on a vermiculated ground of narrow interlaced ribbons incised with niello.

Some of the magnificent pieces of jewelry forming part of the Sutton Hoo treasure provide ample evidence that the English goldsmiths possessed a rare skill in the application of the cloisonné enamel process. They utilized the gold areas to obtain complex openwork effects, as exemplified by the panels with geometric checkerboard motifs and the borders with intertwined zoomorphic motifs of the big shoulder fibula made in two convex hinged parts.

The style that the Celts had brought to a peak of perfection through centuries of consistent expression in ornamental works lived on in England, though in a less rigorous form, until the ninth century. Evidence of this are the rings of Queen Ethelswith of Mercia (836-858) and King Ethelwulf of Wessex (839-858) in the British Museum. The latter is shaped like a bishop's mitre, with the King's name incised on the band and flanked by two Greek crosses; the wide part is adorned with two swans facing each other across a vertical ornamental motif broken by, and ending in, two small rosettes framed by circles. The decoration is in high relief, probably because the ground was nielloed, and the style foreshadows the Romanesque modes. The Queen's ring is decorated with a fantastic animal, a chimera within a four-lobed circle. The various spaces in between are filled with simple foliage ornamentation.

The period from the fourth to the eighth century A.D. was characterized by the great migrations. Central, western and southern Europe and North Africa were overrun by barbarian hordes of various ethnic origins that came from the regions situated northeast of the Black Sea, east of present-day Poland and Hungary, and north and northeast of Germany. Their cultural achievements were limited to metalwork and to a very few sculptured monuments. In this respect they resembled their predecessors, the Scythians and Celts. It was not until they had settled permanently in various regions that their artifacts improved in quality, assimilating stylistic elements of local or Mediterranean origin. As in the Hallstatt and La Tène cultures, which also had their origin in the East, barbarian or Germanic art displays a certain unity of expression and is disseminated over a vast geographic area.

Like their forebears, the great majority of those peoples were accustomed to burying their dead with accoutrements that varied in quality and quantity with the social position of the departed. However, they are far better known today for their prowess in battle and their territorial conquests than for their artistic achievements. The discovery of artifacts of the same style and technique in widely diverging times and places makes it almost impossible to compile a reliable classification of the stylistic trends of the various ethnic groups. Nevertheless, barbarian or Germanic goldwork displays certain common characteristics quite unlike those of the classical Mediterranean world. It bears witness to a clear break with both the realistic vision of the Romans and the idealistic vision of the Greeks. Furthermore, the various influences assimilated from the environment never affected the basic character of that style − even when applied to pieces of jewelry typical of the Roman or Byzantine tradition.

Color had been employed very sparingly in jewelry during the Greek period. Its use became more common during the Roman, thanks to the activities of the Roman-Sarmatian workshops on the Black Sea coast, and it is one of the most widespread stylistic features of barbarian art. This taste for color, already extensively used in the jewelry of India and Iran, shows itself in the setting of colored stones, vitreous pastes, and pearls in cavities that more or less cover the entire surface of the object, producing very lively chromatic effects.

The motifs embrace the shape of the jewel. The design is schematic and linear, rather geometrical, consisting as a rule of curved or broken lines, or a combination of the two, as well as circles and heart shapes, that form a dense network. Very rarely a human head is found reduced to its essentials and closely integrated in the complex ornamentation. In some regions this style appears from the fourth to the sixth century and is peculiar in that the settings in relief constitute the motif, while the metal ground is decorated with concise sinuous patterns in simple, double, or triple filigree.

A different style, considerably influenced by Celtic art and characterized by the almost total absence of color, developed in northern Europe. Jewels decorated in this style are entirely covered with an intricate tracery of curved and broken ribbons in relief, whose convolutions form figures of animals or human heads − always rendered with a strong feeling for schematic decoration. As a rule these jewels display an abundance of openwork with borders, alveoli, and other elements in high relief.

Barbarian motifs were applied on types of jewels derived from Rome or Byzantium (finger rings, earrings, and flexible necklaces) that normally lay outside the scope of the barbarian repertory. The precious ornament most widely disseminated throughout the area covered by the migrations is the fibula. Those that were found in the Petroasa treasure (Rumania), dating from the fourth or fifth century, include a large shoulder fibula in the shape of a bird of prey (Muzeul National de Antichètati, Bucharest). The neck and breast are modeled in the round and the whole object is covered with hollows of different shapes set with gems and pieces of vitreous paste. Fibulae similar in shape and decoration, but flat, have been found in Italy at Cesena and in Spain at Saragossa and Estremadura. (In the Petroasa treasure, there is also a rigid neckpiece in the above-mentioned polychrome style with the front part shaped like a half-moon; the entire surface is covered with heart-shaped hollows, but they are now empty. It further includes a pair of small fibulae with a protuberance on the arch in the shape of a wild beast's head.) The presence of zoomorphic decoration in these articles and in a fibula from Desane (Italy) that has two pairs of heads of birds of prey in the center and at the sides of the arch is a sign that the style originated in the East. The S-shaped fibula at Cividale (Italy) is another example of the polychrome style with zoomorphic details.

Fibulae and disc-shaped or indented bosses with their flat surface decorated in the same polychrome style have been found not only in Italy and Spain, but in Germany and Denmark as well. The fibula from Nagy Mihali (Czechoslovakia) is exceptional for its shape – a triangle with slightly convex sides; attached to the base are three little chains of diminishing length ending in pear-shaped stones. The shape and design of the recesses for the stones, pearls and colored glass paste on the surface of the triangle give this jewel the appearance of an Art Nouveau work.

The rather limited repertory of barbarian precious ornaments in the polychrome style includes belt buckles with decorated plate and ring and a very few pendants.

During the sixth and seventh centuries in the Mediterranean area, Germany and England, the trend went from a more sober polychromy with colored stones set in protuberant bezels, either singly or combined in a pattern on vermicular filigree ground, to jewels entirely of gold adorned with filigree work and embossed with semi-spherical reliefs or concentric circles. This growing taste for filigree seemed to be due, at least in part, to Byzantine influence.

Earlier, in the fifth and sixth centuries, and in the Scandinavian peninsula only, there was a flourishing production of gold medallions for wearing around the neck. They were embossed with the profiles of emperors and empresses in the Late Antique style, apparently copied from Roman models. The origin of this odd, isolated artistic phenomenon has not yet been established.

Production of medallions continued in an entirely different vein as well. In one from Gerete (Sweden) the loop for the thread that went around the neck, worked like a spool and embellished with filigree volutes, encloses an inverted triangle that contains six heads embossed in high relief separated by filigree volutes and covers part of the six concentric borders of the medallion; these latter are adorned with volutes, plaits, and profile heads. In the middle is a human profile with a complicated hairstyle in linear relief. The section of the profile from the nose to the jaw coincides with the outline of the neck and rump of a horned quadruped with open mouth and long flowing tail, whose splayed front hoofs rest on the outer circle of the border. The heads in high relief arranged one above the other should be compared with the third century B.C. Celtic sculpture from Entremont (southern France), which has two heads placed one above the other. The same motif is repeated on one of the bands of the border, which would seem to confirm the belief that the jewel was executed in one of the Celtic workshops that still flourished during the fifth century A.D. The other medallions found at Trollhättan and Söderby in Sweden reveal a certain stylistic kinship with the Celtic gold coins of the first century A.D. that are preserved in the Louvre's Cabinet des Médailles in Paris.

In the sixth and seventh centuries, along the North Sea coast and in northern Germany, a different style evolved that was mostly applied to fibulae, belt buckles, and the hilts of swords and daggers. Its paramount feature is an extremely complex tracery in both the inner compartments and in the openwork decoration around the edge. The majority of these articles are made almost entirely of metal — generally silver gilt — and in some, tracery incorporates highly stylized anthropomorphic and zoomorphic details. This style reveals that the mysterious spirit pervading Celtic ornamental compositions was still an inspiration throughout the entire area at that time.

In the south of Europe, the rich treasure unearthed at Castel Trosino (Italy) contains several pieces of seventh-century jewelry in which the influence of Byzantium is clear. The treasure includes necklaces with coins, disc fibulae, earrings, finger rings, and pendants of Roman type richly decorated with filigree work. A necklace in silver gilt with ornate discs and pendants was found at Zalesie (Russia) at the extreme periphery of the Byzantine sphere of influence.

The Iron Crown in the treasury of Monza Cathedral (Italy) displays a mixture of stylistic elements still partly linked with the concepts of barbarian art, as proved by its schematic forms and design. It dates from the end of the eighth or the beginning of the ninth century and is the first piece of jewelry from that period in which we find elements of classical ornamentation in the shape of gold rosettes arranged so as to form lozenges on the enameled plaques that make up the crown.

The present state of knowledge of the ancient cultures of Pre-Hispanic America permits only very approximate dating, but it is quite certain that they arose a great deal later than those of the Eurasian continent. This might confirm the theory advanced by many scholars (and backed by observations that seem to support it) that Asian colonists reached the western seaboard of the South American continent during the first millennium of our era.

That such an extraordinary achievement was followed by the development of a politico-religious and artistic culture should not come as a surprise. Suffice it to consider the case of Easter Island, a tiny piece of land all but lost in the immensity of the Pacific Ocean, and the grandeur of the many gigantic stone statues found there. We are forced to admit that migrations over enormous distances and almost superhuman achievements were feasible in the distant past.

Therefore, it should not be too difficult to accept the theory (1954-55) of Heine-Geldern suggesting that the methods used for working metal on the American continent in Pre-Hispanic times were imported from China by people of the Dongson culture of Insulindia. However, the proposed chronology in the eighth century B.C. seems rather doubtful.

The natives of the regions in question, like the Chinese and the populations of many ancient civilizations of Asia and Europe, were accustomed to burying their dead with a collection of articles; here the objects consist of articles in gold and jade. These two materials did not represent symbols of either wealth or power to native eyes. Rather, they were associated with certain myths and rites and were viewed as sharing in the sacred nature of Mother Earth. As such they were considered capable of purifying the departed and enabling them, by their very presence, to attain salvation and immortality.

The cultural cycles of Pre-Hispanic America are divided into two broad areas distinguished not only geographically but stylistically as well. They are Middle America, or Mesoamerica, covering approximately the present-day states of Mexico, Guatemala, El Salvador, and part of Honduras and Nicaragua; and the Andean area, which includes Peru, Ecuador and Colombia, with extensions into the eastern regions and the Isthmus of Panama.

The gold was supplied by what is now Colombia, which has always contained large deposits. The alluvial deposits left by the rivers were rich in nuggets and other forms of the mineral, while the mountains are still criss-crossed by auriferous lodes to the present day. Copper is scarce and even in ancient times had to be imported, but emeralds are found in considerable quantities. From that region gold was exported southward to the Cordillera and the Peruvian coast, and northward to present-day Middle and North America.

A logical result of the presence of gold in Colombia was an abundance of jewelry and goldwork in the cultures that succeeded one another in the region. This in turn led to a tradition of technical skill that encouraged the export not only of the precious metal itself but also of the goldsmiths who worked it.

Along the strip of land bordering the Andean Cordillera from the region south of Lake Titicaca to the Caribbean there was a succession of artistic manifestations, starting at a time contemporaneous with the beginning of the Christian era, which were equally important for their variety and aesthetic value. The origin and development of the Andean culture is attributed partly to indigenous peoples and partly to immigrants. The former are believed to have spread from the western limits of the Amazonian forests to the high valleys of the Cordillera and from there to the coast; the latter are thought to have come from the north either by sea or by land. The prevailing opinion is that the Chavín culture, named after a locality in the hills to the north of what is now the city of Lima, dates from the fifth century A.D., while the Mochica and Nazca cultures date from the seventh or eighth. The former has its center in the Moche Valley, the latter in the area that is now southern Peru. The political expansion of the Tiahuanaco tribe, which originated north of Lake Titicaca and then spread through the entire area, took place later. In the fourteenth century it culminated in the Inca empire, with its capital at Cuzco, and the flowering of the Chimú, Chancay, and Inca styles.

The goldwork produced in some of those centers attained a high aesthetic quality, notably in periods when the conditions of the dynasties favored artistic activity – although it could never compare with the Colombian. In addition to lamination, chasing, and embossing (both free and with dies), the Andean goldsmiths discovered at an early date how to weld, cast by the *cire-perdue* (lost-wax) process, produce alloys, and gild copper with the help of plant juices and oxalic acid.

The oldest pieces of jewelry that have come down to us – for instance, those in the Mochica style – have small zoomorphic figures obtained by assembling various elements made of bent sheet gold. By way of example, a fabulous bird or a toucan may have for its beak a curved truncated cone of thin gold plate soldered to the head, which is also a reversed truncated cone with rounded base; the body may be a smooth ovoid form to which are welded lamellae in shapes representing the wings, feet, and tail. Hanging from a wire attached to the tip of the beak may be a small solar disc, a symbol that occurs extremely frequently in all Pre-Hispanic American jewelry. In animal figures the eye is often a single emerald; in the masks it is a row of emerald beads sprouting from the space between the lashes and diminishing in size toward the corners. The figure is sketchily drawn and has a somewhat caricatural appearance, but is very expressive. In the masks the expression often achieves fantastic or demonic effects without losing its highly stylized local character.

Anthropomorphic and zoomorphic representations of this kind, in which expression and physical characteristics are so highly developed, also occur in Mochica and Nazca ceramics and woven fabrics. They display a wide range of variations and interpretations, more or less stylized and enriched with fantastic details, and constitute a permanent feature of all Pre-Columbian art, particularly in the Andean regions.

The simplest and commonest type of personal gold ornament was the solar disc. Large or small, flat or convex, with plain or beaded edge, it was used as earring, nose ornament (nariguera), in necklaces, pectorals, hair ornaments, and other forms.

Many human figures in both clay and gold wear an ornament around the leg, under the knee, or at the ankle, and a bracelet of the same type on the upper arm. These pieces of jewelry seem to be made of hollow cylindrical beads strung on a thread with knotted ends. Beads of this sort, in colored semi-precious stone, baked clay, or even gold, have been found in large quantities. They were used for necklaces in which the colors, shapes, and materials were variously arranged.

Articles of clothing were very often decorated with animal shapes in sheet gold, little bells, and semi-spherical buttons. The finest example of this is a Chimú poncho from Peru on which 13,000 pieces of gold are sewn. On special occasions the high priests wore tunics made entirely of sheet gold in strips interwoven to form a thick fabric.

The Chimú necklaces are very elaborate. They are often composed of embossed heads of deities interspersed with gold beads and other decorative elements. One preserved in the Archaeological Museum at Lambayeque (Peru) has 166 masks set one alongside the other in 7 rows.

The exceptional abundance of gold in the subsoil and waterways of Colombia was matched by an enormous production of jewelry and goldwork in that region. This explains how, in spite of the pillage and destruction at the time of the Spanish Conquest and the intense activity of the guaqueros (unauthorized prospectors and diggers) since then, an immensely greater quantity of Pre-Hispanic goldwork has been preserved in Colombia than in the Andean region and Mesoamerica combined. There are over 7,000 pieces in the Museo del Oro at Bogota. There is also the very rich treasure of the Quimbaya found at two burial sites at La Soledad (Filandia, Cauca district) and presented to Spain by the Colombian government in 1891. It is now in the Museo de América in Madrid.

Unfortunately, accurate study of these works has been hampered by clandestine or unauthorized excavations, with the result that, for the majority of specimens, neither the place nor the level at which they were found is known. This has been made up for in part, as far as the earliest periods are concerned, by the Carbon 14 method of dating. As for stylistic classification, all that it is possible to do is to consult the works of scholars who have specialized in the subject.

From about the fifth century B.C., the upper and middle reaches of the Cauca River were the sites of the earliest Colombian production in the Calima and Tolima styles. Not only were they in close enough proximity to influence each other mutually, but – according to some scholars – they were also related to the art of the San Augustín center, the Maya culture in Middle America, and the Chavín culture in the Andean region.

The Quimbaya style, also located in the upper valley of the Cauca, north of Calima and Tolima, appeared not much later. It persisted over a very long period. For that reason, and still more for the magnificent quality of the goldwork it produced, it is rightly credited with being the most important in Pre-Columbian America. Perez de Barradas, in his monumental work on Pre-Hispanic goldwork in Colombia, says that the Quimbaya style was followed around 500 A.D. by the Coclé style, which developed in the Isthmus (now the Republic) of Panama, and by the other cultures of that nation and of Costa Rica.

At the beginning of the second millennium of our era, the Muisca style developed in the vicinity of the capital of present-day Colombia, at the same time as the Tairona style on the shores of the Caribbean, to the east of the mouth of the Cauca. The Sinú style evolved on the banks of the river of that name and the Darién style in the nearby valley of the Atrato. Barradas suggests the beginning of the first millennium as the approximate date of the important finds in the zone of Popayán. He also distinguishes an "Invasionist" style that originated toward the sixth century during the large scale invasion by people from Amazonia – a style that assimilated various influences and that found expression in a coarse goldwork.

On the whole this complex picture bears witness to the paramount importance of goldwork in the Pre-Hispanic culture of a country that had a wealth of gold deposits and that also produced a great many goldsmiths who displayed an extremely high level of creative imagination and technical skill within the confines of different social groups.

Jewelry, whether made of gold, copper, or tumbago (an alloy of those two metals), was always worked with the same loving care. In all probability the earliest pieces were made of pure gold and the alloy became progressively debased in the course of time by a steadily increasing proportion of copper. This would lead to the inference that there was not only a growing demand for jewelry but also that the extraction of the precious metal became less and less easy.

In the Pre-Hispanic jewelry of Colombia there is no great variety of personal ornaments, but the repertory of forms is virtually endless. The most popular jewel, the *nariguera,* presents the most unexpected forms depending on the period, the style, and the importance of the wearer. The commonest are ring- or disc-shaped, but both types can be embellished with a number of extremely complex motifs. Some resemble horizontal or upturned wings, either plain or decorated, with tips of different shapes; others are crescent-shaped with concentric reliefs and beaded edges, or triangles with the apex pointing downward and the base of various lengths, plain or decorated; others again have the shape of thick rings ending in a disc; many other variations are known as well.

This applies also to earrings: the simplest type, in the form of a ring or a disc, may consist of two elements of different shapes, the first fixed to the ear lobe, the other (or others) hanging from it. The most important, from the decorative viewpoint, are the handsome filigreed Sinú earrings shaped like semi-circles with the small ring for passing through the lobe midway along the diameter. It is embellished with several concentric semi-circles of the same or different width separated by series of circles or alternate bands of circles and tracery, or a regular network in mock-filigree that makes the earring look like a piece of lace. The diameter of the semi-circle is frequently adorned with birds or reptiles. Earrings with anthropomorphic or zoomorphic designs are rarer and at the same time artistically more valid because of the stylization and modeling of the figures and the technical perfection of their execution.

There are gold statuettes that have an ear ornament in the shape of a filigree spiral inserted through holes pierced a short distance apart in the pavilion. The spiral may have ten or more coils, and the pavilion had to be pierced the same number of times to accommodate them.

Another ornament was the *bezote* worn on the lower lip, which had to be pierced for the purpose; sometimes the jewel incorporated a curved lamella that could be hooked on to the lip. The hook broadened on the outside to form a plaque to which a series of long cylinders in sheet metal were attached with little rings or hooks. Other articles of jewelry shaped like spools and still others with zoomorphic heads and hanging tongues are believed to have performed the same decorative function. They may have been worn by inserting an oval aperture in the lower lip.

The ornaments that most tested the skill and imagination of the Pre-Columbian goldsmiths were pendants and pectorals. As a rule the pendants hung from the neck or formed the central part of a necklace, for the reverse is nearly always flat and has a loop for the thread. Except for the large circular pectorals in the Invasionist style, the patterns are seldom edged and nearly always involve anthropomorphic or zoomorphic subjects, or both. The design is executed mostly on the base-plate and marked with low reliefs, fretwork, superposed contoured planes, filigree, and other features. The human or animal head – generally a bird's – the hands, claws or paws, or such accessories as a staff, a headdress or the like stand out in bold relief. These shapes, cast as a rule by the *cire-perdue* process, very often have a row of little rings from which small discs or half cylinders hang. From the stylistic viewpoint, the human and animal figures may display a realistic sculptural aspect, as in the Quimbaya style, but more often the dominant note is an ornamentalism characterized, even in the secondary details, by a clever and highly developed synthesis involving interpretations of quite amazing originality. In other cases the figures are rendered with such essential schematic linearity that they call to mind the modes of expression used by the naïve artists of our own day.

The composition of the necklaces is varied in the extreme. The commonest are made up of spherical, cylindrical, biconical, and annular elements, either all of the same type or combined in different ways. Many, however, are composed of masks, anthropomorphic figures, insects, frogs sketchily or realistically modeled, uniform in size or with a larger one in the middle. Typical of the style are necklaces consisting of elements shaped like the claws of a bird of prey.

The repertory of precious ornaments is brought to a close by crowns and armlets in sheet gold, either plain or decorated solely around the edges. They vary in width and were fastened with laces strung through holes provided for that purpose at the nape of the neck or the inside of the arm.

Pieces of jewelery used by the living were placed in their tombs when they died. But some articles were made specially for funerary use and the gold helmets and masks found in the burial chambers are believed to belong to this type. Some of the helmets are adorned with linear geometric patterns in relief; others have two embossed naked human figures, one at each side, with heads cast by the *cire-perdue* process. A gold mask famous for its exceptionally fine modeling is preserved in the British Museum.

Traveling northward from the strip of land that joins the two American continents, we find that jewelry and goldwork grows steadily rarer until it disappears almost entirely in northern Mexico. The Mesoamerican cultures, so rich in monuments, sculptures, paintings, and pottery, were extremely poor in gold, with the result that artistic achievements in that metal are very rare indeed. Sculptures in clay, with many details in color, can be used as sources of information concerning the personal ornaments worn in that area. Two figures in costume representing a man and a woman (Museum of the American Indian, New York) have the *nariguera,* which was common in Middle America but was certainly imported from the Isthmus region; they have equally ornate earrings. The Olmec mask carved in wood from the Cañon de la Mesa (American Museum of Natural History, New York) and, less clearly, other masks and sculptures, prove that the Pre-Columbian inhabitants of Mexico used to bore a hole in the ear lobe, sometimes of considerable diameter, for the purpose of inserting an ornament in stone, jade, coral, or shell, shaped like a disc or a hollow cylinder flared in front like a trumpet, or a series of rings attached to a disc with a concave groove in the thickness of its rim to keep it firmly fixed in the cartilage. There are clay figures that wear earrings of this type with seven hanging rings. A female figure also has bracelets on the upper arms in the shape of a band to which are applied a series of discs made of jade.

The necklaces were made up of elements in the same materials, mostly spherical and of considerable size. Pottery beads with finely modeled heads, symbols, and attributes were also used. Other ornaments made of fretted shell, flint or obsidian in the shape of stars, wheels, or stylized flowers were probably sewn on garments.

A type of ornament that reveals a high level of artistry was particularly common among the Maya. It is a pendant in jade or jadeite very finely carved with figures of deities. The carving was done in such a way as to make the most of the irregular shape of the mineral. Many of these jades are preserved in the Museum of the American Indian in New York.

Toward the end of the first millennium the State of Oaxaca in southern Mexico saw the rise of the post-classical Mixtec culture on the substratum of the Zapotec culture. In Mexico that period was marked by the practically unique and isolated appearance of some extremely interesting goldwork. The pieces of jewelry in gold, silver, and copper that constitute the major products of the Mixtec culture are viewed as among the most perfect and refined achievements of that ancient region. The repertory of gold jewelry comprises necklaces, bracelets, rings, *narigueras,* anklets, and the like – all worked with the methods employed in the Colombian area, which is not far distant.

The rise and development of this isolated phenomenon in the vast panorama of the ancient Mesoamerican civilizations has been explained possibly by the immigration of groups of goldsmiths from Colombia or the southern part of the Isthmus and by the economic position of the Mixtecs, which enabled them to import the metal not only overland but also by the more rapid sea route. The presence in Mexico at that late date of pieces of jewelry of such highly developed technical workmanship and artistic design tends to confirm the hypothesis that the workshops that produced them were set up by very experienced foreign craftsmen. And in fact some Mixtec jewels dating from the thirteenth to the fifteenth century display characteristics that clearly reveal the Colombian stylistic influence. One is a necklace in the Museum of the American Indian made up of forty convex elements resembling tortoise shells placed side by side, from each of which hang three pear-shaped pendants. The processes used in their execution are mostly die-embossing and filigree.

The same museum has two specimens that are quite out of the ordinary because the ornamentation is of a type seldom met with in Pre-Columbian America. They are rings of extremely refined, complex workmanship. One, in place of the bezel, has a mask with massive headdress and two huge pear-shaped pendants. On another the head of a bird of prey protrudes in high relief from the circlet, which is minutely wrought in mock filigree with a complex interplay of volutes. In these pieces too the inspiration of southern origin is clear to see, but it has led to valid artistic achievements, nontheless.

A truly grandiose work is the pectoral portraying the "God of Death" in the Regional Museum at Oaxaca, which was probably worn in the performance of religious rites. The high level of artistry attained by the Mixtec goldsmiths is evidenced by the expressionistic and plastic naturalism of the gruesome mask and by the rich ornamentation of the headdress. (The Aztecs, whose legendary treasures derived mainly from the spoils of war, made great use of the craftsmen among the conquered populations.)

In the jewelry produced by all the cultures in that vast area during the Pre-Columbian era the predominant ornamental motifs were anthropomorphic or zoomorphic representations, whereas the use of geometric motifs, volutes, and stylized feathers was only marginal. Jewelry probably served a purely magical-religious function and had, it seems, only a tenuous connection with the owner's economic potentialities. It was probably bestowed as a sign of social position, in recognition of a specific activity or as a reward for services rendered, and therefore its nature and iconographic ornamentation may well have been linked with the reasons for which it was conferred.

It may be said, by way of conclusion, that in the vast panorama of artistic activities in the Pre-Columbian cultures precious personal ornaments were predominant in the areas where gold was found in the subsoil. The hypothesis that the goldsmith's art originated there and spread subsequently both in the region of the Andes and in Middle America is highly convincing. That art, in its various forms of expression, reflected (and served as a medium for) the propagation of a symbolism that is still only vaguely understood.

Jewelry is an easily transportable commodity, and a great deal may have been exported from its region of origin very shortly after it was made. The fact remains, however, that the pillage carried on by the *guaqueros,* who still continue their criminal activities, has done much to reduce the material available for scholarly investigation.

Headdress worn by a servant of Queen Pu-abi (formerly read Shub-ad) of the ancient Sumerian city of Ur. Early 3rd millennium B.C. From the Great Death Pit, excavated by Sir Leonard Woolley. Below the gold hair-ribbon are wreaths of lapis lazuli beads with gold beech- and willow-leaf pendants, and a multiple wreath of lapis lazuli beads with lapis lazuli discs mounted on gold spacers. From the back of the head rose a tall comb, its points decorated with gold rosettes. Below the ears hung enormous bold crescent-shaped earrings. Around the neck were layers of beads of gold, lapis lazuli, and carnelian. Ur, c. 2500 B.C.

Pair of gold bracelets which belonged to Nemareth, son of Sheshonq I, founder of the 22nd Dynasty. The bracelets bear a representation of the infant sun-god seated on a lotus, and are inlaid with lapis lazuli. The inscription inside the bracelets says that Nemareth's mother was the daughter of a Libyan chief whose name was Patareshnes, meaning "the land rejoices for her." Egyptian, c. 935 B.C. Ht. 4,1 cm.

Gold finger ring with duck motif. Egyptian, 20th Dynasty, Rameses III (?), c. 1200-1100 B.C. Overall Ht. 2.2 cm.

Gold signet ring. Perhaps a rain ceremony is depicted on the face. Mycenaean, 15th century B.C. W. of bezel 5.6 cm.

Pectoral of Se'n-Wosret II. From Lahun. Found by Sir William Petrie, 1914, in the tomb of Princess Sit Hat-Hor-Yunet. The pectoral is of gold, inlaid with lapis lazuli, carnelian, and turquoise. Two falcons with eyes of garnet support the king's emblem whose hieroglyphs read: "[May the god] Horus give millions and hundreds of thousands of years to [the king] Khai-kheper-Re [Sesostris II]." Egyptian, 12th Dynasty, c. 1880 B.C. W. 4.5 cm.

Broad collar necklace of gold inlaid with carnelian, green feldspar, turquoise, and blue and green frit, with falcon terminals with the name of Tuthmosis III inscribed on the reverse side. These elements have been reassembled, and the arrangement is conjectural. Necklaces of this type are known to have been worn as early as the Old Kingdom. Egyptian, 18th Dynasty. From Thebes. W. 23 cm; L. as strung 35 cm.

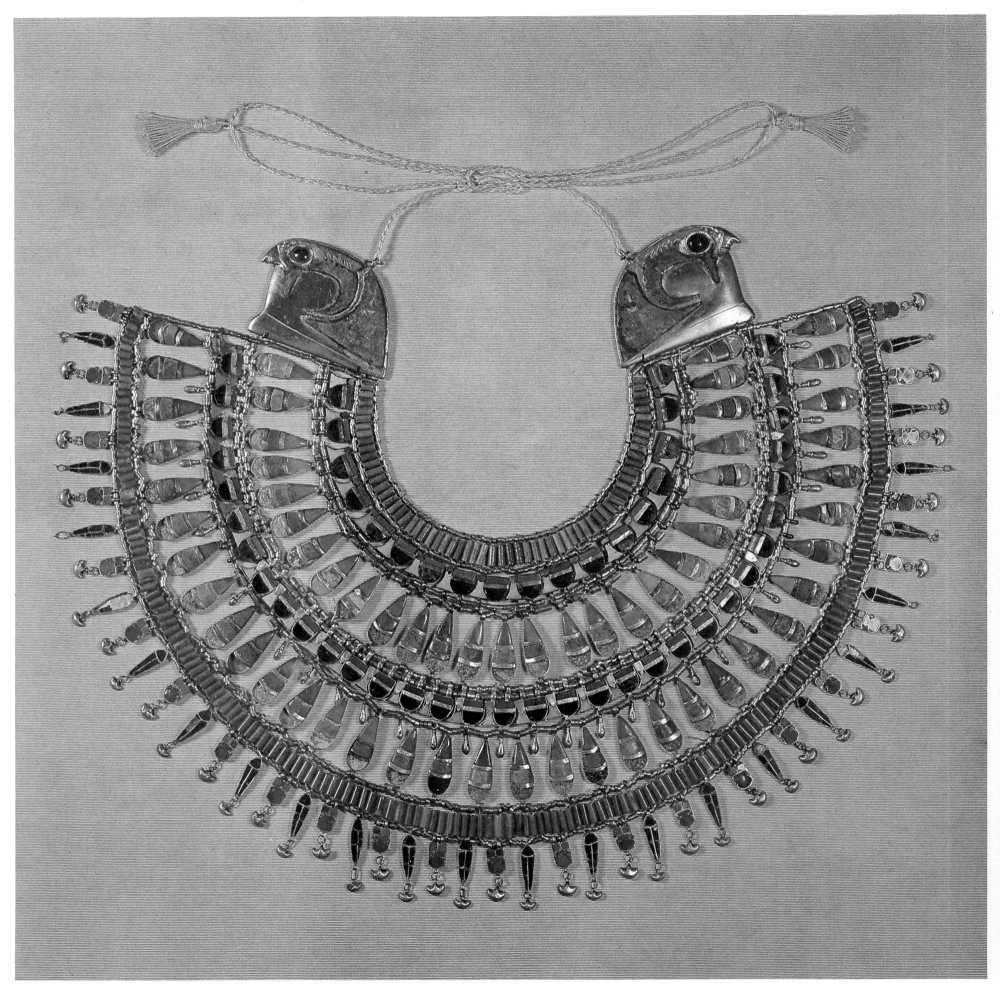

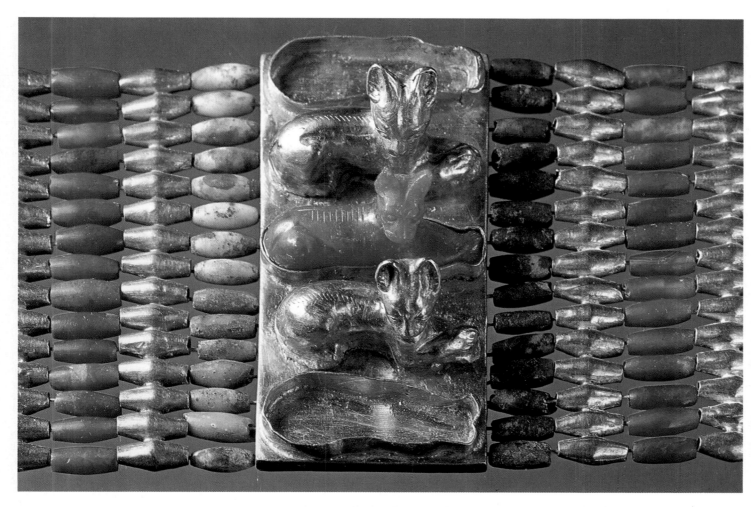

Armlet with cats in gold and carnelian, and beads of turquoise and lapis lazuli. The cats missing from the two empty mounts may have been made of faïence. Cats were very popular as pets in the New Kingdom. The armlet belonged to one of the lesser wives of Tuthmosis III. Egyptian, 18th Dynasty, c. 1450 B.C. From Wadi Gabbanat el Qirud, Thebes. L. approx. 23.5 cm.

Finger ring of blue faïence. This type of signet ring was popular at the end of the New Kingdom and for about a century thereafter. The large cartouche-shaped bezel bears the inscription: "Re and Thoth, Lord of Writing, and Maat, Scribe of the Lesser Ennead [may they] grant a good old age in Karnak to Shemesu." Egyptian, 20th Dynasty, c. 1100 B.C. L. of bezel 6 cm.

A king's ceremonial ring of cast gold. Anatolia, early 2nd millennium B.C. Ht. 4 cm.

Silver bracelet with serpent motif, one of a group of 21 bracelets from Balamun. Egyptian, Ptolemaic Period, c. 300-200 B.C. Ht. 7 cm.

Gold dress clasp (origin unknown, but acquired by museum with a label inscribed "Armagh"). Irish. Bronze Age. 3.8 cm. x 3.8 cm.

Bracelet of electrum. The heads of the wild beasts on the bracelet are an example of the skill of Persian goldsmiths. Persian, 9th century B.C. Total L. 10 cm.

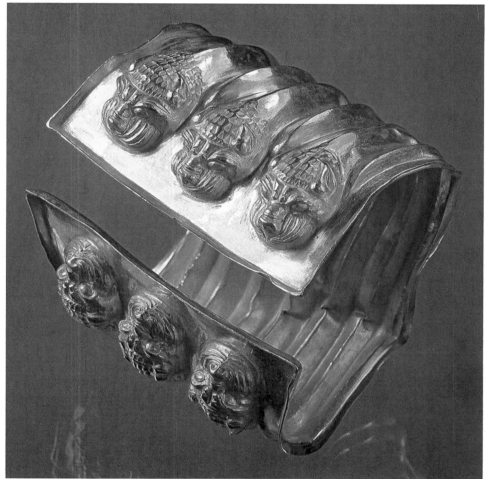

A gold plaque of a lion rending a horse. This ornament, a very fine example of Scythian art, was probably sewn to the clothing of a Scythian chieftain. Among the migrating peoples, the Scythians developed an active metallurgic industry which was highly artistic. The horse, as the nomad's closest companion, appears not only as a decoration, but also as a jewel form in itself. Scythian, 4th–3rd century B.C. 11.5 cm x 16.8 cm.

Gold necklace from the Erstfeld Treasure, Canton Uri, Switzerland. It was found underneath an enormous boulder in 1962; experts believe that a trader from the south was caught in a landslide. This beautiful necklace exerts a special fascination because of the unusual representation of the fabulous hybrid creatures. Note the birds, with their heads turned in the opposite direction to the body. Celtic, 4th century B.C. Diam. 13 cm.

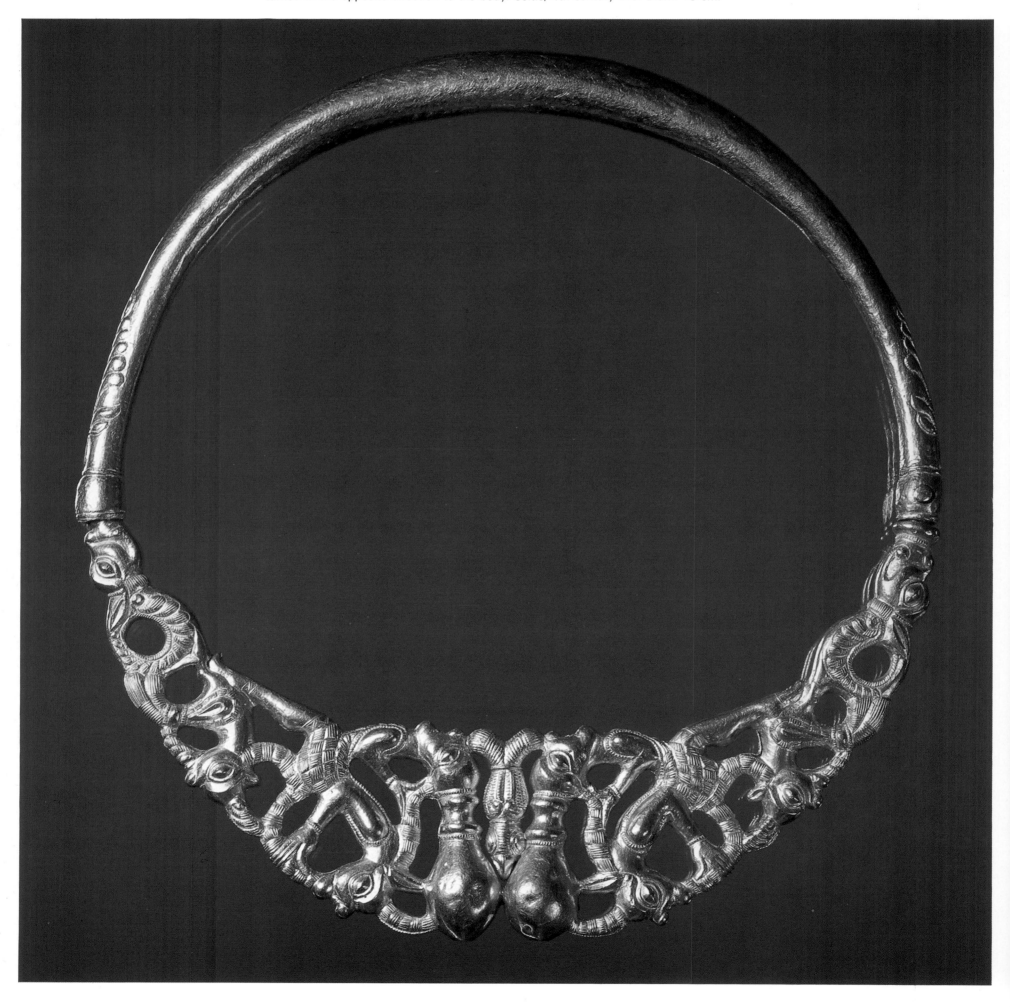

Fibula of gold, silver, and enamel—inscribed with the name of Uffila—found at Wittislingen on the Danube. Barbarian 7th century A.D. L. 17 cm.

Polychrome S-shaped fibula in gold, set with precious stones in cloisonné. The striking feature of such inlaid jewelry at its best is the highly sophisticated geometric and abstract designs created by the gold lines of the cloisons between the colored stones. The S-shaped fibulas found in northern Italy date both from before and after the Longobard invasion of 568 and appear in various forms. A fantastic bird motif is seen in this example. Merovingian, 7th century A.D. Ht. 4.5 cm.

This stylized gold alpaca or llama from Bolivia is a rare example of Tiahuanaco gold. Unfortunately, very few Bolivian gold objects have eluded treasure hunters. This ornament may have been sewn to clothing or suspended from a cord. Bolivia, Lake Titicaca. L. 9.7 cm.

Shoulder clasps from the Sutton Hoo ship-burial. The inlay on the clasps, as on the other gold jewelry from Sutton Hoo, consists of garnets and millefiori glass, set in "cold" (the checkered inlays). The intertwining animals which form the border to the central plaque are also inlaid with garnets in a "false-cell" technique; the stones are set in fairly large cloisons, and gold has then been laid over the top of the stones. Anglo-Saxon, 7th century A.D. L. approx. 12.8 cm. W. approx. 5.4 cm.

A gold disc with a repeated design of filigree-work, showing Byzantine influence. Barbarian, 7th century A.D. Diam. 4 cm.

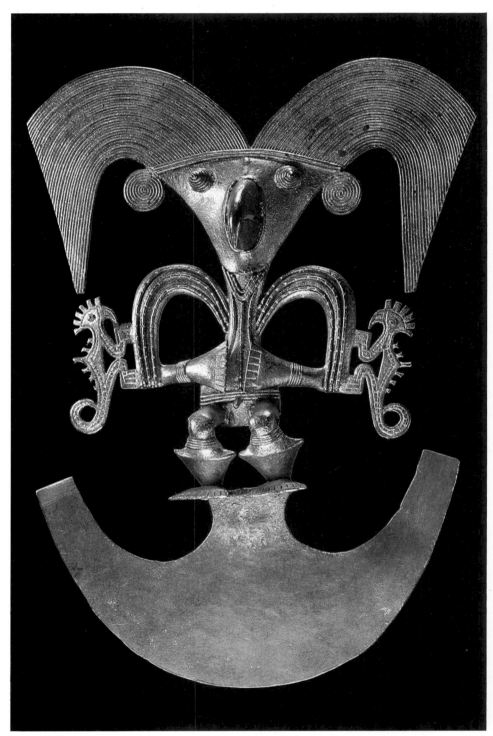

Gold pendant, Veraguas style. The strange figures most likely symbolize a magical context. Note the decorative harmony of the whole composition. Panama. Ht. 8.4 cm.

Gold pendant, Quimbaya style. The Quimbayas produced a very rich collection of gold ornaments, executed with refinement and imagination. Colombia. Ht. 16.5 cm.

Necklace, Tairona style, composed of 25 gold talons with colored stones set between the gold and also forming an outer ring. Colombia. Diam. 40 cm.

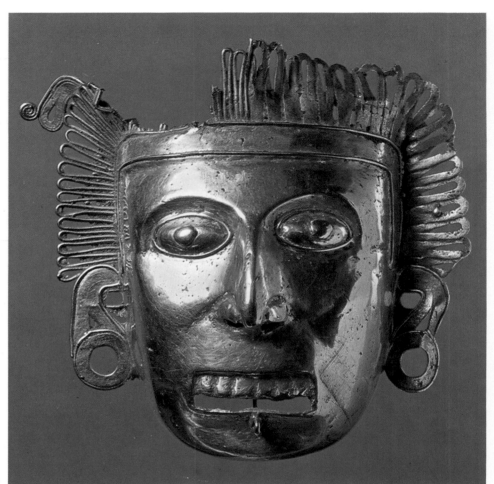

Jade pendant. In the Mayan region of middle America, where gold is rare, most precious ornaments were made of jade. The jade or jadite pendants were finely carved, often with figures of deities, utilizing the irregular shape of the stone. Mayan. Ht. 8.6 cm.

Gold mask, Zapotec style. In ancient Mexico, the use of masks had several purposes, most of them ritualistic or magical. This golden mask probably belonged to a tiny statue of a god, and is typical of the local handicrafts. Mexico, from Monte Alban. Overall Ht. 9 cm.

Gold staff-head, Sinú style. The techniques used to produce this bird, so distorted in its proportions and stylized in its details, consist of the lost-wax process, filigree-work, soldering, and hammering. Colombia. Total Ht. 14.5 cm.

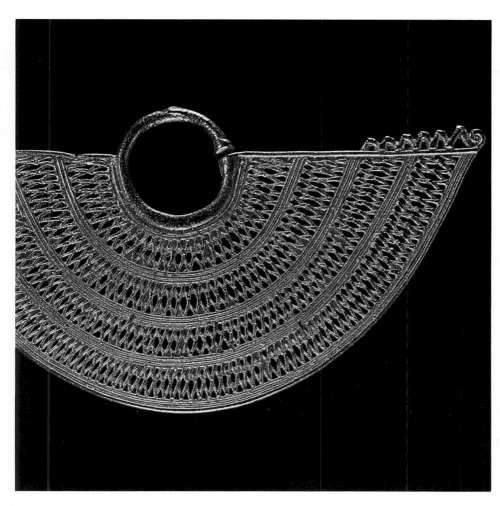

Gold earring, Sinú style. The woven effect on the semi-circular face of this earring is called "mock filigree," because the result is obtained by fusing the gold threads instead of by interweaving them. Colombia. W. 8.1 cm.

Although this Sinu-style jewel seems to resemble a nasal ornament, it is in fact an earring. Similar examples have been found, always in pairs, with many significant variations in size and form. Colombia. W. 8.1 cm.

Pendant of a crocodile with four "danglers" on its back. Cast gold. Diquis Delta, Costa Rica, c. 600-1540. L. 10.5 cm.

Plaque of silver and gold inlay with a design of birds and fishes. The very unusual inlay work should be noted. It is gold inlaid with silver and reversed. Late period, Peru, c. 800-1532. W. 7.9 cm.; L. 18 cm.

Gold necklace, Chimu style. Chimú necklaces are often composed of embossed heads of deities, or masks, interspersed with gold beads and other decorative elements. Some ceramic necklaces have been found. Lambayeque, Peru. 12th century. L. 30.6 cm.

Gold burial mask, late Chimu style. Burial masks were made of wood, pottery, copper, silver, or occasionally of gold. Styles and forms vary by period and area. This one probably represents a deity or a mythological figure being. Peru. Ht. 41.3 cm.; W. 75.1 cm.

Nose pendant, Chimu style. This unusual nose pendant, the so-called *nariguera*, of burnished silver with gold condors, was found in one of the royal tombs in the Lambayeque Valley, Peru, which have yielded quantities of gold and silver objects.

Gold lip plug, or *bezote*. The ornament was worn on the lower lip which had been pierced for this purpose. A fine example of man's instinctive need to decorate himself, the *bezote* was worn purely for reasons of adornment. Mixtec, c. 1300.

Pair of ear ornaments of cast gold. Each is a monster head wearing pendant ear ornaments. Three pendant bells are attached to a rectangle which dangles from the chin. Mixtec-Puebla, Mexico, c. 1200-1521. W. 2.3 cm. L. 6.1 cm.

Double-headed serpent, perhaps worn as a pectoral. The symbol of the double-headed serpent is common in Mexican art; probably it represented the sky. This example could have been worn as a pectoral, as the loops forming the body allow for suspension. The object is carved out of wood and is covered with a turquoise mosaic. The gums and nostrils are picked out in red shell; the teeth are of white shell. Mixtec, c. 1400-1500. L. 43.5 cm.

Helmet, wood with mosaic decoration. Helmets of wood, some gilded, some decorated with mosaic-work, are mentioned in the inventory of treasures that were sent back to Europe at the time of the conquest of Mexico. The mosaic-work is of malachite, red shell, turquoise, and pearl shell. The inside of the helmet is painted green, and there are traces of red pigment on the outer surface. Mixtec, c. 1400-1500. W. 20.3 cm.

Mask, wood with turquoise. This mask is one of the most beautiful and best preserved examples of Mexican turquoise to have survived. It is executed entirely in turquoise, over a cedar-wood matrix, with inset eyes and teeth of white shell. It is usually thought to represent Quetzalcoatl, the god of learning and priesthood; it has also been suggested that it portrays the sun-god, Tonatiuh. At certain festivals and upon the death of a king masks were placed over the faces of effigies of the gods and upon the dead dressed for burial. The holes in the eyes of this mask suggest that it was, in fact, to be worn, probably by the priests during ceremonies devoted to the god. Mixtec, c. 1400-1500. W. 20 cm.

DEVELOPMENT OF STYLES AND FORMS

REYNOLD A. HIGGINS AND
HUGH TAIT CURATORS, BRITISH MUSEUM, LONDON

Ancient jewelry was almost exclusively made of gold and consequently its history is very much the history of the goldsmith's art. The oldest examples are to be sought in ancient Babylonia (modern Iraq). Here, before the Second World War, at the site of the biblical Ur of the Chaldees, Sir Leonard Woolley excavated some fantastically rich royal graves, dating from about 2600 B.C. With the dead was buried jewelry of incredibly high quality for such an early date: hair ornaments of sheet gold cut in the shape of flowers; crescent earrings; finger rings inlaid with lapis lazuli; complicated gold chains; and beads of gold, carnelian, lapis lazuli, and agate. Here too we find the earliest recorded use of two techniques that were to flourish throughout antiquity: filigree and granulation. In the former process, the surface is enriched with patterns made by fine wire, soldered on; in the latter, minute grains of gold are applied in place of wire. Filigree survived as a method of decoration in an unbroken tradition down to our own day. Granulation, however, virtually died out about 1000 A.D., because it could not be done properly by normal hard-soldering methods; this ancient method was revived only just before the Second World War.

From Babylonia the goldsmith's art spread widely, taking root and flourishing in the lands later known as Syria and Phoenicia, and in northwest Turkey on the site of Homer's Troy. Here Heinrich Schliemann uncovered several rich treasures of gold jewelry, which he associated at first with the legendary heroes of the Trojan War. We now know, however, that these treasures, produced between 2500 and 2300 B.C., preceded the Trojan War by at least a thousand years.

This Trojan jewelry was still principally composed of sheet gold, lavishly enriched with filigree and with granulation of much finer quality than was used at Ur a few centuries earlier. The repertoire was amazingly varied. We find complicated diadems made of chains and sheet gold; basket-shaped earrings decorated with attached rosettes or with superfine granulation; hundreds of different kinds of beads; and dress pins with fantastic heads composed of animals or groups of sacred vases.

Not long after these Trojan masterpieces were produced, we find similar, if less elaborate, work in the Cycladic islands, in southern Greece, and above all in Crete, the home of the celebrated Minoan culture, rediscovered and named by Sir Arthur Evans.

A cemetery on the island of Mochlos, off the northeast coast of Crete, yielded the first jewelry that may be considered worthy of the name from this part of the world: diadems embossed with rather naïve patterns; rather more sophisticated pins in the form of flowers for decorating the hair; exquisite chains of astonishing complexity; and beads not only of embossed gold, but also − to provide a dash of color contrast − of steatite, carnelian, amethyst, and rock crystal.

There must have been a continuous development, with constant technical improvements, in Crete, but the thread is tenuous and we do not really pick it up again until about 1700 B.C., when there is suddenly a wealth of material. First, there is the pendant from a royal tomb at Malia in Crete in the form of two bees posed heraldically over a honeycomb. Above their heads is a cage containing a gold bead, and from the lower edge of the pendant hang three discs, probably representing the sun. Seldom have filigree, granulation, and repoussé work – in which the design is hammered into the metal from the back – been combined with such fine effect.

Another pendant, now in the British Museum, is part of a gold treasure said to have come from the island of Aegina. However, to judge from appearances, the treasure is all Cretan work, made between 1700 and 1600 B.C. and in fact may well have been found in the same tomb as the bee-pendant. A river god stands holding a water bird in either hand; at his feet are water lilies. He wears the Cretan costume of a tight-belted loin-cloth, and a tall headdress. The influence of Egyptian art is strong, but the costume and the liveliness of the figure are typically Cretan.

The Minoan culture of Crete was transplanted around 1600 B.C. to the Greek mainland, and especially to Mycenae, the site famous in legend. The Mycenaeans were not Cretans, but their way of life was deeply influenced by Crete, and they seem to have taken over the luxury arts, such as jewelry, of which they had no previous experience, in a thorough-going way.

During the sixteenth and fifteenth centuries B.C., the two cultures co-existed. After the fall of Knossos about 1400 B.C., Mycenaean supremacy succeeded Minoan, but for the next hundred years Mycenaean art was really the logical continuation of Minoan art, to which it bore much the same relationship as Roman art was fifteen hundred years later to bear to the classicism of Greek art.

A silver pin with a gold head comes from one of the shaft graves at Mycenae excavated by Schliemann in 1876, and is dated about 1550 B.C. The pinhead hangs from the top of the pin and takes the form of a Minoan goddess holding a garland in her hand; on her head is an elaborate head-dress with three plumes reaching almost to her feet on either side. She wears the attractive Minoan costume of long skirt and low-cut bodice that leaves the bust exposed.

Later, from 1450 to 1200 B.C., the typical Mycenaean form of jewelry is the relief bead, a calligraphic simplification of Minoan studies of marine and plant life and cult objects. These sophisticated ornaments were worn strung together around the forehead or neck. To add to their charm, they were sometimes enlivened with touches of enamel and granulation. The other Mycenaean specialty was the gold signet ring, in which religious scenes, often of great complexity, were engraved or stamped on the bezel.

Between 1100 and 850 B.C. very little jewelry was made in the Greek lands, for Greece was in the throes of a dark age. The glories of Crete and Mycenae were over and the splendors of Classical Greece were yet to come. All the sophisticated arts such as filigree, granulation, enameling, inlaying, and repoussé work were completely forgotten and contemporary ladies, if they wore any jewelry at all, had to be content with trinkets of gold foil or twisted wires.

Then, around the year 850 B.C., Phoenician craftsmen settled in Greece and reintroduced such luxury arts as ivory-working and goldsmithing. The same techniques as before were used, but the style was different: from Oriental beginnings, jewelry now took on a specifically Greek aspect, comparable with the painting and sculpture of the day.

In the seventh century B.C. the islands were particularly rich in jewelry. A specialty of Rhodes were sets of decorated rectangular plaques worn across the breast. They were embossed with figures from mythology – a winged nature-goddess, a bee-goddess, a sphinx, a griffin, or a centaur – and the finest examples were richly decorated with gorgeous granulation. One such plaque has been calculated to contain no less than 2,600 individual grains of gold.

Closely related to the Rhodian tradition is a class of gold rosettes made on the island of Melos for attachment to diadems of cloth or leather. But this state of affairs was not to last. Around 600 B.C., gold jewelry seems to have almost disappeared from the Greek scene as suddenly as it had appeared. Supplies of gold were no longer available, as they were monopolized no doubt by the rising powers of Lydia and Persia, and the Greeks had to make do with silver.

There was, however, one part of the Greek world where gold jewelry continued to be made in the sixth century B.C. – the Greek settlements of southern Italy, which were always very prosperous. In the absence of Greek models to copy, they looked for inspiration to Etruria. A typical product is a long gold fibula terminating in a ram's head and beautifully decorated with opposed triangles of granulation.

To turn now to Etruscan jewelry, we must go back to about 700 B.C. The prosperous rulers of the Etruscan cities of central Italy were in the habit of adorning their womenfolk with a profusion of gold. Since the Etruscans buried their dead with all their finery in strong stone tombs, much of their jewelry has survived for our edification and enjoyment.

As in Greece, the masters of the new craft were Phoenicians. The techniques they introduced were the same in the two civilizations, but the uses to which they were put were different. Granulation was the decorative process *par excellence,* and the Etruscans explored its possibilities further than the Greeks did. Not only were the grains arranged in simple patterns, but whole scenes were portrayed in silhouette, or embossed in low relief, and the background filled in with granulation. Filigree was used sparingly at first, but on occasion was used in openwork patterns without a background. In the sixth century, Greek immigrants in Etruria, deprived of work in their own country, introduced more specifically Greek motifs, and developed the arts of enameling and inlaying.

Among the finest examples of Etruscan jewelry are elaborate bracelets with superfine granulation and filigree. Earrings at first took the form of enormous gold discs; later, we find the so-called *a baule* type, a strip of gold bent into a cylindrical form and closed at both ends to form a sort of basket. These earrings were richly – perhaps too richly – decorated with patterns in filigree and enamel and with minute gold berries and flowers.

Fibulae for pinning garments together played a much greater part in Etruria than in Greece, and their ornamentation was carried to amazing lengths. One of the finest comes from Vulci. Its basic form is completely encrusted with figures in the round – sphinxes, lions, lions' heads, horses' heads – and everything is covered in the finest possible granulation. To a Greek, such opulence would have been regarded as bad taste, but the craftsman's virtuosity is breath-taking.

To return to Greece proper, the seventh-century tradition continued in areas unaffected by Etruria. In the sixth century many Greek craftsmen emigrated and found work with rich foreign peoples such as the Etruscans, the Celts in the far west, the Thracians to the north, and the Scythians on the shores of the Black Sea. And so, when the Persians were finally defeated and gold was again available (450 B.C.), gold jewelry was once more seen in Greece. The forms were essentially the same as before, but filigree replaced the more laborious granulation, and the popularity of enameling was revived.

During the century and a quarter between the final Persian defeat and the conquests of Alexander the Great (died 323 B.C.) some of the finest jewelry of all times was produced. This jewelry was treated as a sort of miniature sculpture, and subsidiary decoration served only to emphasize the sculptural effect.

Necklaces were not common in this period, but those that have survived are very fine. One of the best comes from Tarentum, a prosperous Greek colony in southern Italy on the site of modern Taranto, where it was made about 380 B.C. It is composed of interlocking rosettes and other ornaments, from which are suspended flower buds and women's heads. The subtle modeling and elaborate filigree decoration are designed to emphasize the play of light and shade on the surface of the gold.

Another masterpiece of this period is a pair of earrings of about 420 B.C. from Eretria in Euboea. From a large enameled rosette hangs a boat-shaped piece decorated with lace-like filigree patterns and with two miniature versions of the principal rosette. A tiny figure of a siren (a human-headed bird) sits on it, and from it dangle cockle-shell pendants on chains. It says much for the goldsmith that the mass of exquisite detail in no way obscures the lines of this perfect jewel.

The conquests of Alexander the Great between 333 and 323 B.C. altered every aspect of Greek life, and jewelry was no exception. The new age came to be known as the Hellenistic period. Thanks to the capture of Persian treasure and the exploitation of new gold mines, jewelry was worn far more extensively than before. No longer an upper-class phenomenon, it spread to the prosperous middle classes. Contacts with Egypt and western Asia created a taste for enriching the gold with brightly colored stones and glass, and with an increased use of enamel. Many stones were used for inlay: rock crystal, amethyst, carnelian, chalcedony, pearls, but above all, garnets. Like the Victorians after them, Hellenistic goldsmiths appreciated the mutual enhancement of gold and garnet.

New varieties of jewelry and of motifs were introduced from the East. The magic reef-knot — sacred to Hercules — set with garnets was a popular centerpiece for elaborate diadems of embossed sheet gold or of intricate gold straps. Other diadems were made more simply of sheet gold, with pictorial decoration of relief work and filigree combined.

In the final years of the fourth century B.C. there was a taste for an elaborate gold disc from which hung an inverted pyramid or cone, equally elaborate in its decoration, and figures of Eros or Victory on chains. The pyramids and cones were later replaced by human or animal forms, frequently winged. Another popular type of jewelry consisted of coils with a human or animal head at one end, the coil often being threaded with gaily colored stones or glass.

Hellenistic necklaces may not be so fine as the best examples of the fifth and fourth centuries B.C., but many are nonetheless very good. One of the most popular varieties consisted of a gold strap from which hung, from a network of chains, pendants in the form of spearheads or jars. Joints in the chains are masked by tiny enameled ornaments. Many other kinds of Hellenistic jewelry mitigate the severity of Classical examples by the addition of a little — but not too much — Oriental richness.

The art of the Roman Empire evolved gradually from that of Hellenistic Greece, and in the course of the first four centuries of our era was gradually transformed into the forerunner of the Byzantine style.

At first, Roman jewelry still favored gold, with inlay of precious stones and glass always being subordinated to the principal forms. By the fourth century A.D., however, increasing emphasis was placed on stones for their own sake and (with certain exceptions) less care was taken in the working of the gold in which they were set. This shift of emphasis was so gradual that there is no precise point at which we can say that the Hellenistic tradition ended and the Byzantine began.

Now for the first time the hardest stones were used in addition to those already found in Hellenistic jewelry: sapphires, aquamarines, and above all, emeralds, from the newly discovered Egyptian mines. One form of goldworking, though uncommon, was very popular toward the end of this period. It consisted of chiseling lace-like patterns into the surface of the gold.

On the whole, the Roman goldsmith was less industrious than his Greek predecessor, and preferred the simpler processes. Granulation was virtually abandoned, and filigree used sparingly. Enameling gave way to an almost universal use of inlay. Stones were seldom cut to regular shapes, and emerald crystals were used in their natural hexagonal form.

Earrings were very common among the Romans. The Hellenistic hoop was replaced by a horizontal bar hanging from a stone; from the bar, in turn, hung two or three drop pendants. Bracelets were apt to be fairly substantial. A number have been found at Pompeii (destroyed in 79 A.D.) cast solid in the form of coiled snakes. The finest pieces of Roman jewelry were the finger rings. Massive gold rings were set with one or more brightly colored stones, producing a remarkably modern effect – which, finally, is the impression left by Roman jewelry in general. At last, the Roman goldsmith was able to break away from the classical mode and to move in an entirely new direction.

This brief survey has attempted to cover some three thousand years of development – a spasmodic development at that – for jewelry, being a luxury art, reflects the prosperity, and its absence the poverty, of a particular age. Though there were both lean and prosperous periods, it is fair to say that Minoan, Mycenaean, Greek, and Etruscan jewelry at their best can stand comparison with the art works of any civilization and any age.

*
*　　*

In the sphere of jewelry, the transitional period between Antiquity and the Middle Ages is not marked by any decline, either in technical skill or in inventiveness. New styles and forms evolved as a result of the upheavals experienced by the civilized world which gave rise to a whole series of mutually felt reactions.

As might be expected, there is no clear line of demarcation between Late Roman and Byzantine jewelry following the division of the Empire and the rise of the Byzantine state in the fourth century A.D. The same trend toward a polychromatic style of jewelry – the amassing of large, intensely colored stones (cabochons) such as carnelians, sapphires and garnets with gold of ever-increasing lightness and fragility – is discernible both in the Western and the Eastern Empires. The importance of the Middle East (Sassanid and Achaemenid Persia) as the source for new styles, particularly the polychromatic and the cloisonné styles (in the latter semi-precious stones are cut flat, polished, and laid in cloisons, or small cells, created by soldering thin strips of metal, usually gold, at right angles onto a metal base), has long been recognized. Undoubtedly, Georgia and southern Russia, then inhabited by the Sarmatians, also played a very important role in the elaboration of the polychromatic style. With the commencement of the great barbarian or Hun invasions in 375 A.D., the Goths reached the Black Sea area, taking the art of cloisonné jewelry from east to west as they swept across Europe. Through the agency of other tribes – the Franks in Gaul, the Lombards in Italy, the Visigoths in Spain and the Anglo-Saxons in Britain – this style of jewelry was introduced into every part of western Europe, though, of course, each area developed its own distinctive variants.

The stone most used in this type of jewelry was the garnet: there are over 4,000 individually cut garnets set in the jewelry found at Sutton Hoo (England). The rich red glow of this jewel, often heightened by using patterned gold foil as a backing, contrasts vividly with the occasional cell filled with lapis lazuli, cobalt-blue glass, transparent green glass or – rarest of all – with colored *millefiori* glass. The most striking features of this inlaid jewelry at its best are the highly sophisticated geometric and abstract designs created by the gold lines of the cloisons between the colored stones. Where the latter are not used, an even more extensive reliance upon abstract ornamental patterns, whether engraved or in relief – especially elaborate interlacing, often composed of stylized animal motifs – characterizes much of the jewelry. Indeed, in Viking jewelry it continues for more than 700 years, into the twelfth century.

The pagan custom of burying the dead with the equipment appropriate to their station in life – the weapons of a soldier or the trinkets of a wife – did not cease immediately with the advent of Christianity. By far the greater part of the barbarian jewelry known to us has been recovered from tribal burial grounds and the graves on those sites. The pagan women clearly wore brooches and pins of metal and bone. They also wore earrings, though it is interesting to note that in western Europe, unlike Byzantium, earrings went almost completely out of fashion after the pagan period, remaining in disuse until the Renaissance. Garnet-studded necklaces of gold, sometimes with an attached inlaid pendant, were worn by the rich, while beads of multi-colored glass and semi-precious stones were common among those less well-to-do. Bracelets, so much worn in prehistoric and classical times, were less in favor, perhaps because the long sleeve fastened at the wrist was almost universal. Indeed, in western Europe, the bracelet reappears only in the fifteenth century, though it continued to be popular among the Vikings and in the Byzantine Empire. Finger rings, on the other hand, are frequently found in pagan graves and range from the simple bronze and silver twisted-wire variety (to allow for expansion) to the solid gold version enriched with garnets or niello decoration. Most common of all were the brooches worn on the breast or shoulder to fasten the tunic or cloak, and the belt buckles and other girdle fittings that both sexes of all classes wore.

By the end of the sixth century, Byzantine jewelry reflected almost completely a Christianized empire: the cross, figures of Christ, the Virgin, saints, and peacocks (symbolic of Paradise) became popular motifs that replaced the old pagan repertoire. The classical tradition of cameo carving continued unabated and, in fact, some of the surviving finger rings, brooches, and pendants are set with cameos that now rank among the greatest of Byzantine treasures. The subjects are virtually all religious. Using different alloys, Byzantine craftsmen created red, green, and yellow golds, which they used with great subtlety for setting the variously colored gems. They favored the use of thin gold for a lighter effect, adopting the Roman *opus interrasile* (openwork technique) and developing equal skill with gold filigree and granulation.

The ancient niello technique was used extensively in Constantinople, particularly for wedding rings and for rings bearing the insignia of officials at the imperial court. Even more important, the Byzantine goldsmiths created the art of cloisonné enameling on gold, fusing colored vitreous glazes (enamels) at high temperatures onto the gold within cloisons, the walls of which could be shaped to form the desired outline – be it figures, animals, flowers, or an abstract pattern. In a sense, cloisonné enameling on gold creates the effect of a mosaic in miniature; in the realm of jewelry, the application of cloisonné enameling greatly extended the polychromatic range, which was wholly in keeping with the Byzantine taste for extravagance and sumptuous display.

The wealthy classes, in the manner of the imperial court, dressed in stiff, richly embroidered robes (sewn with pearls, gems, and even enameled gold medallions), over which they wore jewelry that would attract attention from a distance, partly by its violent contrasts of light and color and partly by its sheer size. No longer was it necessary to follow the ancient Greek tradition of fine modeling and perfection of detail in order to create jewelry that the discriminating eye could linger over. Furthermore, there is evidence from several texts that in the streets the rich did not wear their valuable gem-studded gold jewelry, but rather cheap "costume jewelry" made of gilt bronze and set with inferior stones.

In western Europe, Byzantine culture was to become the admired model for the highly aristocratic society of the Ottonian Empire in the years around 1000 A.D. Consequently, jewelry assumed a position of new importance in the episcopal and imperial palaces and monasteries. One of the most outstanding collections of Ottonian jewelry — belonging to Empress Gisela and thought to have been worn at her wedding to Conrad II, which took place (1027) in Rome amid the utmost pomp and splendor – reveals a deliberate copying of Byzantine imperial forms. For example, the great pectoral ornament comprising six tiers of gold chains and antique engraved gems and pearls is directly derived from the Byzantine *maniakion,* or collar with symmetrically arranged jewels. Ottonian jewelry is frequently enriched with fine cloisonné enameling and elaborate filigree decoration, but unlike Byzantine jewelry, in which the plain raised setting or collet was used, Ottonian jewelry frequently employed the device of holding the gem as if it were between claws so that the light might pass completely through it – a technique that endured throughout the Middle Ages.

The airy, almost fragile, Ottonian jewelry gradually gave place to more solid and compact forms from about 1100 onward. Cloisonné enameling died out, and the use of the champlevé technique of enameling was still very limited; otherwise there are no significant developments in jewelry until the thirteenth century. During this period, male and female attire became virtually indistinguishable and the simple cut of the heavy ankle-length woolen clothes – the dress with its long sleeves, the plain tunic over it with its shorter sleeves, and the full-length cloak – provided little scope for the jeweler's artistry. The belt buckle was increasingly ornamented, sometimes richly modeled in high relief with a truly sculptural effect. The brooch, often large and set with pearls, rubies, and sapphires, was the major item of personal adornment, used principally to fasten either the cloak or the slit in the neck of the dress. There was often no catch for the pin of the brooch, since the natural pull of the cloth being pierced would hold it in place against the outer ring of the brooch; these "ring-brooches" remained popular throughout the thirteenth and fourteenth centuries.

Gothic jewelry reflects the principal preoccupation of the culture of the Middle Ages – the concept of chivalry, which had as its focal point the worship of woman. The jewel, as a gift exchanged by lovers, assumed a new and a highly personal significance for the wearer. Finger rings and ring-brooches are frequently enriched with amatory inscriptions and mottoes, praising woman's beauty as a divine gift and acknowledging the quality of pure love. By the end of the thirteenth century, French and Italian gold-smiths were again using enamel to decorate their jewels, but in a totally different way and with a totally different result. The new technique, known as basse-taille enameling, consisted of cutting away a design or figural composition in low relief on a sheet of silver or gold, and flooding the area with colored translucent enamel. Because the highest point of the relief is below the surface of the surrounding metal, the enamel lies in varying thicknesses over the whole area, and because the enamel is translucent not only does the composition of the low relief show through, but the light is reflected back from the silver or gold through the varying thicknesses of the enamel — thereby adding a brilliant tonal quality to the enamels and creating an impression of three-dimensional modeling ranging from the bright highlights of thin enameling to the rich tones of the deep recesses of the engraved relief. Inspired by French and Italian models, this art of translucent enameling reached a very high level in the Rhineland. Medallions, to be worn as pendants or sewn on the dress, as well as small reliquaries (designed to be worn around the neck), were enameled in this technique with both secular and religious scenes. Devotional jewels came more and more into fashion during the fourteenth century and before the end of the century most countries in Europe had introduced laws restricting the wearing of jewels, which had now become a clear sign of rank. In England, Edward III's Statute of 1363, while forbidding craftsmen and yeomen (as well as their wives and children) to wear gold or silver jewelry, also denied to knights the right to wear rings and brooches made of gold or studded with precious stones.

In contrast, royalty and the nobility wore more and richer jewelry over finer and more colorful silks, brocades, and costly furs. Elaborate dress and jewels were to remain the marks of privilege until the French Revolution. The divorce of jewelry from its function as part of an overall costume marks the commencement of the story of jewelry as purely fashionable ornament for purposes of extravagant display.

The ever-growing luxury of fourteenth-century European courtly society reached its zenith at the French courts of Charles VI (1380-1422) and of his uncle, Jean, Duc de Berry (d. 1416), though for sheer opulence the Burgundian courts of the Netherlands under Philip the Good (1419-67) and Charles the Bold (1467-77) were unrivaled. In 1454, at a pageant in Lille, the Duke of Burgundy wore jewelry valued at over one million thalers – but Burgundy was by then the wealthiest country in the world and this princely treasury of jewels was also a form of capital to be realized in times of emergency.

Gold and precious stones were now the essential ingredients of the new fantastic fashion. The increased supply and demand for precious stones led to laws forbidding the use of paste gems and false pearls: in 1355, French jewelers were forbidden to use river pearls mixed with Oriental pearls or to put tinted foil under amethysts and carbuncles to enhance their color. The Duc de Berry is known to have broken off important discussions of state affairs with the King (his nephew) in order to receive two Venetian merchants who had just arrived with precious stones for sale. The discovery of an improved method for diamond cutting at about this time and the creation of table-cut diamonds with simple faceting led to a sudden rise in the popularity of the diamond in the fifteenth century. Soon other stones were no longer left as simple polished cabochons. And in this period the skilled stone-cutters of the Netherlands started to lay the foundations of their future eminence in gem cutting.

Quality of craftsmanship and originality of design in the use of gold and precious stones was never more appreciated or encouraged than by these courtly patrons. Great use was made of a new enameling technique known as *émail en ronde bosse,* or encrusted enameling, which in effect consisted of creating a miniature sculpture in gold, either in the round or in very high relief and covering it with layers of differently colored enamel. The brilliant realism of the treatment of the human form in miniature is often combined with a tender lyrical quality that does not outlast the fifteenth century. The new pictorial quality of these brooches and pendants was to open up an entirely fresh approach to this type of jewel, which in the hands of the Renaissance goldsmiths during the sixteenth century was exploited to the full.

The need for necklaces and pendants became imperative as the neckline steadily began to fall during the second half of the fifteenth century – despite the laws that forbade a "display of the neck and shoulders." This trend culminated in the true décolletage of the sixteenth century, when the brooch was almost completely replaced by the pendant. For a brief period, in the Italy of the Renaissance, jewelry ceased to be used as a symbol of rank and became instead a means to enhance the beauty of the female body. The discovery of human beauty and the nude – like the discovery of man as an individual, whose accomplishments and merits were more important than his origins – was made in fifteenth-century Florence and spread through the courts of Ferrara, Mantua, and Urbino to the great cities of Italy. Suddenly, the hair, for so long hidden beneath coifs, wimples, or elaborate headdresses, was left uncovered; whether braided and gathered up to reveal the beauty of the neck or left in flowing tresses, it was entwined with strings of pearls and aigrettes of precious stones, of which the ruby was the most preferred. The gentle curve of the high forehead was stressed by a thin headband with a sparkling gem placed in the center, and the slender column of the neck was set off by a single row of pearls or a necklace with a pendant that emphasized the soft beauty of the breast. Earrings, especially those using pearls, were once more in fashion, and for the first time bracelets reappeared. However, finger rings were worn sparingly – no more than two or three, unlike the Late Gothic fashion that favored several on each finger and even on the thumb. While there was in no sense a rebirth of classical jewelry in the Renaissance except in cameo carving, the repertoire of ornamental motifs (putti, dolphins, satyrs, scroll work, etc.) was entirely different from the Gothic and was derived from the new vocabulary of the Renaissance artists. For men, the wearing of jewelry was even more restrained, but the gold enameled hat medallion became very popular; some portrayed religious subjects, many more depicted scenes from classical mythology. Benvenuto Cellini (1500-71) describes, in his technical *Treatise,* with what painstaking skills he modeled and enameled these miniature sculptural scenes in high relief to vie with the creations of his great rival, Caradosso (d. 1527).

The interlude of free harmony between body, dress, and ornament during the early Renaissance was soon to be replaced for both sexes by an era of unprecedented formal splendor – a style dictated by the Spanish court, grown rich from its possessions in the New World. Bare skin disappears beneath stiff heavy brocades and velvets (mainly of black, purple and deep violet), until only the face and hands remain visible, and even these are constricted within the starched ruffs and high lace collars and cuffs from which pendant jewels hang. The rigid façade of the remote and dignified grandee had to be encrusted with a profusion of pearls and luxurious jewelry indicative of rank. In England, for example, James I (1603-25) was no less bedecked in jewelry than his predecessor, Queen Elizabeth I. Heavy gold enameled chains with table-cut emeralds, pearls, diamonds, and rubies were perhaps the most prominent element in the "Spanish fashion," which prevailed from around 1540 to 1630.

The greatest scope for creativity lay in the massive pictorial pendants – those little miracles of inventive skill – that not only hung from the chains but were also fastened to the dress and pinned to the sleeve. Using large irregularly shaped "baroque" pearls as the torso, the goldsmiths would create fabulous creatures (mermaids, tritons, hippocampi, seadragons, etc.) by adding the rest in gold, enameled *en ronde bosse* and studded with gems. This imaginative marriage of natural phenomena with the technical perfection of the goldsmith's art was characteristic of this age of exploration and discovery.

As the Netherlands, and later the France of Louis XIV (1638-1715), replaced the Spanish dominance of Europe in the seventeenth century, so all stiffness (including the iron hoops and hip-pads) disappeared in favor of the deep décolletage and soft flowing draperies adorned with relatively few jewels – usually a parure (a matching set comprising a necklace, earrings, pendants, bracelets, etc.) or ropes of pearls. In this century, the jeweler became quite distinct from the goldsmith and the diamond was acknowledged as the finest stone. The riches of the newly discovered diamond deposits in India, at Golconda and in Hyderabad, were brought to Europe by the Dutch trading companies. Parures became fashionable; the designs were increasingly naturalistic, with a marked preference for flowers and a total rejection of figural subjects. For men, the finger ring was only sparingly worn, but buttons – especially rose-cut diamond buttons – were the great luxury. Louis XIV is said to have had as many as 1,824 diamonds on one waistcoat.

By the beginning of the eighteenth century, the formal Baroque dress became lighter and more flimsy as the Rococo style developed; less and less jewelry was worn, except in the evenings, when it was exclusively an adornment of the ladies. Aigrettes, the parure, and the Sévigné brooch (worn on the bodice) were all set with diamonds, since colored stones were completely out of fashion by 1720. The Brazilian diamond mines yielded vast quantities from about 1725 and the new techniques of cutting resulted in the brilliant, which radiates with a thousand reflections. Instead of gold, silver was used for the setting in order not to compete with the diamond; enameling was hardly ever used now. The *pavé* setting enabled the jeweler to achieve a dense massing of diamonds so that only the ensemble – rather than the individual diamond – dazzled with its endless glitter. For men, the jewels of the insignia of orders and societies were the only real complement to the ladies' flower-sprays of diamonds (and, after the middle of the century, of colored stones), though their shoe buckles were generously studded with diamonds.

Toward the end of the eighteenth century, jewels of semi-precious stones were as much owned by the rich for use in the daytime as by the middle classes, perhaps reflecting changes in fashion more rapidly than the diamond parures of the ladies at court, which were designed to be seen by candlelight. Memorial jewelry (plaited hair, funeral motifs, the use of jet and Berlin ironwork) had a long life: Queen Victoria even had a bracelet set with the first teeth of all her children. Romanticism also influenced nineteenth-century jewelry – the mock Gothicism of Fromet Meurice's *style cathédrale* in France was rivaled by that of Pugin in England. Again, a conscious revival of Scottish and Celtic jewels in England was paralleled by a wave of Neoclassicism in France soon after the middle of the century. Design was eclectic, ranging from "Etruscan" to "Renaissance" and from "Egyptian" to "Louis XVI." Only with Lalique and the Art Nouveau style at the end of the nineteenth century was originality reintroduced into jewelry.

Detail of the dazzling gold headdress worn by an attendant of Queen Pu-abi (formerly read Queen Shub-ad) of Ur (in ancient Sumer). From the "Great Death Pit," which was excavated by Sir Leonard Woolley. Ur, c. 2500 B.C.

Gold earring (of hoops of wire with subsidiary spirals) from Shaft Grave III, Mycenae. 16th century B.C. Ht. 3.6 cm.

Gold finger ring of penannular form from a pre-Etruscan (Villanovan) culture. Found in Vulci, Italy, c. 800 B.C. Diam. 2.2 cm.

Pale gold rosette with six rounded petals, each outlined with twisted wire. Eastern Greek, 7th century B.C. Diam. 4.3 cm.

Gold earring of the so-called a baule type, richly decorated with patterns in filigree. Etruscan, 6th century B.C. W. 2 cm.

Gold earring with granulation. Originally inlaid, probably with amber or rock crystal. Greek, c. 8th century B.C. Diam 3 cm.

Gold ornament in the form of a griffin's head with open mouth and protruding tongue. Greek, 7th century B.C. Ht. 2.5 cm.

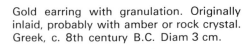

Satyr's head pendant decorated with granulation. From Cerveteri, Italy. Etruscan, c. 5th century B.C. Ht. of pendant: 3.6 cm.

Gold finger ring in the form of a snake. This was a very popular design. Roman, 1st century A.D. Diam. 2 cm.

Gold finger ring with two clasped hands, a portrait of Marcus Aurelius and Faustina. Roman 2nd century A.D. Diam. 1.8 cm.

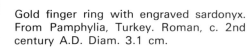

Gold finger ring with engraved sardonyx. From Pamphylia, Turkey. Roman, c. 2nd century A.D. Diam. 3.1 cm.

Gold finger ring with a large scarab, with figure of a woman on the reverse. Greek, 4th century B.C. W. of scarab: 2 cm.

Gold bull's head which was once an ornament on a necklace. In order to show the granulation, the object has been magnified approximately seven times life size. From Thessaly. 6th/5th century B.C. Ht. 3.5 cm.

Gold mask of a Mycenaean King from the Vth Royal Tomb on the Acropolis of Mycenae. Discovered in 1876 by Schliemann. Mycenae is supposed to be the legendary residence and burial place of Agamemnon. Whether or not the mask covered the face of Agamemnon (as Schliemann believed) it shows the face of a warlike king. Mycenae, 16th century B.C. Ht. 26 cm.

Gold hairpin in the shape of a flower. Early
Minoan, c. 2200-2000 B.C. Perhaps from
Mochlos. Diam. 3 cm.

Detail of a diadem from Melos with a Hercules Knot. Greek, c. 3rd or 2nd century
B.C. Total length: 27.9 cm.

156

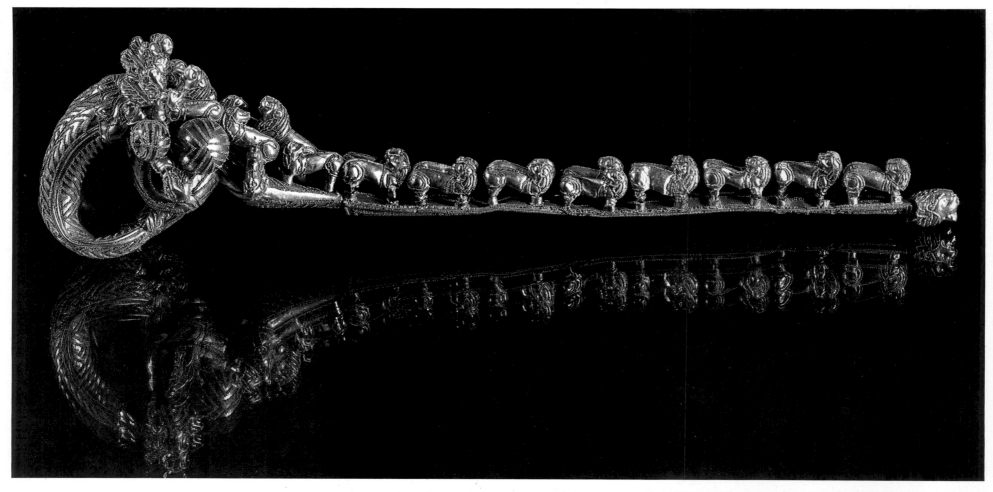

Gold votive fibula brooch with serpentine bow. This fine fibula, or safety pin, was found in a tomb in Vulci. Its basic form is completely encrusted with figures of animals in the round, and everything is covered with very fine granulation. Etruscan, 7th century B.C. Length: 18.6 cm.

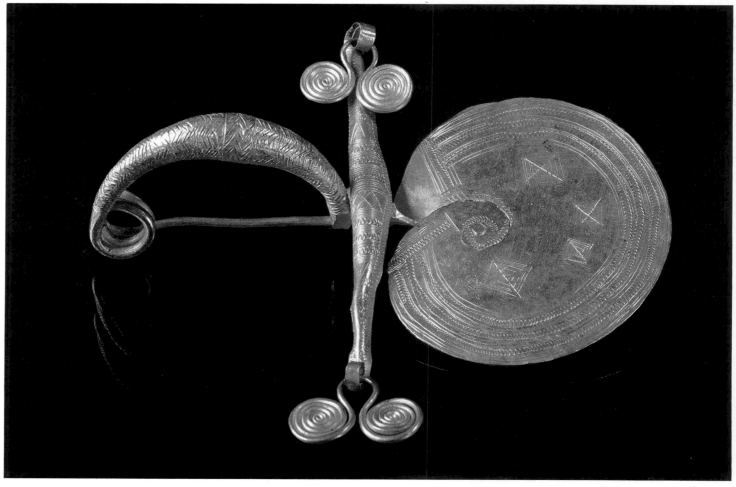

Gold fibula. The bow is of the "leech" type, decorated with incised chevrons and zigzags. There is a cross-bar similarly decorated with zigzags and lines, while from either end are suspended double spirals in wire. The sheath is a large flat plate curving spiralwise from the cross-bar. Its upper surface is decorated with zigzag lines within plain lines and inside are four incised groups of "labyrinths." The loop-bow is prolonged until it joins the cross-bar. On this loop rests the pin, which springs from the farther end of the bow, where it is twisted into a double spiral spring. Etruscan, c. 8th-7th century B.C. L. 7.4 cm.

Gold ivy wreath. Although wreaths are mentioned in accounts of the 5th and 4th centuries B.C. from the Parthenon, surviving examples are few. They were made of gold, silver, bronze or wood covered with gold leaf, and they closely resemble wreaths made of actual leaves. In the Roman army, wreaths were the highest military decorations, awarded exclusively to victorious generals and to those who had saved the life of a Roman citizen. Greek, 5th century B.C. W. 29.2 cm.

Gold pendant found in a tomb in the region of Sardis, the ancient capital of Croesus, a king of Lydia in the sixth century B.C., whose name is synonymous with vast wealth. It was most likely worn over the chest and perhaps had some symbolic significance. Lydian, 6th century B.C. Diam. 7.3 cm.

Gold armlet, penannular, the loop almost solid at the back and tubular towards the ends, which are in the form of winged monsters – the hind quarters and legs being represented in relief upon the surface of the hoop. The Treasure of the Oxus, Persian or Elamite, 5th century B.C. Ht. 12.3 cm.

Gold hair ornament with two long pointed projections at the back. The front is a con-cave-convex gold plaque, representing a lion-griffin couchant, embossed and chased, the head alone being completed in the round. The legs are bent without regard for anatomy, but with an ardent feeling for decorative effect; the tail forms two loops and ends in a leaf; while pellets of gold are placed in the ears and at the extremity of the horns. Persian or Elamite, 5th century B.C. Ht. 6.15 cm.

Gold pectoral, or breastplate, of horseshoe ▷ or crescent shape. The pectoral is made of a single sheet of gold, not thicker than three-tenths of a millimeter. It may have been fastened to a tunic by bronze fibulae. The entire surface is decorated with narrow rows of animals and ornaments in low relief; these were embossed by stamping the gold sheet, which was placed over pitch. The gold is very pure. Etruscan, early 6th century B.C. Ht. 33.7 cm.

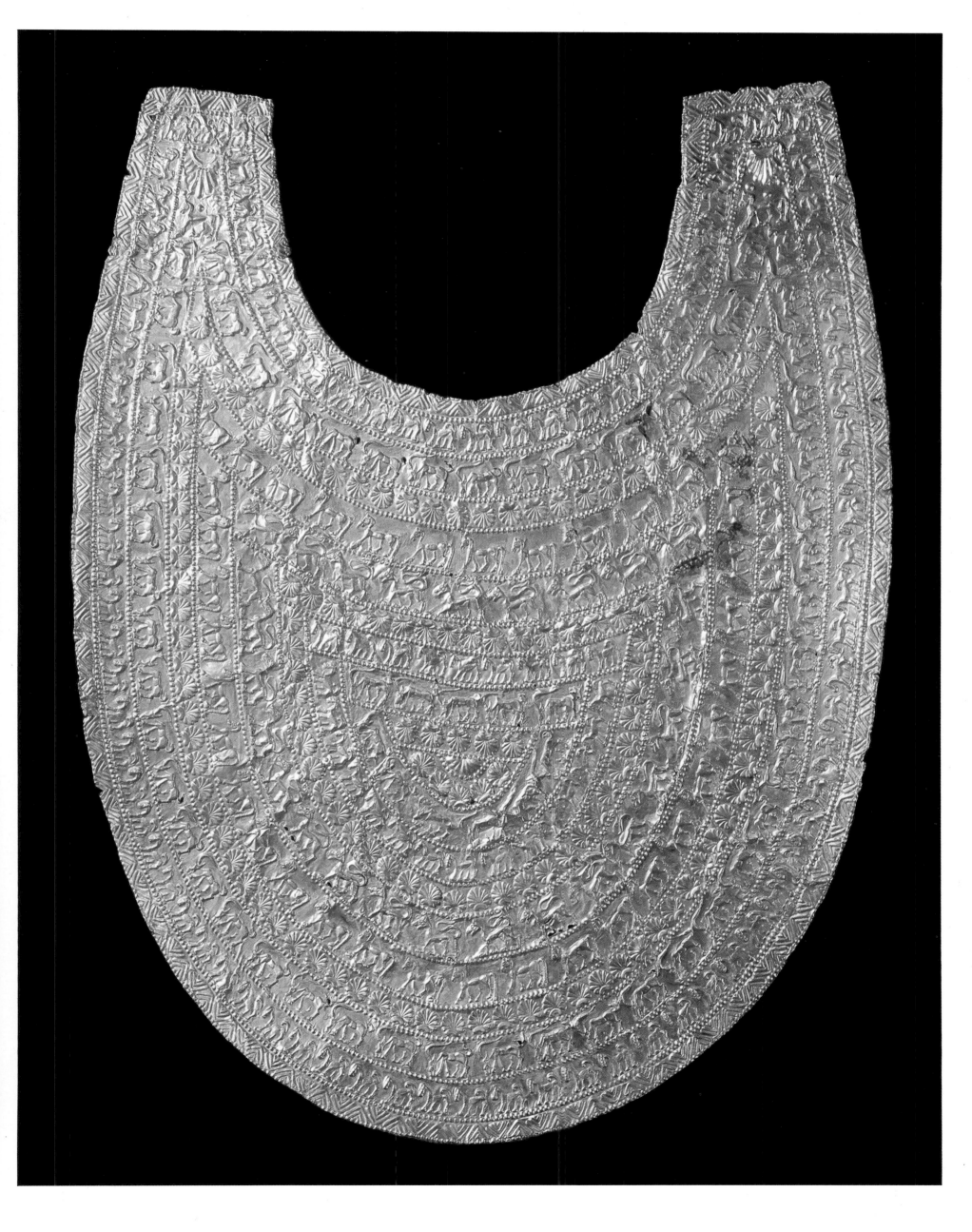

Pair of exquisitely detailed gold earrings. These earrings are one of the masterpieces of this period. Greek. From Eretria in Euboea. About 420 B.C. Ht. 6 cm.

Gold necklace composed of rosettes and other ornaments, with suspended flower-buds and women's heads. Greek from Tarentum, 4th c. 380 B.C. L. 30.6 cm.

Detail of the gold Crown from Armento in Lucania, an ancient district of Italy. This precious ornament is composed of an oak wreath exquisitely decorated with ivy leaves, blossoms and bees. Above the center is the inscription: ΚΡΕΙΘΩΝΙΟΣ ΗΘΗΚΕ ΤΟΕΙ ΣΤΗΦΑΝΟΝ, "Kreithonios consecrated the crown." On top is the Goddess of Victory, Niké, flanked on each side by an elf. She is dressed in a beaded tunic and mantle and wears a wreath topped by a single flower. She holds a flower in her right hand, and in the left, a drinking saucer. Greek-Italian, 4th century B.C. Ht. of Crown: 37 cm. Ht. of Goddess: 10 cm.

Gold serpentine spiral bracelet with Hercules knot. Spiral bracelets, mostly in the form of snakes (usually worn on the arm above the elbow) appeared in the Classical period and enjoyed great popularity during the Roman era. On the famous example shown here the tails of the two serpents form the Hercules knot, which is embellished with a large garnet. According to Pliny the Hercules knot (similar to a reef knot) was treasured by the Greeks and Romans for its power of healing wounds. Greek. From Eretria. 3rd-2nd century B.C. Ht. 12 cm. Ht. 12 cm.

Chalcedony cameo with busts of Diocletian and Maximian Herculius. The cameo, yellowish white to deep orange with flecks of brown, is mounted in a gold frame with three pendant beads and two loops at the top for a chain. An incised inscription, "Diocl Maxim Aug" on a gold plaque inserted below the busts, identifies the two emperors, who ruled jointly; Diocletian (284-305) and Maximian Herculius (286-305). The identification is supported by the resemblance of the busts to portraits in other media, particularly in the case of Diocletian. Roman, end of the 3rd century A.D. W. of cameo: 4.3 cm.

Silver-gilt radiate headed brooch with niello inlay, said to have been found in Tuscany, Italy. Lombardic type, date about 600 A.D. Ht. 16.3 cm.

Eagle fibula of bronze, originally inlaid with stones. Gold inlay around breast shield. Found near Saarbemünd, Germany. Barbarian 6th-7th century A.D. Ht. 9.5 cm.

Gold finger ring with pierced inscription, ACCIPE DVLCIS MVLTIS ANNIS "Accept it, sweet one for many years". Found in Egypt. Italian, 4th century. Total Ht. 2.7 cm.

The Castellani Brooch of gold, enamel, and pearls, and cloisonné work. Found at Canossa, South Italy. Probably Italian, 6th or 7th century A.D. Diam. 6.4 cm.

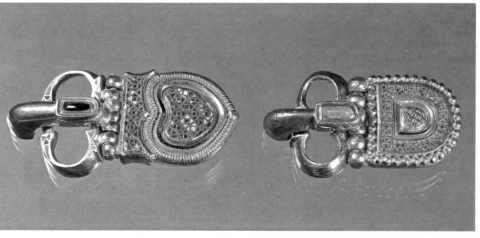

Two buckles said to be part of a treasure from Constantinople. Left: The buckle and belt plate are cast in gold, with glass and glass paste inlay. Length: 7.5 cm.

Gold necklace with openwork pendant containing pearls, emeralds, and sapphires. Found in Egypt. Byzantine, about 600 A.D. W. 7.2 cm.

Right: The buckle and belt plate are of the same type. However, the buckle has no punched decoration. Constantinople, 7th century A.D. Length: 6.2 cm.

Pair of gold earrings with pearls, emeralds and sapphires. Found in Egypt. Byzantine. About 600 A.D. Total Ht. 12.5 cm.

Detail of a breast chain of gold medallions, said to be found in Egypt. Byzantine, about 600 A.D. Diam. of medallion: 7.8 cm.

Gold pectoral cross, enameled and with a Greek inscription identifying the Mother of God with St Basil and St Gregory. Byzantine, Constantinople, 12th century. Ht. 6 cm.

The Towneley Brooch of enameled gold, a fine example of a round brooch employing the technique of enamel. Probably German, early 11th century. Diam. 6 cm.

Gold earring, decorated with pearls, rubies and turquoise. Found in Thrace. Byzantine, 7th/9th century Ht. 3.2 cm.

Silver-gilt brooch, ornamented with lions and eagles on foliage. Swedish, 15th century (?) Diam. 7.6 cm.

166

1 Silver-gilt finger ring with prominent cone-shaped bezel set with a ruby. Romanesque, 12th century. Ht. 2.4 cm.

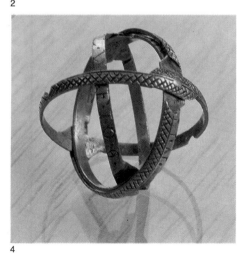

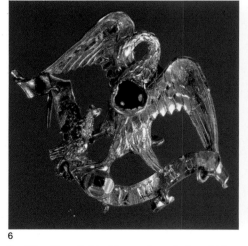

2 The Dunstable Swan Jewel. A gold jewel in the form of a swan covered with enamel for the plumage. English or French, early 15th century. Ht. 3.4 cm.

3 Gold Jewish cult finger-ring. Example of High Gothic architectural form, the symbol of the ark of the covenant. German (?), c. 1500. Ht. 4.3 cm.

4 Astronomical folding finger ring of silver-gilt. It is constructed of four round, narrow hoops. German, early 17th century. Diam. 2.2 cm.

5 Gold finger ring, a so-called love ring with a Hercules knot on the bezel. Probably English, 14th or 15th century. Ht. 2.6 cm.

6 Gold jewel in the form of a pelican, set with a ruby. The scroll is decorated with a smaller bird, a diamond, and the letters Y.M.T.H. Flemish, 15th century. Ht. 3 cm.

7 Silver earring, one of a pair, decorated with large and small granulation. Probably made by Serbian artisans, 13th century. W. 5.8 cm.

8 Silver finger ring. The design is a reflection of the decorative ornamentation of churches of the period. Serbian, 15th century. Ht. 3.5 cm.

Gold jewel in the form of a crowned imperial double eagle. The white and red enameled crown is decorated with diamonds, rubies and pearls. On the breast are the Austrian arms, composed of two rubies and diamond rosettes. Viennese or Italian, c. 1550. Ht. 15.6 cm.

Gold enameled Tudor pendant jewel depicting the story of Joseph in the well. The back has a design in the style of Etienne Delaune, the French engraver, who was active about 1550. W. 6.4 cm.

169

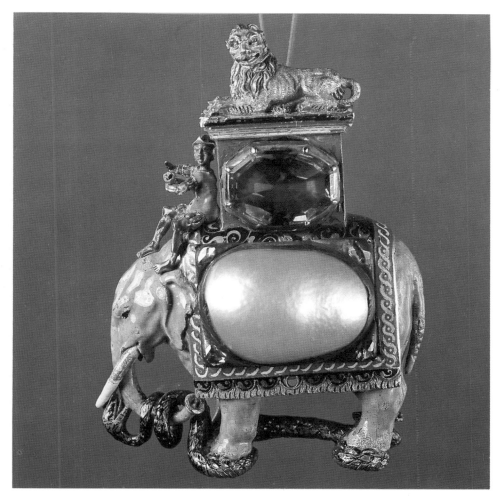

A pendant of gold and enamel in the shape of an elephant with a serpent twined around its feet. Over its back is a cloth which is decorated with a large baroque pearl on one side, and the other, the Bavarian arms in enamel. Munich, c. 1560. Workshop Hans Reimers? Ht. 5.6 cm.

A pendant of gold, enamel and table-cut diamonds. The discovery of an improved method for diamond cutting and the creation of table-cut diamonds with simple facets led to a sudden rise in the popularity of the diamond in 15th century. Munich, c.1600. Ht. 8.4 cm.

A gold and enamel pendant bust of Cleopatra with the asp in her bosom. Her head is adorned with a six-pointed diamond diadem. The face and hands are of cut hyacinth and she holds a green enamel viper twisted around her arm against her bosom. Her dress is of blue enamel. German, 16th century. The stone cuttings are probably of Italian workmanship. Ht. 8.7 cm.

Ring-watch of gold and enamel bearing the monogram IHS. Possibly Augsburg, c. 1580. The fine details of the shoulders of the ring, of the actual watch case, and of the lid, show the tremendous skill of the maker, a skill for which Augsburg was well-known. Perhaps by Jacob Wittmann, a watchmaker from Antwerp working in Augsburg. Diam. of watch: 1.7 cm.

A collar-type necklace of diamonds, topazes and amethysts. The flowers and ribbons are made of topaz and are surrounded by small diamonds; the leafage is in amethyst. It is set in silver. Italian, 18th century. Ht. 21 cm.

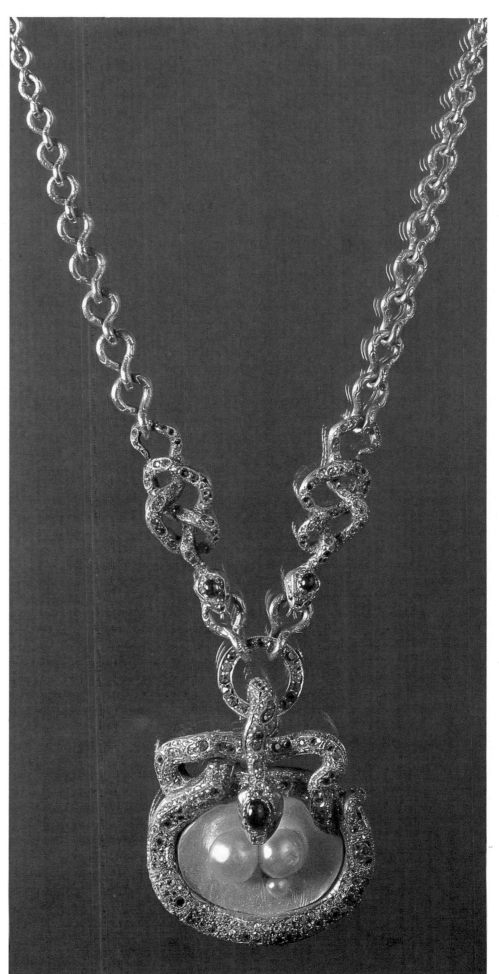

Chatelaine and watch in mother-of-pearl, gold, and enamel. The upper portion, for pinning on the dress, is shell-shaped in mother-of-pearl, with the Russian double-headed imperial eagle carved in gold and enameled in black, red, and white. Below this, and in reverse, is a gold shell. From the top shell hangs another mother-of-pearl shell with the Danish royal arms, with a smaller shell repeated below it carved in gold. A drop pearl hangs from the crown, as do two chains holding the watch, which has a mother-of-pearl case. The watch was a present from the Tsarevich Alexander Alexandrovich to Princess Dagmar of Denmark. French, 1866. Ht. 15 cm.

Lorgnette of gold and enamel in the form of a lizard by René Lalique, the Art Nouveau goldsmith. Paris, c. 1900. Ht. 16 cm.

Gold necklace with emeralds, diamonds, and rubies. In 1918, Kaiser Wilhelm II, known for his love of unusual stones, gave an order to Professor Lucas von Cranach, the Berlin goldsmith, to create a piece of jewelry out of a pearl's shell. German, 1918. W. 3.6 cm.

Gold brooch in the form of two peacocks, made of blue enamel, glass paste, and sapphires. The peacock was a popular subject of the Art Nouveau artist-jewelers. This brooch was exhibited at the Salon d'Automne, Paris, 1902. René Lalique, Paris, 1902. W. 22 cm.

Pendant with chain, a rare Fabergé Art Nouveau work of gold and enamel with chrysoprase and diamonds. The mistletoe, the storks, and the lettering ''L'an neuf,'' a shortening of ''Au gui l'an neuf,'' a New Year's wish are all enameled on gold. Peter Carl Fabergé. W. 4.8 cm.

THE SACRED JEWELS

CANON CHARLES J. LEDIT CURATOR, TROYES CATHEDRAL TREASURE

The sacred is distinct from the magical and the symbolic.

To have faith in an object – for example, to wear an amulet for protection – is to live within a magic circle.

To see a sign of wisdom in the structure, form, and color of an object, and to link it with immaterial truths, is to confer on it a symbolic role.

To evoke, by means of a symbolic object, the presence of another is to cross the threshold of the sacred. This implies a tangible link with the unique, and the object becomes sacred.

These three levels of significance have existed constantly, in varying degrees, since man came into being. The frontiers between them are not absolute, and it is worthwhile to examine some characteristic examples before embarking upon a more general description of sacred jewels.

From a work of art to a sacred jewel

In China, recent archaeological discoveries have brought to light the tomb of the princess Tou Wan (second century B.C.) and her burial shroud, an elaborate garment made of 2,156 jade tablets sewn together with threads of gold. The existence of such shrouds is mentioned in ancient texts: "On the death of an emperor, use was made of a jade container *(yu-hia)* in the form of armor *(k'ai-kia)* which was held together with gold thread." Was this simply a burial garment, or did it have magical significance? We do not know, and this jade shroud has for us no other function than the solemnization of the funeral of a princess.

Among examples of Egyptian jewelry is the pectoral that the ancient priests placed on the breast of the young pharaoh Tutankhamen. In the middle of the breastplate is a warm-colored chalcedony: it is a scarab which will help the young god as he stands at the gates to the other world. This scarab is none other than his father, the god Amon, whose outstretched wings bear the ship of soul on its journey. Protected by the uraeus of Buto – the cobra symbolic of divinity – as well as the eye of Horus *(ondjat)*, the dead man is ensured health, fecundity, and perspicacity in the eternal life. Three reversed lotus flowers scent the night. A counterpart to this pectoral is a magnificent ship holding the rising sun; a beetle pushing a vermilion carnelian – a symbol of resurrection – with its claws. Other scarabs, maneuvering other gems, decorate the necklace from which the jewels hang. Thanks to the magic of this amulet, all the forces of the other world would recognize Amon's son, and the pharaoh could walk with confidence down the paths of darkness.

Moses remembered the Egyptian wisdom on which he had been nurtured when he described the breastplate of judgment which should be worn by the high priest: "Thou shalt make... of gold... And thou shalt set in it settings of stones, even four rows of stones: the first row shall be a sardius, a topaz, and a carbuncle... And the second row shall be an emerald, a sapphire and a diamond. And the third row a ligure, an agate, and an amethyst. And the fourth row a beryl, and an onyx and a jasper; they shall be set in gold in their inclosings. And the stones shall be with the names of the children of Israel..." (Exodus 28:15-21, King James Bible). Inspired by Jehova, and worn in his presence, this jewel had only the remotest connection with its material value: devoid of all magical properties, it remained the testimony of the alliance between God and a beloved people. For this reason, the jewel was sacred.

According to Indian tradition, Buddha has a "third eye" in the middle of his forehead. In India and Nepal, it is represented by a semi-precious Himalayan stone. Certain people think that this eye-stone represents the pineal gland and symbolizes wisdom. There is another interpretation, suggested by the pious chant: "Om mani padme hum"–translated as "Hail to the jewel in the lotus." The jewel ensures communion with the invisible; it refers to immanent wisdom, to the presence of the eternal. The lotus is the heart of man. The jewel in the lotus is therefore wisdom in the heart of man through which he may achieve deliverance. Man must rivet to his heart the violence and tenderness that are the two faces of the divine. It is not only the eye-stone of Buddha that is sacred, but the whole statue.

No object – precious or otherwise – is sacred of itself; it becomes so by the faith and love with which men surround it and by which it acts as a bridge between the divine and the human.

Why is it, then, that sacred jewels are so often precious objects? It is because no natural or manmade object will be rare enough, precious enough, or beautiful enough to fill this privileged role, to serve as a prop to the highest spiritual aspirations. To this may be added the belief that precious metals and stones, being more subtle than mere chalk and lead, are predestined for this office. Each shape, each color, will evoke – by mysterious symbolic connotations – the Christian virtues, the richness and beauty of the souls of God's servants, the radiant splendor of the celestial Jerusalem.

Non-temporal riches

Born poor among the poor, the early Church possessed few precious objects; only a few onyx chalices have come down to us from those times. The Venetians had found them among the treasures of Constantinople and although they were exhibited in St Mark's Basilica, such objects were not important for the first Christians.

The early Christians entered the period of the persecutions with the spirit of conquerors, nourished by their reading of the Apocalypse. They saw God as seated on a throne glittering with emeralds, handing a dazzling precious stone to the conqueror, an intaglio carved with a name of eternity. And again it is the Apocalypse which promises the chosen one that he shall enter the heavenly Jerusalem, the city of gold, vast as the sky: "And the building of the wall of it was of jasper: and the city was pure gold, like unto clear glass. And the foundations of the wall of the city were garnished with all manner of precious stones. The first foundation was jasper; the second, sapphire; the third, a chalcedony; the fourth, an emerald; the fifth, sardonyx; the sixth, sardius; the seventh, chrysolite; the eighth, beryl; the ninth, a topaz; the tenth, a chrysoprasus; the eleventh, a jacinth; the twelfth, an amethyst. And the twelve gates were twelve pearls; every several gate was of one pearl: and the street of the city was pure gold, as it were transparent glass." (Revelation, 21 : 18–21, King James Bible).

St Agnes, when a young woman thirteen years old, replied to an aspiring lover: "I am already betrothed... He has adorned me with bracelets and necklaces of precious stones. My earrings glitter with priceless gems. As a wager for my dowry he has given me a wedding ring and crowned me like a bride. He has clothed me with a tunic threaded with gold." St Agnes died a Christian martyr.

The liturgy talks of Mary Magdalene, the converted sinner, in the same language: "See how the lost drachma returns to the king's treasury. Free of its mud, the gem surpasses the brilliance of a star." The real jewels of the new-born Church were its first members, not its material objects.

The sacred jewels of Western Christianity

Very early in their history, Christian communities preserved relics of the saints, not so much in memory of them as people or as personalities, but more for the profound belief and precious testimony to which they had consecrated their lives.

To preserve and honor the saintly remains, Christians developed the custom of enshrining and glorifying them with a reliquary. This reliquary had the dual function of exhalting the glory of God through the saints, and of inciting the living to serve God. The reliquary is sacred because it is intimately involved with the dialogue of man with God. These reliquaries are innumerable; the faithful were content with their proliferation, as was the Church which did not, however, encourage suspect fervor.

It can be readily understood that the reliquaries enclosing parts of the Cross or the thorns of Christ's crown were constructed with great piety. Examples of different types, each of great beauty, will be discussed.

Charlemagne had a great predilection for sacred jewelry. When he died in 814 at Aachen (Aix-la-Chapelle), he was buried reverently with his favorite jewel—known now as Charlemagne's talisman—placed on his chest. It is a two-sided jewel, a sort of breastplate in the form of an ampulla, of which the central stone, which has been lost, has been replaced by a cabochon of blue glass, showing a relic of the True Cross. Around the edge, eight emeralds and garnets are separated by baroque pearls. On the other side is a pale sapphire surrounded by a similar decoration. In being buried with this piece of jewelry, the old emperor wanted his death to be transfigured by the cross of Jesus Christ. The value of this jewel for him lay not in the emeralds, garnets, and pearls, but in the relic of the True Cross, which for Charlemagne was the sign of his faith and the pledge of his well-being. Today this precious jewel is part of the treasure of Reims Cathedral.

At the emperor's side was a casket, richly ornamented with precious stones. It was a reliquary, for tradition says that the wooden box contained some earth steeped with the blood of the first martyr, St Stephen. St Stephen's Burse is a reminder that the offering of his own blood is the Christian's supreme gift. Charlemagne, unable to give his own blood, made it clear that he offered his life and his death by having laid beside him the sacred chest. Today this reliquary is to be found in the Kunsthistorisches Museum in Vienna.

The French King Louis IX was renowned for his great piety and Christian virtues. He brought back several relics from his crusades in the Holy Land, notably Christ's crown of thorns, fragments of the True Cross and the sacred spear. The king built the Sainte Chapelle to hold these precious objects. In addition, he gave presents to members of his family and to religious communities. In this way a king of Aragon became owner of one of the sacred thorns and preserved it in a pendant reliquary which as a sacred jewel is comparable in importance to Charlemagne's talisman, though in style it is less barbaric: it belongs to the peak of the Gothic style. Among the gifts St Louis gave to the religious communities of France was the reliquary crown that he gave to the Dominicans at Liège. It is composed of eight plaques of vermeil, overlayed with fleurs-de-lis and linked by eight angels. The plaques and fleurs-de-lis are ornamented with pearls and precious stones. Since the end of the Second World War, after a very eventful history, this jewel has been preserved in the Louvre.

Among the reliquaries belonging to churches and monasteries, two in the treasure of the Abbey of St Maurice d'Agaune in Switzerland merit mention. The first, a sardonyx vase, was an object of pagan origin, belonging in form, decoration and execution to the Hellenism of the Ptolemaic age (second or first century B. C.). It was mounted on a pedestal in the seventh century, bordered with gold, and adorned with cloisonnéed enamel, pearls, and cabochons. This vase would be but a precious object if legend had not made it a reliquary. According to a tradition still alive in the west of France, St Martin made a pilgrimage to the place where Maurice and his companions of the Theban Legion had been decapitated toward the end of the third century, having preferred death to the denial of their Christian faith. On arrival at the field of martyrdom, Martin is said to have obtained the miracle of a dew of blood and to have filled four vases given him by an angel, one of which he presented to the monks of Agaune. The pagan origins of the vase were unknown to the pilgrims who made the journey to the abbey. Having become a reliquary, the vase was sacred.

In the same treasure of St Maurice, and also a reliquary, is Theodoric's casket, named after the person who "commanded that it should be done in honor of St Maurice," according to an inscription beaten into the lozenge pattern on the back of the casket. It seems to have been executed in the seventh century in the Rhine area. The perfection of this work seems to be unrivalled in Merovingian goldware. This casket, as a final adornment of mortal remains, is a doubly precious testimony, in its beauty and its significance, to the cult of the saints.

The Majesty of St Foy, belonging to the treasure of the ancient Abbey of Conques in France, is also a reliquary. St Foy was a young Christian who was martyred at Agen in the year 303. The martyr's body was stolen from a church in Agen by a monk from Conques, who had sworn to build an abbey with the help of the saint.

Originally, the statue and the chair were carved in the same wood and covered with gold. The reliquary attracted many pilgrims to Conques, and in the year 985 the first miracle was performed: the saint restored the eyesight of one Guibert, who was thenceforth called the Enlightened. Conques rapidly became a local center of pilgrimage, all the more frequented for the fact that it was a resting place on the great route to Santiago de Compostela. On the road to the shrine of St James as on the road to paradise, the Majesty of St Foy brought hope and a friendly presence to the humble and the poor.

Reliquaries have existed in all ages and all Christian nations. Whether offered by princes or by groups of the faithful, they have one thing in common: they belong and will belong to the whole of Christianity as long as the faith is a living one, uniting and uplifting souls. If the reliquary survives simply as a precious object, it is no longer sacred—it becomes merely a museum piece.

Among the mass of sacred objects are the numerous images of Christ. Their function is to inspire contemplation and action, even to inspire participation in the life of Christ. "The image that you see there," said

Theodorus Studita (A.D. 759-825), "is that of Christ; it is Christ himself, at least according to the name ... Those who prostrate themselves before it honor Christ: those who refuse him this honor are his enemies ..."

Christ is given many iconographic forms. Two, however, recur the most frequently, and these forms are, in fact, complementary—Christ as teacher, and the crucifix.

Christ as teacher is seated in majesty; his right hand is raised in blessing and he holds the book of the Gospels in his left hand. He is painted in frescoes and on cathedral spandrels for the edification of the masses. In order to bring Christ close to the faithful, His statue is individualized and takes on a precious character—for example, the sober and noble brass statuette covered in gold which, toward the end of the Middle Ages, stood next to the tomb of Saint Peter in the Vatican basilica (see page 185).

The crucifix bearing Christ or the empty cross remind the Christian of Christ's death and of Christianity's great lesson of love. The treasure of the Cathedral of Monza near Milan includes the Berengar's Cross (see page 187). The cross is a ninth-century Carolingian work, studded with precious stones: four dozen in the arms, and eight in the central crown around a large sapphire. The cross has been a sign of victory since the time of the Emperor Constantine; here again, the jewel is a testimony of the alliance between man and God.

Certain objects—notably altars, chalices, and monstrances—used in religious services are considered sacred because they are used in the liturgy. Each altar, in turn, can be reduced to a stone and its relics; in effect, the sacrifice of the mass is always celebrated on a reliquary.

All altars are equally sacred, but some are also great jewels. Two examples are especially arresting. First, the portable altar of the Emperor Henry II: it is a slab of crystal set between two rows of precious stones: amethysts, sapphires, emeralds, and pearls.

The second example is the Pala d'Oro in St Mark's, which is more of an altar decoration than an altar in itself. It is, however, a sacred jewel, because it serves as the basis of solemn ceremonies, and because, by the brilliance of its gold and gems, it evokes the celestial Jerusalem.

The Pala d'Oro consists of 84 enameled panels on a base of gold, scattered with 300 pearls, 400 garnets, 90 amethysts, 300 sapphires, 300 emeralds, and 80 rubies. This prestigious assemblage, which was made at Constantinople in 976, relates the life of Jesus.

St Mark's Basilica is enriched with other treasures; more than 300 pieces of goldware and silverware are crowded into two small rooms and piled up one on another, as if they had just been unloaded from gondolas. Not all of these pieces were made in Venice, however. A large portion was brought from Constantinople, where the Venetians, during the crusade of 1204, helped themselves abundantly.

Among the pieces from the crusaders' pillage of Constantinople is a goblet chiseled from a semi-precious stone, the sard. One cannot fail to reflect on the mystic vessel, the chalice–the hidden Grail Parsifal saw carried by a virgin and guarded by footmen; Christ used the chalice at the Last Supper, and the one Joseph of Arimathea used to wash and embalm the body of Christ. This chalice of sard in Venice is not the Holy Grail, but, by the consecration of the wine, it becomes the sacred depository of He who, at the end of his life, said "This is my blood...".

The use of the monstrance dates back to the second half of the thirteenth century when Pope Urban IV instituted the feast of Corpus Christi (1264). The last of the sacred vessels to come into use, the monstrance is a transparent disc – the receptacle of the host – framed by golden rays and placed on a pedestal. The function of the object is well explained by its name: it shows the consecrated host during ceremonies involving large numbers of people. This function is comparable to that of a reliquary because the monstrance preserves, at least for a certain time, the sacred host.

The golden rays that emanate from the glass or crystal lunule containing the host give the object a solar aspect which has inspired a variety of forms and has given rise to symbolism which may be summarized in this way: just as there is only one sun, the source of all life in the temporal world, so, in the spiritual world, there is only one source of life – Christ.

There are countless beautiful monstrances: one finds them in cathedral treasures, in convents, even sometimes in country churches. Among the most beautiful is the one called the Sun, belonging to the church of Notre Dame of Loretto in Prague. The body of the object is made of vermeil; its ornamentation comprises 6,222 diamonds. Their fiery brilliance can be imagined, either within the church reflecting the light of hundreds of candles, or outside, glinting in the sunshine as if the heavenly body had been added to the dazzling manifestation of the sacred mysteries.

The Christian Church, repository of eternal truths, is tied to the temporal world. It insinuates itself into the social structure in order to give witness and teach the truths that transcend historical realities. Indications of this dual role of the Church are found in certain objects destined to confer dignity on the great of this world, but also to remind them of the responsibilities of their position and their duties as Christians.

Thus it is that the imperial or royal crown, the tiara, the sword and the orb – the emblems of temporal power – and the papal ring and the episcopal cross are sacred objects, whether rich or rustic, because they were intended to remind God's chosen one that he was there to realize the reign of God, of justice and love. That this duty has not always been respected, that these emblems have been taken over by political powers, through pride or cupidity, detracts nothing from their sacred character.

In the West, the first royal crown dates from the end of the fourth century: it is the Iron Crown of the Lombard kings, today preserved in the Cathedral of Monza, near Milan. According to tradition, this crown, which was originally a simple circle of iron made with a nail of the True Cross, was given to Queen Theodolinda, who died in A.D. 626, by Pope Gregory the Great. The circle of iron was then plated with gold and ornamented with precious stones. It was transformed several times in the seventh and ninth centuries, and exists today as a gold diadem studded with precious stones. Now it is only a valued historic relic, but for centuries it assumed great significance: made with a nail which had pierced a part of Christ's body, given by the Pope, the vicar of Christ, it conferred on its owner and her descendants the mission of leading the Christian people, and it imposed upon the people the respect due to God's chosen one. That the crown was used for political purposes by Charlemagne and other emperors does not lessen the profound significance of the jewel.

In his state apparel, the emperor of the Holy Roman (Germanic) Empire carried, apart from his crown, a terrestrial globe in his left hand, and a sword in his right. The symbolism is obvious: the emperor reigned over the temporal world; the Church reigned over the spiritual order. He is, with the pope, God's representative on earth. The globe is the manifestation of his juridical power and the sword confers upon him the power and the duty to protect justice and to defend Christianity.

The crowns that were intended for statues had an evident symbolic value. There is, for example, the celebrated Crown of the Andes, destined to adorn a statue of the Virgin Mary, venerated as Queen of the Andes. More than an offering, the crown is a pledge between the Mother of Christ and Christians; it is the materialization of a mystical tie. This crown did not have to be a fabulous jewel, but its wealth—it has 453 emeralds weighing 1,521 carats—symbolized the inestimable value that the donors attributed to their gesture and to the mystic reign and the protection of the Virgin Mary. Times have changed: today the Crown of the Andes is part of a private collection.

Sacred jewels provide not only an interesting example of the goldsmith's or the jeweler's work, but also the underlying importance of the realisation of their historical significance and, as images of the soul, of their departure from the concrete level of craftsmanship into the abstract realm of symbolism. Thus the sacred jewel finds its profound significance and link between the soul and the unique.

The statue of Christ enthroned, which stood originally at the altar of St Peter's tomb in Rome. Gold-plated copper and precious stones. Italian, 13th century.

The reliquary statue of St Foy at Conques is a wooden figure covered with sheets of gold and silver, wearing a crown consisting of a circlet and two arches of joined plaques with fleurs-de-lis between, set with antique cameos, pearls, and gems. These gems are the uncut stones typical of the Middle Ages. St Foy, in addition to her crown, wears earrings of gold decorated with granulation and filigree, the pendants hung with pearls, crystals, and garnets. French, late 10th century. Total Ht. 85 cm.

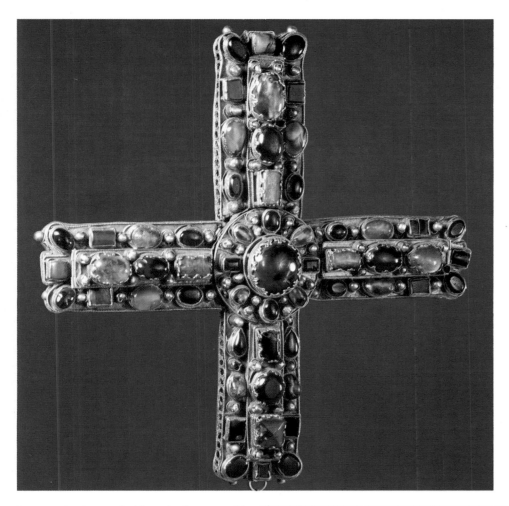

Berengar's Cross, fashioned of pure gold studded with 126 precious stones—garnets, hyacinths, emeralds, and pearls—set symmetrically around a large central cabochon sapphire. Carolingian, 9th century. Ht. of cross 22 cm.; W. 22.3 cm.

The Imperial Orb and the Imperial Sword of the Holy Roman Empire.

The Imperial Orb is a hollow ball composed of 6 golden plates soldered together. The encircling vertical bands are ornamented with gems and filigree work. German (Cologne?), last quarter of the 12th century. Ht. 21 cm.

The Imperial Sword. The blade is steel; the pommel and cross-bar are slightly gilded; the hilt is bound with silver wire. German, c. 1198-1218. L. of sword: 110 cm.

The Talisman of Charlemagne, one of the most famous amulet jewels. It was buried with the emperor in 814 at Aachen, exhumed by Frederick Barbarossa in 1166, and conserved in the cathedral treasury until, in 1804, the canons presented it to Empress Josephine in order to thank Napoleon for bringing back the imperial treasure from Paderborn; The Talisman consists of two large oval cabochon sapphires, 32×27 mm., back to back, through which a relic of the true cross is visible.

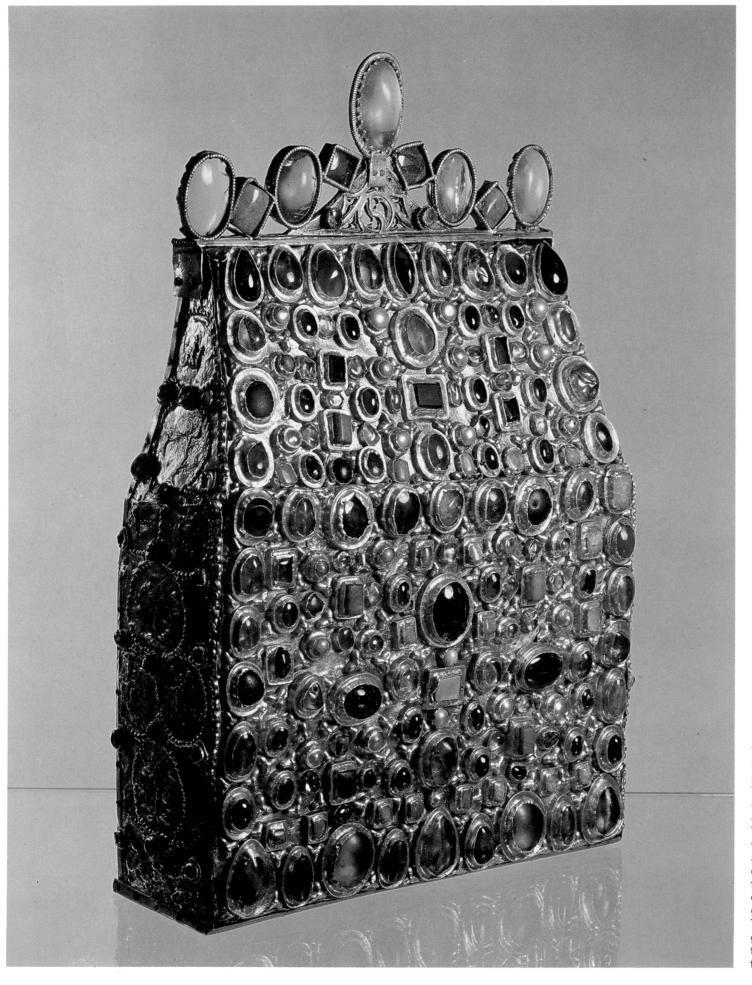

The Burse of St Stephen, a reliquary which according to tradition contained earth soaked with the blood of the arch martyr. The wooden core of the case does in fact contain cavities; they are, however, empty except for one compartment at the bottom. There lies a relic, a white fragment of cloth wrapped in a yellow-brown piece of sheet, and authenticated by a seal of the Cathedral Chapter of Worms, dating from the first half of the 12th century. The Burse is of gold foil on wood (except for the back of gilded silver), precious stones and pearls. The sides show stamped medallions of a goddess of Vengeance, a fisherman, a falconer, and a bird-trapper. Reims (?), first third of the 9th century. Ht. 32 cm.

The sardonyx vase, called the Vase of St Martin, chiseled (probably in Alexandria, 50 B.C.), from a single onyx stone. Cloisonné work is Merovingian. Ht. 22.3 cm.

Crook of an abbess' staff with realistic figures of St George about to kill the dragon. St George's Cloister, Prague Castle. Bohemian, 1st half of the 16th century.

The Crown of the Andes. The lavish crown was commissioned in 1593 for the statue of the Virgin Mary, Queen of the Andes, to whom the inhabitants of the city of Popayan gave full credit for saving their families from the scourge of the plague. Twenty-five goldsmiths worked without interruption for six years to complete it. The whole population donated more than a hundred pounds of pure gold and the patrician families of Popayan, whose ancestors had been with Pizarro and Benalcazar during the downfall of the Peruvian empire, donated the precious emeralds their families had hoarded from the earliest days of the conquest. The crown is decorated with 453 emeralds—the world's oldest and largest emerald collection—with a combined weight of 1,521 carats.

A detail of the Pala d'Oro (golden alterpiece) which still serves in St Mark's Basilica as a background for solemn ceremonies on great feast days. The story of Jesus is told in some 84 enameled panels on a gold ground interspersed with an immense number of gems: 300 pearls, 400 garnets, 90 amethysts, 300 sapphires, 300 emeralds and 80 rubies. Byzantine and Italian, 10th-14th centuries.245×365 cm.

The celebrated Iron Crown of the Lombards. It consists of 6 gold plates connected to each other by hinges and forming a ring. It is adorned with 26 rosettes in gold relief, 22 precious stones, and 24 enameled ornaments, which consist of a sprig with white leaves and round blue rosettes on a green ground. Inside is an iron rim said to have been made from a nail of the true cross brought by the Empress Helena from Palestine. Lombardic, c. 9th century. Diam. 15.3 cm.

The Casket of Theodoric is a very fine example of gold cloisonné. Note the perfect harmony of the net-work and its design, the classical intaglios, the medallion in the middle which is such a puzzle to experts, and the lines of pearls. Merovingian, 7th century. Ht. 12.6 cm.

A two-handled chalice with a semi-circular cup of sardonyx. Gold mount encrusted with gems. Probably from the imperial workshop in Constantinople and presumably brought back to Venice as plunder by the Crusaders in 1204. Byzantine, 10th - 11th centuries. Diam. 20 cm.

The reliquary known as the Crown of St Louis, after the saintly king who gave it to the Dominicans of Liège. It is composed of 8 silver-gilt plaques with fleurs-de-lis terminals linked by 8 winged angels. The plaques are decorated with oak leaves and are set with cabochon stones. Paris (?), c. 1260. Diam. 21 cm.

Detail of the portable altar of Emperor Henry II. The altar stone is a rock crystal tablet framed by two rows of amethysts, sapphires, emeralds and pearls. From Metz or Reichenau, c. 1010. Ht. 43 cm.

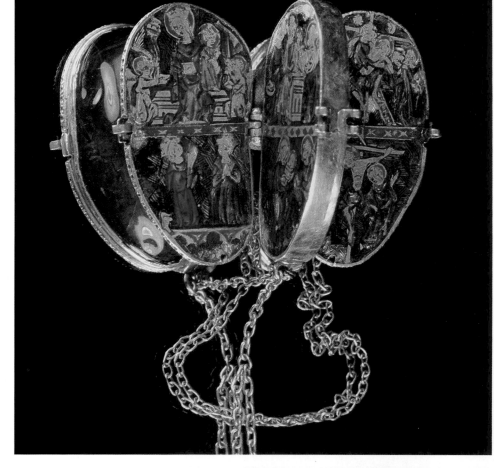

Gold reliquary pendant of the Holy Thorn set with two large amethysts. It is said that St Louis detached a few single thorns from the Crown of Thorns he purchased, with other relics, about 1239 from Baldwin II, Emperor of Constantinople, and gave them to members of his family. Later by order of the King of Aragon, one was mounted between two large cabochon amethysts set in gold and decorated with scenes from the life of Christ in translucent enamel. North French, c. 1330-1340. Ht. 3.9 cm.

A so-called papal ring of gilded bronze with an amethyst set over red foil. On the hoop in relief are the four evangelistic symbols—a tiara, the name of Pope Pius II (PAPH PIO), crossed keys and the arms of Piccolomini. Italian, 15th century. Ht. 4.5 cm.

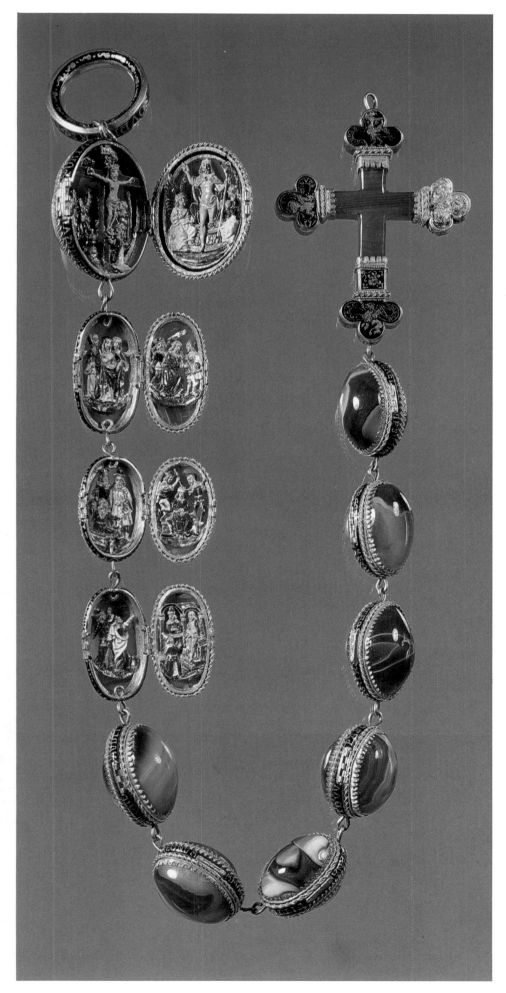

A splendid surviving example (most were melted down) of the rosaries of the late 15th and early 16th centuries, which were formed of beads, each opening like a reliquary pendant to show two carved or enameled reliefs. This beautiful rosary has agate beads which open to reveal enameled reliefs of the life of Christ. Probably Italian, early 16th century.

The Diamond monstrance, often called the Sun monstrance, which is the most valuable monstrance in Prague. It bears the following engraving: "Made in Vienna by M. Stegner and J. Khünischbauer, 1699". It was a gift from the Countess Eva Ludmila von Kolovrat. It is silver, gold-plated, and contains 6,222 diamonds. In 1699 it was taken from Vienna to Prague in a closed coach, and for safety, it was accompanied by five horsemen of the imperial guard. Viennese, 1699. Ht. 89.5 cm.; weight 2 kg.

Detail of the Diamond, or Sun, monstrance.

St Peter enthroned. The statue of St Peter, a 5th-century bronze, formerly stood in the old basilica, placed there by St Leo the Great in the year A.D. 445. Through the ages, this statue has been the object of such veneration that the kisses of the faithful have polished and worn the right foot. In this photograph, the statue of the fisherman to whom Jesus entrusted the keys of the kingdom of heaven reigns in splendor, wearing the pontifical robes and jewels – among them a tiara of silver-gilt – reserved for his feast day, which is celebrated each year in June. This practice is thought to have begun in 1736, and the tiara dates from the 18th century.

REGALIA
AND CEREMONIAL
JEWELRY

R. W. LIGHTBOWN ASSISTANT CURATOR, VICTORIA & ALBERT MUSEUM, LONDON

From the most ancient times jewelry has been used not only to adorn man's dress but also to proclaim his rank and wealth. In the hierarchical society of medieval and Renaissance Europe the classes were sharply separated in manners, customs, and pursuits, and the distinctions in degree between them were as sharply expressed in the costumes and jewelry they wore. So dearly did rulers value these external symbols of the fixed order of society that they constantly made attempts to enforce the observance of sumptuary laws on those audacious enough to wear dress and ornaments above their station. Such laws, at once a definition of the theory and a description of the practice of society, are now a priceless source of information about both. We know more about the jewelry of the past from documents than from surviving pieces. Changes in fashion, the scarcity and the intrinsic value of the metals and gems with which jewelry is wrought—these have caused a vast destruction of precious ornaments from generation to generation. Most of the old jewelry that still exists in modern times owes its survival to special circumstances – loss or concealment by an early owner, the special sentiment attached to venerable historical insignia or to a royal gift, and (perhaps most important of all) the guardianship of the Church, which preserved the votive offerings of jewels made by the faithful to relics or shrines. Of the Renaissance and Baroque jewels in London's Victoria and Albert Museum, for example, a goodly number once belonged to the Spanish shrine of the Virgin of the Pillar in Saragossa, which only sold them during the political troubles of the 1870s.

With evidence of this kind, as will be obvious, we have very little material for establishing a continuous history of the jewelry worn by the lower orders of society. We are consistently well informed only about the jewelry of the court and the higher nobility. We can assume that the precious crowns, necklaces, brooches, pendants and girdles described in inventories or still surviving here and there in museums and church treasuries were worn largely on ceremonial occasions, at feasts and balls, at receptions for important visitors or during the great ceremonies of Church or State.

Let us consider first the history of the greatest ceremonial ornament of all, the crown. The gold crown of the Holy Roman Empire still survives in the Schatzkammer at Vienna as witness of the ceremonial magnificence with which the Ottonian emperors, anxious to assert themselves as the true heirs of Charlemagne and the Caesars, surrounded themselves. It is composed of eight arched plaques enriched with filigree and set with precious stones – sapphires, rubies, emeralds – and pearls, and decorated with cloisonné enamel in imitation of Byzantine cloisonné enamel. The crown's design is modeled on that of a Byzantine imperial crown, and, as on Byzantine crowns, the central plaque is surmounted by a cross that is also set with gems and pearls. The subjects of the enameled plaques, four in all, are Christ as Lord of the World; Isaiah telling the ailing Hezekiah that God has answered his prayer and added fifteen years to his reign; King David as symbol of royal justice; and King Solomon as symbol of royal wisdom. Each of these four plaques has an inscription taken from the liturgy of the imperial coronation. Above the figure of Christ the inscription reminds kings that it is through Him that they reign; above Hezekiah it promises an addition of years to god-fearing kings; above David it declares that the love of justice is the honor of kings; and above Solomon it warns the emperor to fear God and forsake evil.

It will be seen that the crown is a symbolic admonition to those who wore it at their coronation that they must acknowledge God as the source of their power, fear Him, and rule justly and wisely. It is now thought that the crown in Vienna was made for the coronation of Emperor Otto the Great in Rome in 962. The cross on the front is thought to have been added by Otto III (983-1002) late in his reign or else by his successor Henry II (d. 1024). Originally there was also a cross on the central plaque at the back. The pendant strings of gems that hung at the side are now missing. The single arch of this crown was an imperial prerogative; it was designed so that it could be worn over the mitre the emperor also wore to symbolize his role as priest and king. The present arch was added by Emperor Conrad II (1024-1039) and it has been suggested that each of the emperors before Conrad may have substituted a fresh arch with his own name for that of his predecessor.

The great reliquary statue of St Foy at Conques—a wooden figure covered with sheets of gold and silver—also wears a crown, together with the other pieces of ceremonial jewelry that late-tenth-century France thought proper for the image of a greatly venerated saint. Her crown is a closed one, consisting of a circlet and two arches of jointed plaques with fleurs-de-lis between, set with antique cameos, pearls, and gems. These gems, like those of the imperial crown, are the uncut gems of the Middle Ages, which when first seen seem disconcerting to modern eyes, accustomed as we are to the smooth, sharp planes that cutting imposes on precious stones, and to a precise realization of a few geometric forms, creating the hard clarity of water. After a little experience, the modern eye comes to value the irregular form and clouded color of medieval gems, and to be drawn by their gentle polish, which preserves the accidental form while revealing the intrinsic nature of the stones. We then come to understand how such gems appeared to possess that mediatory power between the earthly and the spiritual—at its highest mystical, at its lowest magical—which medieval eyes discerned in them.

The gems on both these crowns possess a symbolic meaning that we cannot now understand. The reader will have noticed that the most prominent plaques of the imperial crown are those set with gems and pearls, not those decorated with enamel. It is highly probable that the crown of St Foy is a true crown, one that was really worn, for it has been reduced in order to fit the saint's head and it has no hoops for suspension such as are found on the votive crowns customarily offered to churches in the Dark Ages and Carolingian times. The two arches indicate that it is probably a royal rather than an imperial crown, and to understand how these crowns acquired their form we must turn eastward to Byzantium.

The Byzantine imperial crown had evolved from the imperial Roman diadem, a circlet fastened at the back with ribbons. Under Emperor Justinian the diadem had become the *stemma*, a complete circlet with pendant strings of pearls and gems *(cataseistae)*. Within was a tall cap. During the eighth century it became customary to make the crown from a number of arched plaques fastened by pins instead of a single circlet. To this the Macedonian emperors (863-1056) added arches over the cap enclosing the crown, and a cross—the great emblem of a Christian emperor. The crown thus formed was known as the *kamelaukion*; this is one version of its evolution. According to another theory the *kamelaukion* was evolved from the ceremonial helmet of the later Roman emperors, which was surmounted by an arch.

There still survives a crown that gives some idea of a Byzantine crown of this type—the celebrated crown of St Stephen, the Holy Crown of Hungary, traditionally said to have been sent by the Pope to King Stephen. The crown has been variously dated (it seems to be of composite origin), the dates ranging from c. 1000 A.D. to the late eleventh or early twelfth century. But it is clear that it must be largely or at least in part of Byzantine origin. By contrast the crown of the Byzantine Empress was always open, for a closed crown was the privilege of the emperor alone. The tradition of the Byzantine crown survived in Russia where legend, probably arising in the sixteenth century, claimed that the twelfth century "Cap of Monomachus" (now in the Kremlin Museum) was none other than the imperial crown of the Byzantine Emperor Constantine IX Monomachus (d. 1055) which he had presented together with other imperial insignia to his grandson Vladimir II Monomachus (reigned 1113-25), Grand Duke of Kiev. A copy of this cap was made in 1682 for the double coronation of Ivan V and Peter the Great; it also influenced the design of other Russian seventeenth-century crowns. This was only natural, for after Ivan IV had taken the title of Tsar of All the Russias at his coronation in 1547, the Russian emperors regarded themselves as the direct successors to the Byzantine emperors. It was once the custom of the Byzantine emperors to send crowns to kings on the borders of their empires, as symbols both that they derived their authority from the emperor and that the emperor recognized their sovereignty–a custom imitated by the Western emperors and by the Popes. There was a curious revival of it in 1605, when the Mohammedan ruler of Constantinople, Sultan Ahmed I of Turkey, sent a crown to Prince Stephan Bocskay of Transylvania, who had rebelled against the Emperor Rudolph II and offered his submission to Turkey. Shortly afterward, the Sultan's gift was captured by Archduke Mathias and sent by him in 1610 to Vienna, where it is still preserved in the Schatzkammer, a strange intrusion of light and gay Oriental splendor into the heavy magnificence of so many ancient and illustrious relics of the Holy Roman Empire.

We have seen that Byzantine imperial crowns provided the inspiration for the Western imperial crown. Closed crowns of the same general type with two arches such as that of St Foy were worn by kings of the West, following the example of the German emperors. So too were imitations of another type of Byzantine crown in which each plaque of the circlet was surmounted by a trefoil ornament of gems or pearls, said to have been first used by Constantine on his imperial helmet. A German example of this type of crown dating from the eleventh and early twelfth centuries still survives on the reliquary bust of St Oswald in the treasury of Hildesheim Cathedral. It is made of gold set with pearls, gems, cameos, and enamels. This type of crown developed in the West into the familiar crown surmounted by fleurs-de-lis, or fleurons as they are usually described. Emperor Charles the Bald is shown wearing a crown of fleurons in his Gospel book, executed between 846 and 869. The crown with fleurons was copied in England as early as the third quarter of the tenth century and its influence can be seen in the design of the crown of St Foy. An early example of a fleur-de-lis crown is that on the head of the tenth-century Golden Virgin in the Minster at Essen. It seems possible that this is the crown once worn by Emperor Otto III and later given by him to the Minster of Essen, then an Imperial Abbey (his sister Matilda was its Abbess).

From the time of King Louis VI (1108-37) the fleur-de-lis was adopted as the symbol of the French kings and a circlet with the fleur-de-lis became the standard design for French royal crowns. In the thirteenth and fourteenth centuries, when French Gothic culture prevailed, it became the standard form for European royal crowns in general. It was also used by princes of lower degree than king, and it seems that at least as early as the twelfth century the distinctions in rank that ought to have been indicated by the use of different forms of crowns were becoming blurred through misuse. In indignant reaction against such practices Emperor Lothair II (1125-37) replaced the low arch of earlier imperial crowns with the tall arches known as imperial arches. At the summit of these Conrad III (1138-52) set an orb, surmounted by a cross symbolizing his right to universal supremacy as the Christian Emperor. Crowns with imperial arches of this type remained the distinctive prerogative of the emperor until the fifteenth century, when they were again taken over by lesser rulers, first by the kings of England from c. 1416, later by the kings of Portugal (from 1481), then by the kings of Scotland and France. During the sixteenth century the kings of Sweden and Denmark also added arches to their crowns, thus completing the process by which the closed crown displaced the old medieval circlet with fleurons as the symbol of royal or sovereign rule.

From the crown, the great symbol of sovereignty and rank, let us now turn to jewels that, though worn only on great occasions, were more purely ornamental in their splendor. St Foy, in addition to her crown, wears earrings of gold decorated with granulation and filigree, the pendants hung with pearls, crystals, and garnets. They are probably Byzantine or else Western imitations of Byzantine earrings, for the fashions of the remote imperial capital were eagerly imitated in the aspiring courts of the West. Yet strangely enough, there is little evidence from the twelfth century onward that earrings were at all common in feudal Europe during the Middle Ages. The most important single ornament was the clasp or brooch, which fastened the mantle worn by men and women alike.

Two very important examples of brooches worn by the great ladies of the Ottonian Empire were discovered at Mainz in 1880. These were the two gold eagle brooches associated with Empress Gisela, wife of Conrad II. Both are designed as eagles set in circles. The larger brooch, now in the museum at Mainz, is decorated with cloisonné enamels, and the eagle wears a little crown of sapphires. In the smaller brooch (in Berlin's Schlossmuseum prior to the Second World War), the eagle is decorated with cloisonné enamel, deep blue stripes alternating with green, with a ruby at the top of the tail. The circle enclosing the eagle is set with cloisonné enamels imitating precious stones. With these two brooches was found a splendid gold breast ornament of hanging chains divided into oblong pieces by cross links set with cameos and gems, a large stone at each of the crossings with the vertical chains and a small one between, with a chain hanging from it set with a gem or a cameo at the end.

In general, however, we know little about jewelry from the twelfth or even from the thirteenth century, since few pieces survive and the practice of keeping inventories of jewels began only with the fourteenth century. Perhaps the most splendid of thirteenth-century jewels is the great brooch known as the Schaffhausen Onyx. Made in the second quarter of the thirteenth century for Count Ludwig III or IV of Frohburg, its central feature is a great antique Roman onyx cameo carved with an allegorical figure personifying the blessings of imperial rule. This is mounted in a three-dimensional interlaced display of stylized plant motifs and collets set with precious stones—lions marching around the edge in alternation with the high collets of the gems. This intricate setting is patterned by four large stones set at the top and bottom and at the mid-point of each side. The four divisions thus created are divided yet again by smaller gems set on the mid-point of the edge of each of them and framed in collets set with leaves so as to make them stand out. On the back there is an image of the Count, which is identified by an inscription; he holds in his hand the eagle that was the heraldic charge of his shield.

The change from the majestic style of the Schaffhausen Onyx, still gravely Romanesque in feeling, to the elegance and delicate fantasy of Gothic art can be seen in the late-thirteenth century golden pendant, shaped like an ivy leaf, now in the museum at Cividale del Friuli. It is enameled on the front with a design depicting a leafy spray with birds perched on its branches and on the back with the lozenge-shaped coats-of-arms of Filippo of Taranto, second son of King Charles II of Naples, and Tamar, daughter of Nicephorus I, Despot of Epirus. We know that the pendant must have been made between 1294, when Filippo and Tamar were married in Naples, and 1309, when the Greek princess was sent away in disgrace from her husband and from the Neapolitan court. In all probability it was made in Naples, perhaps by one of the French goldsmiths attached to the court of Charles II, for the heraldic patterning is closely related in style to two French objects of the same date, the so-called Valence Casket, now in the Victoria and Albert Museum in London, and the enameled lid of a nautilus cup in All Souls College at Oxford.

From the beginning of the fourteenth century it becomes progressively easier to learn from surviving objects and from inventories something of the splendors of ceremonial jewelry in the later Middle Ages. As we have just seen, the stylistically significant lines and motifs were in general those of the Gothic style—of all the great European styles perhaps the best suited to jewelry because of its preference for elegant pointed shapes and clear geometric patterns. The sapphire was the Gothic stone par excellence: its blue was constantly imitated in the translucent enamel (basse taille) with which fourteenth-century goldsmiths decorated jewels and plate, chasing and engraving the metal to varying depths so that the coating of enamel would not only echo the light and shade of reality, but evoke the shifting colors of the precious stone. It was of sapphires such as those in the brooches now in the Museo del Castelvecchio, Verona, that Dante must have been thinking when he wrote of the *"dolce colore d'orientale zaffiro."* They have been attributed to Venice, but the splendors they call up are those of the great court of the Scaligers at Verona. Rubies, emeralds, and pearls were the other stones most prized.

In fourteenth-century western Europe the center of fashion was the royal court of Paris. We can form some impression of the jewelry worn by a French king from the short inventory of very personal possessions that had belonged to King Jean le Bon. The list was drawn up after King Jean's sudden death in London on 8 April 1364. By far the largest part of his collection of jewels consisted of rings. His remaining ornaments were few and simple—some brooches, mostly set with gems, usually of cluster form (smaller stones arranged around a larger central stone, of which at least one was a cameo); a gold chain from which hung a signet set with another cameo, several paternosters; and two ambergris balls, better known as pomanders. At this period, and for some two centuries more, the distinction between the sexes in the nature and quantity of the jewelry they wore was far from being so great as it became afterward, though of course differences in costume brought with it some differences in the type and design of jewelry. Brooches, belts and chains were worn by both men and women; perhaps the fillet and coronal were the only exclusively feminine pieces of jewelry, since noblemen wore their coronets and kings their crowns only as symbols of rank on great occasions.

The jewelry worn by a great queen of the same period can be seen from the inventory of King Charles V of France, drawn up in 1379-80, in that section describing the personal jewels of the King and of Queen Jeanne de Bourbon (d. 1378). The most distinctly feminine pieces are the ornaments for the head, the fillets and coronals just mentioned. The Queen had several fillets (cercles) that consisted of a number of jointed oblong pieces, set with precious stones, and several coronals in the form of a band of jointed oblong pieces from each of which rose a fleuron. Some fourteenth-century coronals still survive; two that are probably German are in the Collezione Carrand in the Bargello (Museo Nazionale) in Florence. The other large body ornament was the belt, which might be short and worn tightly clasped around the body or long and worn hanging down in front like a girdle. Those recorded in the inventory were of gold, made of jointed pieces—up to sixty in one case. For their decoration pearls were preferred, either large or small; sapphires, rubies, emeralds, and diamonds are also mentioned, but seem mostly to have been reserved for the clasps. Only one necklace is mentioned in the inventory of Charles V. It had five large and four linking sections; each of the large sections was set with twenty-four large pearls, two rubies, and two emeralds around a central sapphire. Although such elaborate necklaces were rare, pendants were often worn, probably hung from slender chains. The cross was, of course, a favorite motif, as it had always been in Byzantium and western Europe from Early Christian times, but images of saints, fleurs-de-lis, and animal motifs are also recorded in the inventory. Suspended from her girdle a fourteenth-century lady might also carry a small mirror. This could be of gold set with gems, or like that of Queen Jeanne, which had a "C" and a "J" on the outside (the initials of the royal pair) and on the inside an enameled scene of the Annunciation. The main decoration for the neck remained the clasp or brooch, still all-important as the fastening for the mantle or the top of a dress. It might be a pattern of jewels set in gold, like those of Queen Jeanne, or have imagery such as was found on many of those owned by the King, who had a number of *fermeaux* shaped as fleurs-de-lis; one in the form of an Agnus Dei set with rubies, diamonds, pearls and a great sapphire in the center; and others in the form of eagles, griffins, stags, and swans. A fleur-de-lis clasp, dating from the late fourteenth century and which was once part of the French regalia, still survives in the Louvre.

Often the brooch would be inscribed with a device, in courtly circles frequently amorous, promising fidelity and eternal love. Often too its function as a clasp would be ingeniously allegorized into an emblem of love and its design fashioned with appropriate symbols such as the age-old motif of two clasped hands. Devices might also be prophylactic, and many medieval brooches and clasps were inscribed with an AVE MARIA GRACIA PLENA or a IESVS NAZARENVS REX IVDAEORVM or a CASPAR MELCHIOR BALTASAR, all mottoes believed to ward off harm and protect the bearer. It was also a medieval habit, which indeed like many others has persisted almost into modern times, to wear relics (or pieces of such) in jewelry for the same purpose. Great numbers of reliquary pendants and brooches are recorded in inventories; some of the pendants were fastened by a screw stopper that allowed the relics to be removed or changed at will. Another jewel was the ball of musk or ambergris, which we noted was worn by King Jean; those of Charles V were mounted in gold and most were suspended by a silk ribbon, fastened by a button of pearls.

Perhaps the most beautiful of all Gothic ladies' crowns is the late-fourteenth-century gold crown, now in the Schatzkammer of the Munich Residenz, which was brought to Germany in 1402 by Princess Blanche, daughter of King Henry IV of England, as part of her dowry upon her marriage to the Elector Palatine Ludwig III of Bavaria (son of Ruprecht, King of the Romans). This crown later became known as the Crown of the Palatinate. It is almost certainly identifiable as the crown described in 1399 as being one of the older possessions of the English crown, and it is now thought to have been made around 1370-80. The circlet is composed of twelve links, each of Gothic sexfoil form and pierced with elegant Gothic tracery. The links are enameled red and blue alternately, and set with a central sapphire, surrounded by rubies and quatrefoils of pearls. Above each of the links soars a fleuron, alternately low and high. The stems of the taller fleurons are set with quatrefoils of pearls and are topped by triangles of pearls, while the shorter fleurons have single pearls on their stems and at the top. From the leaves of all the fleurons gems—sapphires, rubies, emeralds—stand out like flowers in high collets. On the leaves of the larger fleurons they are so disposed that three sapphires shine around a ruby; on the smaller ones three rubies set off a central sapphire. The whole design is a sophisticated Gothic transposition of nature into an abstract formality of pattern and color, the forms of nature being evoked by symbolic correspondences rather than by realistic depictions. The enamel that decorates the links of the circlet adds an additional decorative note of color echoing the rubies and sapphires glowing in the pattern of jewels. How similar a man's crown might be appears from a record of the sale in 1415 by Charles, Duke of Orléans, a French royal prince, of his great crown of gold and gems. This had six tall fleurons, enameled in green and blue on the back. The central fleuron at both front and back was set with five sapphires and five rubies; the other fleurons were set with pearls, thirty-five on each of the larger ones, and five on each of the smaller ones, which were set with two emeralds in addition.

It has been suggested that Princess Blanche wore her crown as a bridal crown. We might expect royal ladies to wear crowns at their weddings, but in the Middle Ages young girls of lesser degree also wore crowns or chaplets on their heads and ornaments on their dresses on the occasion of their wedding. The poet Chaucer mentions such a custom in late-fourteenth-century England, and it still survives at weddings in Norway and Sweden, where so many of the customs and styles of medieval Europe persisted long after their disappearance elsewhere. Two other customs have led to the making of crowns of great artistic splendor. One was the practice of crowning reliquary statues or busts with magnificent crowns, such as we have already encountered in the case of St Foy. Naturally, the reliquaries given crowns were usually those of royal saints. In the late thirteenth century King Philip IV of France gave a crowned reliquary bust of his grandfather, St Louis, to the Sainte Chapelle in Paris which Louis had founded (the bust was destroyed in the French Revolution). The famous fourteenth-century reliquary bust of Charlemagne in the treasury of the cathedral at Aachen wears a beautiful Gothic crown. Figures of Christ were also shown crowned in the medieval period, to symbolize the monarchy of Christ—the bronze crucifix figure in the cathedral at Vercelli is still crowned with a real crown of imperial type dating from the late tenth century. Statues and even paintings of the Virgin were (and still are) often crowned to show that she is the Queen of Heaven.

Internal dissension and the English occupation of much of France in the first three decades of the fifteenth century brought a brutal end to the brilliant and sumptuous life of all the Valois courts, with the exception of that of the dukes of Burgundy. It was the great cities of the Netherlands with their flourishing crafts that made the Burgundian dukes the wealthiest and most important patrons of their age. The Netherlands had produced important artists in the fourteenth century, but they had been drawn to Paris and to the other royal courts of France. With the settlement in Flanders of a ducal court which was determined to maintain the splendid sumptuary and artistic traditions of the French royal house from which it sprang, there began in the Netherlands those three marvelous centuries during which the region was one of the most creative artistic centers of Europe. In jewelry the Burgundian court continued and developed the traditions of late-fourteenth-century Paris, though with a rather heavier splendor. Thus the Burgundian brooch of c. 1430-40 in the Schatzkammer at Vienna in which two lovers hold hands in a frame of leaves continues the tradition of émail en ronde bosse. This naturalistic technique of coating gold figures with opaque enamel, notably a brilliant white, had been invented in late-fourteenth-century Paris. The cameo portrait of c. 1440 that used to be regarded as a portrait of Philip the Good of Burgundy, but that is now thought to represent Robert, Seigneur de Masmines (who was admitted into the Order of the Golden Fleece in 1431), is another example of Burgundian work in a genre originally Parisian.

It was in the fifteenth century that there arose the fashion for wearing chains and necklaces that was to make them and the pendants hanging from them of singular importance for two centuries. As we have already seen, the necklace had not been an important ornament in the fourteenth century, but now the neckline of women's dresses plunged, creating a frame for the display of a sumptuous ornament. A beautiful German late-fifteenth-century necklace is in the possession of the Hohenlohe family. The motif of the links is the typical Late Gothic naturalistic one of interlacing leafless twigs; between each link is a sapphire set in a delicate frame of leaves. The pendant is a double rose, enameled white, on which with true fifteenth-century love of irony and surprise there rests the head of a fool. In the second half of the fifteenth century, there was a fashion for making the close-fitting collars known as *gorgerins* in precious metal. Sometimes these were decorated with letters, usually those of the wearer's Christian name. In 1467, the Duchess of Burgundy had one of gold mesh set with two plates each enameled with two "C"s. In 1493, Anne of Brittany paid a goldsmith for one made with thirty-two double strands interwoven in checkerboard fashion and set with thirty-two twisted "A"s partly enameled red and white and framed in black beads. The whole was fixed on a ground of burnished gold.

The reasons for the new popularity of chains among men are not so clear. Already in 1413-16 the Duc de Berry owned a collar of twisted gold wire

212

decorated with his device of little bears in white enamel and with rosettes in white enamel, each rosette set with a diamond, alternating with lozenges. Another of his collars was also decorated with little bears in white enamel. Yet a third was composed of lozenges, while two more had the broom-pods of the royal order of the King of France. A sixth had links like those of a chain and was set with a square ruby and a great diamond between two bears enameled black. From its front hung two broom-pods, one of emerald and one of mother-of-pearl, and from its back, which was set with another ruby, hung two more broom-pods, one enameled white and the other green. For most of the century the chain was an emblem of knightly dignity. In this, the last age when dreams of chivalry still shaped the ceremonial forms of court life, orders of knighthood proliferated in every state, from large kingdom to small duchy. Each order had its own distinctive badge and many a distinctive collar, worn by its members as a sign of fraternity and allegiance. Some, like the Order of the Golden Fleece of the Dukes of Burgundy, were destined for a long and illustrious life; others disappeared almost immediately after their foundation. In one instance—the English collar of interlinked "S"s, which was the badge of the House of Lancaster—is still worn by certain English dignitaries.

It was in the fifteenth century too that it became customary for emperors, kings, and other rulers to present gold chains as a sign of favor or as a reward for bravery, merit, or faithful service. King Louis XI of France gave a gold chain to Raoul de Lannois at the end of a tournament with the joking words that since Raoul was so furious a fighter he needed a chain to keep him alive for the King's service. Until 1614 and even later, French kings regularly gave a gold chain to the colonels of the Swiss regiments they took into their service and another to the Swiss ambassadors every time they renewed their alliance with the Cantons. As late as 1679, the Republic of Venice could still give the Italian poet Antonio Caraccio a gold chain as a token of its appreciation of his epic poem in praise of the city, *L'Imperio Vendicato*. A number of chains with gold medals bearing portraits of German rulers and princes of the early seventeenth century suspended from them were probably such gifts. Only in the eighteenth century did the snuff box finally oust the chain as the favorite token of princely esteem and gratitude.

Partly of heraldic significance was another typical article of fifteenth century male jewelry, the hat badge. The origin of this particular type of jewelry was probably religious. From the twelfth century at least it was the custom for pilgrims to buy images and tokens, usually made of lead, at the shrines they visited and to wear them afterward on their clothes. As early as 1183, there is a reference to the wearing of such badges on the chaperon, the usual covering of the head in the early Middle Ages. In the fourteenth century they seem to have been worn as pendants or brooches when it was desired to give them prominence. The first references to political and heraldic badges come from this century. In 1358, for instance, the rebellious citizens of Paris swore to wear little enameled silver brooches with the words *"à bonne fin."* And from at least as early as the later years of the century, badges with the arms of princes and great noblemen were made to be worn by their retainers. Obviously religious, armorial, and political badges of this kind could be (and were) worn as pendants. The fashion for elaborately fanciful hats that arose during the fourteenth century inaugurated the custom of wearing such badges prominently on the hat. They were worn only by men, for women did not begin to wear hats until the sixteenth century. One of the finest of surviving hat badges is the gold and enameled one in the Schatzkammer at Vienna, showing a half-length figure of the young Emperor Charles V.

The English regalia still contains a curious survival from the Dark Ages in the form of royal bracelets. Bracelets or armlets of gold were royal ornaments in the ancient East, but were rejected by the Greeks and Romans as ornaments fit only for women. By contrast, among the Northern peoples they were regarded as emblems of royal and noble rank and they retained their ancestral prestige into Carolingian and Ottonian times. Charles the Bald wore armlets at his coronation in 875, and later armlets were included among the insignia of the Holy Roman Empire. The custom of delivering them to the emperors at their coronation seems to have disappeared by the eleventh or early twelfth century, but a pair of bracelets was kept among the insignia of the emperor at Nuremberg until they were lost between 1796 and 1800, during the invasion of Germany by the French Revolutionary armies. The fashion for wearing bracelets as personal ornaments seems to have begun in the late fourteenth or early fifteenth century, a period during which, as will already have become obvious, a number of rich and elaborate types of jewelry were introduced. They were worn by both men and women. The wedding trousseau of Marie de Bourgogne in 1415 included a gold bracelet set with six sapphires and six pearls. It was enameled with little flowers on the outside and on the inside was set with little beads of white, green, and silver gilt. These early bracelets, as we learn from Philip the Good's inventory of 1420, often had little chains hanging from them to which rings were attached. Perhaps because of its form and its position near the pulse, the bracelet frequently had an amorous significance. In 1428, the King of England owned one showing two ladies (enameled white) each holding in her hand a flower of four diamonds with an ouch (clasp) above her head. Jehan de Saintré, the hero of Antoine de la Salle's romance, written in 1451, was ordered by his lady to wear for love of her a gold bracelet enameled with her device and his, and decorated with six good diamonds, six good rubies, and six good and large pearls weighing 4 to 5 carats.

The jewels of great ecclesiastics were no less splendid than those of the laity. The Papal tiara or *regnum* with which a Pope is crowned after his election was as splendid as any secular crown. This was only proper, for it was the symbol of his temporal sovereignty. Originally it had been a linen cap which in the eleventh and twelfth centuries became taller and was stiffened at the base by a rim of precious metal set with gems. The imperious Boniface VIII (reigned 1294-1303) added a second circlet around the middle of the cap, at which time it began to be referred to as a tiara. A third circlet was added by 1315 and from this time onward the Papal crown acquired its name of the *triregnum* (literally, "triple kingdom"). The three crowns have been accounted for allegorically and mystically, but the most probable explanation of their origin is that they were adopted by the popes in rivalry with the emperors, who from the thirteenth century onward were crowned, more often in theory than practice, with three crowns—the golden crown of the Holy Roman Empire, the silver crown of Germany, and the iron crown of Italy. With the first, the Pope himself had to crown the Emperor in Rome, with the second he was crowned at Aachen by the Archbishop of Cologne, and with the last by the Archbishop of Milan at Milan, Pavia, or Monza. The famous, if historically rather dubious, Iron Crown is still preserved in the last named; only in the eleventh century did Monza first claim that the kings of Italy must be crowned in its cathedral. The rich mitres (*mitrae pretiosae*) worn by the Pope and higher clergy were often enriched with gold and silver, precious stones, and enamels. In 1419-20 Lorenzo Ghiberti made one in Florence for Pope Martin V of gold decorated with eight half-length figures, and in the 1430s another, even more elaborate, for Pope Eugenius IV, ornamented in front with Christ seated on the throne surrounded by small angels, and at the back with the Virgin, also enthroned and surrounded by small angels. On the base were figures of the four Evangelists and more small angels. A silver-gilt mitre set with gems which in 1457 belonged to the Venetians was also decorated with figures of the Evangelists and was studded with pearls, relieved by sapphires and rubies. On the pendants of the mitre were the images of St Peter and St Paul and silver-gilt tabernacles, set with rubies and sapphires.

The morse that fastens the cope across the breast of the priest was often as rich as the most elaborate secular brooches. It too might be of gold and silver, set with precious stones and enameled or decorated in relief. Of those belonging in 1295 to St Paul's Cathedral in London, one was set with cameos, precious stones, and pearls; another was decorated with scenes of the Coronation of the Virgin, with St Peter and St Paul standing to either side with angels above, and also set with gems and pearls; while yet another had a lion in the middle, encircled by gems and turquoises. Later, in the second half of the fourteenth century, we find such fanciful devices as gold morses in the form of an "M" (for Mary, the Virgin). In 1379, one of these belonged to the royal chapel of King Charles V of France, and it is likely that the so-called brooch that William of Wykeham, Bishop of Winchester, gave or bequeathed in or before 1403 to his foundation, New College in Oxford, where it is still preserved, is in fact a morse. It is decorated with the Annunciation scene between the bars. In 1379, the French royal chapel also had a morse decorated with the Nativity in relief. Ghiberti is known to have made a gold morse with the Pietà on it for Pope Martin V. One or two beautiful morses decorated with sculptural scenes still survive from the fifteenth century.

It was not until the end of the fifteenth century that the Renaissance style made an impact upon the design of European jewelry. Even in Italy for much of the century the splendor and prestige of French and Burgundian court fashions influenced the costume and jewelry of the aspiring lords and merchants of Italy, though the simpler domestic styles are those most often represented in Italian fifteenth-century portraits and paintings. Is it accidental that in an inventory of the treasures of the Este Dukes of Ferrara, drawn up in 1493-4, twelve of the fifteen jewels listed are described as *"alla tedescha"*, that is, in the German fashion? All were of enameled gold set with precious stones. The subjects represented on them scarcely suggest the Renaissance: a man stretching a bow, a man holding a mace, a fool, a mermaid sounding a horn, a griffin seated in front of a tree with a monkey at its feet, a siren playing a harp, another holding a mirror, a fountain with two children, an eagle and the Este badge. Imagery and symbolism are still Gothic even in the most elaborate of these jewels, in which six griffins supported a mountain of enameled silver, set with castles and trees, on top of which was a two-headed eagle, the heraldic device of the Estensi, with a crown on each head and a collar around its neck. At the foot of the mountain was a grotto, underneath which was a fountain enclosed in a towered wall, with a child standing on top of the fountain and a unicorn beside it. To judge from the evidence of portraits, simple strings of pearls and delicate chains were principally favored by Quattrocento ladies. But since most surviving portraits of the period show ladies who were only merchants' wives, we cannot expect them to display the elaborate jewelry of court ladies. Piero della Francesca's portrait (c. 1470) of Battista Sforza, wife of Federigo da Montefeltro, shows her wearing a *gorgeret,* a rich neck-lace and pendant, and a jeweled headdress—all of which amply proclaim her princely rank as Countess of Urbino.

Classical jewelry, probably because it was little known, influenced neither the forms, the decoration, nor the techniques of Renaissance jewelry, which instead used classical forms and motifs borrowed from other arts, either in miniature form or from classical gems. There was no adoption, as there was to be three centuries later under the French Empire, of classical fashions. Indeed it is obvious that Renaissance jewelry is the result of an application of general Renaissance stylistic motifs (and at times of Renaissance imagery) to types of jewelry were already current in the early fifteenth century. Thus the importance of the chain or necklace in no way changes, but its links are designed with Renaissance rather than Gothic ornamental motifs.

Enamel continued to be the paramount decorative technique and was applied according to High Renaissance canons of coloring, though in contrast to the previous age, the preference now was for a stately balance between enameled areas and uncolored gold. We may note here some changes and also some curiosities of fashion. The medal became a frequent constituent of jewelry from the second half of the Quattrocento—most medalists were in fact goldsmiths until the end of the Baroque age. The coronal or chaplet was no longer worn by ladies of rank, perhaps because a gold-embroidered headdress was now the fashion. In the sixteenth as in the fifteenth century certain sorts of objects were still worn by women suspended from the girdle or belt, a custom that often meant they were transformed into works of jewelry. The pomander, also worn by men, was still carried in this way. Another fashion, that of suspending a favorite small book—usually, but not alas always, so moralists lamented, a book of devotion—appears to have been a Renaissance innovation. Some splendidly worked silver-gilt bindings that survive, in some instances richly enameled, were probably made for wearing from the belt or girdle. Perhaps the custom developed from the Late Gothic motif of pendants in the form of books. At her death in 1517 Queen Catherine of Navarre owned a small *matines* (matins book), which when opened showed two scenes of the Nativity and Pietà, one on each of the covers.

The brooch fell completely out of fashion in the late fifteenth century because of the universal adoption of décolletage by woman, and of the close fitting tunic by men. By the 1520s, when Benvenuto Cellini received his first important commissions, the usual items of jewelry were the hat badge for men, chains or necklaces, pendants, the belt or girdle, the bracelet, and the ring. When Italian styles spread to the rest of Europe, as they did increasingly from about 1500, their adoption was made all the easier because they brought no innovation in genre, but merely in design.

We are much better informed about sixteenth-century sources of designs and production, much better indeed than about the jewels themselves, for sixteenth-century jewels are only relatively less rare than medieval ones. What we know certainly suggests that, if anything, the appetite for jewelry grew during this period, and that the consequence was a tendency to standardization of designs and production methods, even at the level of ceremonial jewelry. Cellini tells us that in Rome in the second and third decade of the century, the Milanese goldsmith Caradosso found it difficult to meet the demand for his "excellent works" and so took to making bronze models with motifs in relief for hat badges and medals. He hammered and chased his sheet of gold over the model so that the motif was embossed on the gold, then removed the gold and put it through various other finishing processes. A few years later this practice must have begun to spread, for a number of sixteenth-century copper and bronze models for jewelry survive; there is a famous collection of them at the Historisches Museum in Basle. It would, however, be wrong to give the impression that jewelry became a mass-produced product in the Renaissance: many important jewels are known to have been unique works of art that were specially commissioned and designed.

Yet the sixteenth century was also the first great age of the international jewelry designer, now for the first time often not a practicing goldsmith. His rise was probably stimulated by the swiftly spreading popularity of the Renaissance style in the courts and among the great and learned personages north of the Alps. This style was totally unfamiliar to all Northern goldsmiths, the vast majority never having visited Italy. Dürer, who brought the Venetian Renaissance to the Gothic city of Nuremberg, made drawings of belt-ends and clasps for goldsmiths, and the German-born Holbein, who settled in England in 1526, designed pendants and chains in the German Renaissance style for his patrons at court. Engraving, the essential technique for reproducing such designs, thus making them a marketable commodity, was already in existence, and in its origins was exclusively a goldsmith's technique.

The style of nervous elaboration that developed from about 1515 onward and that is known to art historians as Mannerism was soon reflected in jewelry. From the 1540s the old, serenely spacious manner begins to disappear. Although there is no change in the choice of motifs selected for pendants (the type of jewel that has survived in greatest numbers), their treatment is now languidly decorative, a tendency implicit in the impersonal figural style favored by the Mannerists. The Mannerist tendency to reduce the figurative elements in a composition at the expense of the architectural framework is also expressed in jewelry. Frames now assume an exaggerated importance in many pendants. Intricate, sometimes even including architecturally treated figures, these frames often detract from the motif they enclose. Smooth planes and contours are rejected in favor of surfaces richly decorated in low relief and with broken outlines. Like the High Renaissance style, the Mannerist style in jewelry was diffused through engraved designs: among the most important are those of Etienne Delaune and René Boyvin, representing the School of Fontainebleau, and those of Hans Collaert whose designs are typical of the even more influential Antwerp Mannerists.

The staccato effects in the general design of Mannerist jewelry were paralleled in the treatment of color: the broad, almost heraldic boldness of earlier enamel with its few smoothly applied colors is replaced by a wide range of colors applied in small patches, in elaborate patterns of changing tints, sometimes almost achieving the effects of "shot" color beloved by Mannerist painters. Stones are usually small and are absorbed into larger patterns of color; if large, they tend to be worked into the general color scheme, if only by supplying its key. There was one exception to this tendency: the Mannerist age saw an apotheosis of the pearl, above all of the irregular "Baroque" pearl, whose iridescences and asymmetrical form gratified its taste for the caprices of nature. It was the triumph of every great jeweler to incorporate them into ingeniously constructed figures, mythological monsters, birds, or animals. This taste for conceits assembling different materials and techniques into a single composition also appears in a group of jewels, possibly made in Milan, of which the most famous is probably the hat badge depicting Leda and the Swan (Kunsthistorisches Museum, Vienna). In these jewels (often called *commessi*), carved gems or stones form an integal part of the scene represented, while the rest is carried out in traditional techniques. Thus the body and foot of Leda are in white agate, and the other parts of the badge are executed in enameled gold, producing a very splendid effect.

Engraved gems and carved stones were the delight of Mannerist princes, who saw in difficult techniques a means of penetrating the secrets of Nature. In the middle decades of the sixteenth century the technique of porphyry carving was rediscovered in Florence by no less a personage than Cosimo I de Medici; and a little later, and in the same city, came the invention of the technique of *pietra dura*. Hence it is not surprising to find that cameo cutting and the working of semi-precious stones flourished even more extravagantly than in the past. Milan was an important center of these crafts. The Saracchi and Miseroni were famous practitioners in crystal carving there during the second half of the century, and it was from Milan that the Emperor Rudolph II brought cameo cutters to his court in Prague, the most important center of late international Mannerism.

It was for the Emperor Rudolph that one of the most beautiful imperial crowns was made. It is of a special imperial type, called the mitre-crown. From the time of the Ottonians, it was an imperial doctrine that the emperor, like the kings of Israel, was both king and priest. It was known from the Bible that the High Priest of the Jews has worn a golden crown over a mitre and the Emperor Otto I and his advisers chose for his coronation a form of crown with a single arch because it could be worn over a mitre. Later the Popes, ever anxious to reduce the pretentions of the emperors, granted other kings the privilege of wearing the mitre, but the emperors nonetheless continued to wear one throughout the Middle Ages. It seems to have been the Emperor Frederick III who introduced the innovation by which mitre and crown were combined into a single mitre-crown; the new imperial regalia he ordered from Nuremberg in 1452 included the mitre-crown that he is shown wearing on his tomb effigy in St Stephen's Cathedral in Vienna. The high pointed sides of the mitre were formed of bands of precious metal enclosing panels decorated with pearls. Within was a cap for wearing under the crown. Although Frederick's son Maximilian and Emperor Charles V are also known to have had imperial mitre-crowns, Rudolph's is the only example of the type extant. It symbolizes his triple dignity as Emperor, as King of Hungary, and as King of Bohemia in three scenes embossed on the sides of the mitre around the circlet. In one Rudolph receives the crown of the Holy Roman Empire in Frankfurt Cathedral, in the second he rides in the Hungarian coronation procession on the coronation hill at Bratislava, and in the third he goes in procession to his coronation on the Hradschin in Prague. A fourth scene is an allegory of his greatest achievement as a Christian Emperor, the defeat of the Turks. In addition to its reliefs, the crown is decorated with enamel, diamonds, and rubies. A single sapphire, perhaps symbolizing Heaven, surmounts the hoop, and above it rises the cross. Rudolph commissioned the crown because in 1423 the Emperor Sigismund had handed over the insignia of the Holy Roman Empire to the custody of the city of Nuremberg. They were taken from Nuremberg only when they were carried to Frankfurt on the occasion of the coronation of each new emperor. Hence Rudolph had need of a splendid crown to symbolize his dignity. It was made in 1602 in his imperial court workshop in the Hradschin. Its designer is unknown, but it seems very likely that he was Rudolph's court goldsmith, Jan Vermeyen. In 1804, when Austria became an independent empire, the Emperor Francis I chose this crown as the Imperial Austrian crown.

With the advent of Baroque costume the great age of ceremonial jewelry was over. The Baroque age preferred vast flowing and spreading effects of rich materials to the tight-fitting, somber fashions relieved only by splendid lines of gold and gems that had been the preference of the previous period. Already in the 1640s the French court, which was to set European fashion in costume and jewelry for the next century and a half, regarded it as vulgar to wear jewels, or at any rate to be heavily adorned with them. Instead the French courtiers preferred to deck themselves out in ribbons. Madame de Motteville, describing the entry of a Polish ambassador and his retinue into Paris in 1645, was struck with admiration for the rich costumes of the Poles, strewn with diamonds and precious stones, and commented: *"En cette occasion, la mode des Français de ne porter que des rubans fut trouvée chétive et ridicule"* ("On this occasion, the French habit of wearing only ribbons seemed paltry and ridiculous"). Later Louis XIV might appear in a coat spangled with diamonds, but the subordination of jewelry to the decoration of costume implied in this fashion was symptomatic of the changed attitude of the new age to ceremonial life. Tradition demanded that crowns and other ceremonial jewels be made, in order that ancient rituals and time-honored distinctions of rank might be maintained. But in the Age of Enlightenment their role became formal and conventional, and they were no longer endowed with a living symbolism of a universally accepted earthly hierarchy. This change in the role of jewelry is clearly reflected in its design, which becomes purely frivolous, or else a pale and timid imitation of traditional designs.

Portrait of Henry VIII by Hans Holbein the Younger. The King's costume makes clear his flamboyant taste in jewelry. He is wearing the smaller of his two famous great collars; it has 9 great balas rubies and collets of gold with 10 knots, each containing 16 round pearls. In this portrait, as in others, we note that the jewelry also includes pieces which form an integral part of the king's clothing, such as jeweled buttons to fasten his doublet. The forms and colors of the jewels match the fabrics.

The splendid Eagle brooch (also known as the Gisela brooch) of enameled gold from the treasury of the Empress Gisela, wife of Conrad II. This imperial brooch is a very important example of the brooches worn by the great ladies of the Ottonian and Swabian Empires. The eagle in the center, decorated in cloisonné enamel, breaks through the encircling ring, which is adorned with 8 flowers enameled in translucent green, blue, white, and yellow. The eagle wears a little crown of sapphires. Ottonian, c. 1025. Ht. 9.6 cm.

A delicate Gothic golden pendant, shaped like an ivy leaf. It is enameled on the front with a design depicting a leafy spray with birds perched on its branches, and on the back with the lozenge-shaped coats of arms of Filippo of Taranto, the second son of Charles II, King of Naples, and Tamar, daughter of Nicephorus I, Despot of Epirus. Late 13th century. Probably by a French goldsmith working in Naples. Ht. 7.5 cm.

Brooch of pearls and precious stones, attributed to Venice. Northern Italian, mid-14th century. W. 10.5 cm.

Brooch in the shape of a star set with pearls and precious stones. Northern Italian, mid-14th century. Diam. 15 cm.

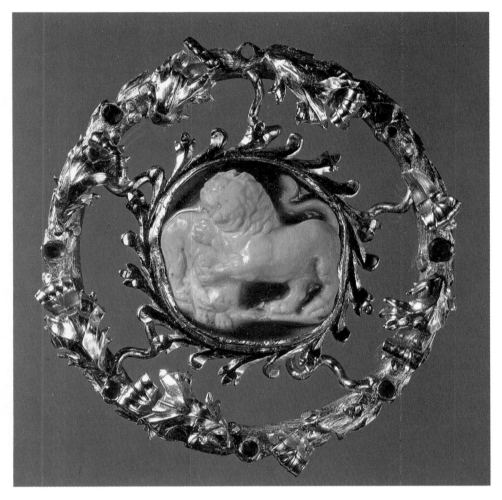

Gold brooch set with an onyx cameo of a lion rending its prey, and rubies. Spanish, late 14th or 15th century. Diam. 5.2 cm.

Gold ring-brooch set with rubies and sapphires; the back is decorated with a wreath in niello. French, 13th century. Diam. 5 cm.

Cameo, formerly supposed a portrait of Philip the Good of Burgundy. Burgundian, c. 1440. Diam. 9 cm.

Gold brooch, partly enameled and set with pearls and precious stones, showing two lovers holding hands in a garden of flowers and foliage. Between the lovers' heads is a triangular diamond and beneath it is a cabochon ruby. This splendid brooch (probably the finest example of 15th century brooch extant) was part of the treasure of the House of Burgundy and came into the imperial collection at Vienna through the marriage of Mary of Burgundy to Maximilian I. Netherlands, 1430-1440. W. 5 cm.

Hat medallion of enameled gold bearing a portrait of the young Emperor Charles V about 1520, shortly after his coronation. During this period cameo portraits were very much in fashion. Francis I and Henry VIII as well as other famous personalities (such as members of the Medici family) had their portraits cut by the leading cameo cutters of the time. The jewelers, not to be outdone, produced rival portraits in enameled gold. Netherlands, c. 1520. Diam. 4.9 cm.

Detail of the Hohenlohe necklace showing an enormous sapphire in a frame of leaves and the pendant which is a double rose in white enamel on which rests the fool's head.

Necklace of gold, enamel and sapphires in the possession of the Hohenlohe family in Germany. The motif here is of interlacing leafless twigs; between each link is a sapphire set in a delicate frame of leaves. The pendant is a double rose, enameled white, on which there rests the head of a fool. German, second half of the 15th century.

The Phoenix Jewel, which shows a bust of Queen Elizabeth I, cut from the Queen's Phoenix medal of 1574, framed in a wreath of Tudor roses executed in enameled gold. English, 16th century. W. 4.6 cm.

Ring of gold, the shoulders ornamented with flowers and leaves once enameled. The oval bezel contains a chalcedony with the arms of Mary, Queen of Scots. French, 16th century. Diam. 2.1 cm.

Agate cameo by Jacopo di Trezzo – one of the most famous cameo cutters of the Renaissance – in a frame by Jan Vermeyen (goldsmith to the court of Rudolf II). Prague, c. 1600. Ht. 3.5 cm.

230

Gold pendant in the form of a Bohemian Lion, possibly from a design of Hans Mielich. The lion holds in its forepaws an open circlet of emeralds and wears a crown decorated with rubies and pearls. His neck-ring is set with diamonds. German, c. 1570-80. From the Palatine Treasury. Ht. 8.8 cm.

Mermaid pendant jewel of wrought gold, enamel, precious stones and pearls. Using large irregularly shaped pearls (so-called baroque pearls) as the torso, the 16th century goldsmiths created fabulous creatures (mermaids, tritons, sea dragons) by adding the rest in gold, enameled *en ronde bosse* and studded with gems. Style of Benvenuto Cellini. Italian 16th century Ht. 14 cm.

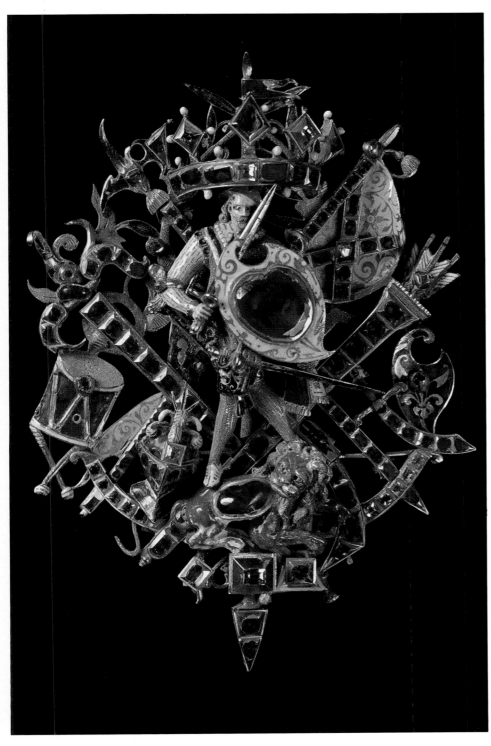

Trophy-jewel of enameled gold set with rubies, said to have been lost by Charles I of England on the battlefield of Naseby in 1645, during the English Civil War. This splendid ruby-set jewel shows a knight armed with sword and shield surrounded by a trophy of arms. A flag bears the St Andrews Cross of Scotland, and a lion crouches at his feet. German, c. 1615. Ht. 9.2 cm.

A Golden Fleece of oriental garnets, brilliants, rubies and gold. The order was founded in Burgundy, and later passed to the House of Habsburg. The insignia of the Golden Fleece, worn by sovereigns, was a great fashion for jewelry in the 18th century. The most splendid gems in the royal collections were mounted in magnificent compositions which became luxurious symbols of distinction. German, 1760-70. Ht. 15.7 cm.

The Imperial Sword of Bavaria, made of gold decorated with chased ornamentation. The hilt and guard are set with rubies, sapphires, brilliants, and a large emerald. The clasps bear the maker's mark, "M.G. Biennais Paris 1806." Total L: 95.5 cm.

Diamond sword designed by Everard Bapst and executed by Charles Bapst for the coronation of Charles X of France in 1824. It contains 1,576 brilliants, weighing 330.75 carats, chosen from stones in the crown jewels. French, 1824. L. 93.5 cm.

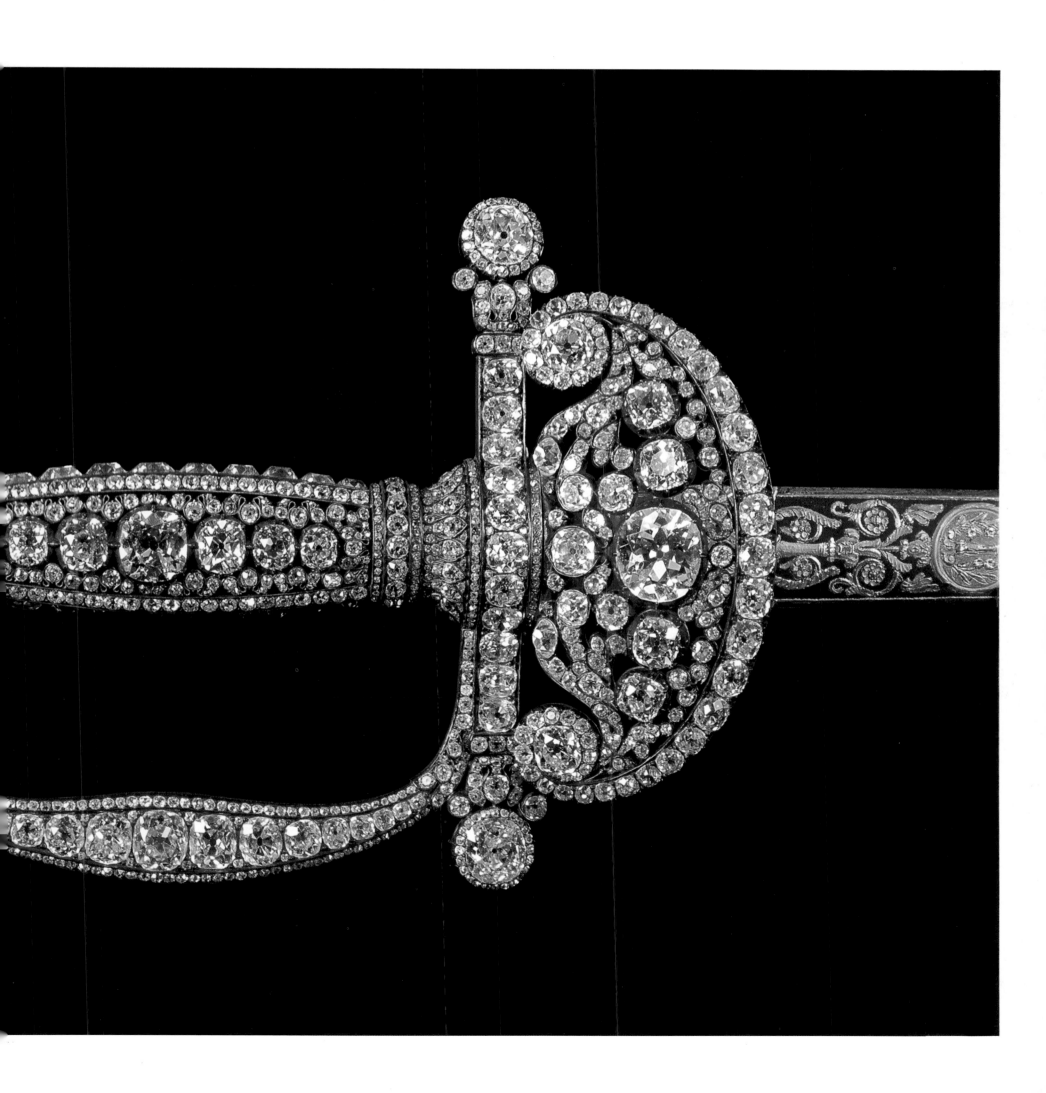

Theodolinda's Crown—one of Italy's two historic Lombardic crowns. Her crown consists of a gold circlet, the upper and lower borders of which was originally decorated with 38 pearls. Later, they were replaced with pieces of mother-of-pearl; only one of the original pearls has been left. The center of the circlet was decorated with sapphires and emeralds but most of these were removed when the crown was stolen by Napoleon's soldiers in 1804. Lombardy, 6th century. Diam. 19 cm.

Crown of the Empress Kunigunde, daughter of Siegfried, Count of Luxemburg, and wife of the Emperor Henry II, known as Henry the Saint. Both of them were renowned for their devotion to the Church and they were both canonized. The gold circlet consists of five rectangular plates decorated with filigree and set with sapphires, rubies, amethysts, pearls, topazes, and chrysolites. The five plates are joined together with hinges. Probably from Lorraine (Metz?) c. 1010-20. Diam. 19 cm.

Silver-gilt crown consisting of 11 rectangular plates, each of which is surmounted by a fleur-de-lis. The front fleur-de-lis is considerably larger than the others and is surmounted by a stylized cross which is set with a fine sapphire. The crown is richly decorated with rubies, pearls, sapphires, and amethysts. At one time this crown and the Crown of the Empress Kunigunde were joined together so as to make one crown. German, 1350. Diam. 19 cm.

Gold crown, one of the most beautiful of all Gothic crowns, brought to Germany in 1402 by Princess Blanche, daughter of King Henry IV of England, as part of her dowry on her marriage to the Elector Palatine, Ludwig III of Bavaria. The crown is elaborately decorated with sapphires, rubies, emeralds, and pearls. It is almost certainly the crown that was described in 1399 as being one of the jewels of the English crown and was made c. 1370-80. French or English. Diam., 18 cm.

The Crown of the Emperor Rudolph II of Habsburg – after 1804, the Austrian Imperial Crown. Made of gold, enamel, diamonds, rubies, pearls, and a single sapphire surmounting the hoop, perhaps symbolizing Heaven, it is one of the most beautiful of imperial crowns. The crown is the principal achievement of the workshop that Rudolph II established at the Hradschin. It is assumed that Rudolph's court goldsmith, Jan Vermeyen, is responsible for this crown. Prague, Imperial Court Workshop, 1602. Ht. 28.6 cm.

The Crown of the Holy Roman Empire. It is thought to have been made in a German gold-smith's workshop for Emperor Otto the Great in the year 962. This crown, which is one of the most venerable and most historic royal ornaments still preserved in Europe, is some-times referred to as the Crown of Charlemagne. The cross on the front is thought to have been added either by Otto III late in his reign or by his successor, Henry II. Ht. of the front plate; 15.6 cm. Ht. of the cross 9.9 cm. German, 962.

So-called Crown of Emperor Henry II (St Henry). It is a Gothic crown of silver gilt, consisting of 6 plates carrying a large fleur-de-lis. The plates and fleurs-de-lis are decorated with a foliage pattern and precious stones in claw settings. The fleur-de-lis are divided by pinnacles of angels. The central stones in the front and back of the crown are cameos, the front is a sardonyx, bearing the head of Minerva, dating from the late Roman Empire – the back is of 16th century origin. South German, from Bamberg, c. 1280. Diam. 20 cm.

Crown of Prince Stephan Bocskay of Transylvania. Gold with niello, rubies, emeralds, turquoises and pearls – a strange intrusion of light and gay oriental splendor into the heavy magnificence characteristic of so many of the relics of the Holy Roman Empire preserved in Vienna. This crown was a gift to the rebellious prince from the Sultan Ahmed of Turkey, but was captured by the Austrians. Turkish, 1605. Ht. 23.5 cm.

Portrait of Queen Elizabeth I of England. Elizabeth, like her father, Henry VIII, was inordinately fond of jewelry. From King Henry she had inherited splendid rubies and she was renowned for her great passion for pearls. Elizabeth probably best demonstrates the shift that took place in the wearing of jewelry, for up until this time jewelry had been worn in greater profusion by men than by women.

MODERN JEWELRY

RENÉE S. NEU CURATOR, MUSEUM OF MODERN ART, NEW YORK

The period from the turn of the century until the present day has been marred by two global wars and violent political upheavals. Rapid developments in technology and radical changes in the structure of society, the economic fabric, and the philosophical outlook have touched every aspect of life. Thus, the making as well as the wearing of jewelry has been greatly affected.

The period began as one of great elegance and splendor, often reaching luxurious ostentation. The imperial and royal houses provided the pattern and the focus for most of the high social life. The jewels that graced the numerous formal occasions were abundant, flamboyant, and often ostentatiously expensive. Many ladies had parures (or demi-parures) that consisted of matching sets of earrings, necklace and/or choker, pin, bracelet, and hair ornaments; they would wear all of these, and even more, on a single occasion. After the opening of the South African diamond mines in 1867, and thanks to the spreading use of electric light, which enhanced the sparkle of the gems, diamonds came greatly into fashion. The style of the jewelry, however, in this tradition-bound society was mostly an adaptation of what had been fashionable in the late eighteenth century.

Fabergé's success had its roots in this situation. He combined great elegance and great craftsmanship, with results that pleased his aristocratic clientele, primarily the Russian court – known for its love of dazzling jewels – but he contributed nothing to the development of design. The upper bourgeoisie imitated the example set by the courts and nobility and, in their efforts to identify with them, also demanded jewelry of conservative taste. In countries without a royal court, such as France, the upper class on the whole followed the same conservatism. In the United States the moneyed aristocracy complied with the general trend by often buying their jewelry in Paris or London.

Formal receptions or balls were not the only opportunities to wear important jewelry in abundance. The same elegance and formal wear were displayed at premières of the opera, theater, and ballet. The public at these events was a mixture of the nobility, bankers, industrialists, merchants, artists, and demimondaines, who together represented a lively segment of society, and not all of whom were conservative in taste. By 1900, many of them had accepted the graceful, sinuous line of Art Nouveau and considered it fashionably chic.

The style, considered revolutionary by the public at large, and intended by its practitioners to shock the masses, was the result of a combination of aesthetic and ethical principles. In the late 1880's, William Morris, Walter Crane, and Lewis Day had militantly advocated the integration of arts and crafts to create a better environment. As part of this "aesthetic movement," Morris founded an interior decoration firm, in which many well-known artists collaborated with craftsmen. Simultaneously there was a trend toward religion and mysticism, with William Blake, Aubrey Beardsley, Oscar Wilde, the Vienna Secession, and the Symbolists as its exponents.

Far Eastern art, particularly the Japanese print, was also among the many influences in this complex period, and it had great impact on the visual arts. Art Nouveau design in jewelry also shows Renaissance, Rococo, Celtic and Gothic inspiration. As the new style was not based on structural changes but on ornamentation, it was particularly suited to the applied arts. Its unifying characteristics are the flaming, undulating line and the motifs taken from nature that occur in virtually all Art Nouveau works.

During the prosperous reign of Queen Victoria, England had been the leader in jewelry design. The emergence of René Lalique transferred the center of creativity to Paris. After having exhibited anonymously at the Paris Exposition of 1889, he provoked a stir in 1891 with jewels designed for Sarah Bernhardt. At the Salon du Champ de Mars, Lalique was represented by seventeen jewels, and his work was hailed by judges and critics as a great revelation. From then on he continued to delight—and shock—the public. The number of his admirers grew, as did his influence on other designers.

Nonetheless, Lalique was not the originator of a new style. Rather, he represented the culmination of Art Nouveau in jewelry with a flamboyance and flourish unsurpassed. His creative imagination triumphed in both the lines of the design and the choice of materials. Rejecting valuable gems and using semi-precious stones in soft, subdued colors, as well as opaque glass, bone, silver, and gold, he succeeded in changing, at least temporarily, the common standard of jewelry. Lalique's pieces were judged as works of art because of the imagination and magnificent craftsmanship they displayed, not because of the size, quality, or value of the gems. His imagery was largely borrowed from nature: dragonflies, snakes, flowers, and plants (particularly those that twist and cling), the human figure, and heads with flowing hair.

This vocabulary was already known, but Lalique's use and interpretation were his own. In some pieces, he achieved a unique freedom of expression; many of them have a quality that today would be called surrealist. This holds true for some of the jewels bought by Calouste Gulbenkian, one of his earliest patrons, which are now on view at the Gulbenkian Foundation in Lisbon. The large orchid adorning a comb, made of ivory and horn, is very naturalistic, yet partly hidden in the flower is a little head. The stems of another orchid end in snake heads. More formal in design, but showing Lalique's great craftsmanship and color sensibility, is the necklace shown at the Paris Exposition of 1900. Nine large perfectly matched opals alternate with nine plaquettes, each with a nude female figure in gold set in plique à jour enamel in a milky color. Decorative elements are used in a functional manner: the locks of hair, in black enamel, end in symmetrical round curls, to which links are attached to hold the plaquettes with the opals.

Several of Lalique's contemporaries contributed beautiful pieces in the Art Nouveau style. Eugène Feuillâtre, with his skillful handling of enamel, belongs to this group. From 1898 to 1905, Alphonse Mucha designed a collection of jewelry that was executed by Georges Fouquet. Mucha's rich decorative talent, which made him one of the best graphic designers of his time, expressed itself in compositions in which the vivid colors of the enamels were juxtaposed with gold, ivory, and semi-precious stones and which achieved an almost barbaric feeling of opulence. The hand ornament designed for Sarah Bernhardt is an outstanding example of Mucha's art. The curly tail of a snake in champlevé enamel encircles the wrist several times; the head – of carved opal, enamel, and gold, with flashy ruby eyes – rests on the back of the hand, while holding the head in position are delicate chains that join it to another snake's head.

In Paris, Paul and Henri Vever, and Georges and Jean Fouquet were also working at this time; in Belgium, Philippe Wolfers. All were members of well-established firms of goldsmiths and jewelers. The design of their elegant pieces and the use of valuable materials, in contrast to Lalique, resulted in delicate but somewhat mannered and formal works. In England, the better known designers were Sir Alfred Gilbert and C. R. Ashbee. The London department store of Liberty & Co., Ltd., offered mass-produced jewelry in the Art Nouveau style to its clients. In Spain, there was the rather severe work of Luis Masriera; in Italy, V. Miranda's pendants of smiling, frolicking ladies with flowing hair displayed a more lighthearted approach. In Germany, the popular designers were Hirzel, Möring, and Carl Gross; in Austria, Theodore van Gosen, Prutscher, and Hauptmann, produced attractive pieces.

In the United States the most outstanding representative of Art Nouveau was Louis C. Tiffany. He made a limited amount of jewelry, the style of which is not consistent, ranging from uncannily realistic pieces— particularly hair ornaments of branches of flowers or berries, even dandelions gone to seed—to those of more decidedly Art Nouveau design. Among them is a pendant depicting the sea animal called a medusa, with the body made of large opals and the twisting and curling tentacles made of gold with stones. His more elaborate "peacock necklace," in a rather formal arrangement, is a mosaic of opals, amethysts, and sapphires.

Another necklace, in the Metropolitan Museum of Art in New York, is generally referred to as belonging to the Secessionist style (after the Viennese practitioners of the Jugendstil). Although the design is simple, its colors make it opulent and fully reflect Tiffany's preference for rich, iridescent shades.

Because of the trend toward integration of the arts and crafts, important exhibitions were frequently held in which the works of leading painters and sculptors were shown alongside those of the most talented craftsmen. As a result, well-known artists tried their hand at jewelry design. One of the most successful among these "part-time" jewelers was the Belgian Henri van de Velde, who, though originally a painter and later an architect, was now devoting his talents to the applied arts. His powerful work is characterized by a unique form of abstraction. Dynamic lines energize the rational structure inspired by organic forms. A play of positive and negative shapes is created, wherein the active line, often rich and sensuous, gives an impression of motion and controlled energy. Van de Velde's style was extremely influential in the development throughout Europe of jewelry of abstract linear design. Also influential in this direction were Josef Hoffmann and J.M. Olbrich of the Wiener Werkstätten, an arts and crafts center in Vienna that was similar in concept to William Morris's. The commercial center of Pforzheim, in Germany, was influenced by this style, which suited its technological requirements, and produced works of stylized geometric design that anticipated later developments.

In Denmark, Georg Jensen, together with Johan Rohde and Eric Magnussen, brought Nordic stylization to Art Nouveau. For his silver jewelry, Jensen used hand-chased relief work with such natural motifs as acorns and fish scales, a kind of work that continued for many years. There exists, although not to a high degree, a stylistic affinity between his work and Van de Velde's.

Around 1910, the world of fantasy and the representation of romanticized nature was fading. Many new influences, which at first may seem remote, started to have an impact on jewelry. In 1909, Diaghilev's Russian Ballet, which performed in Paris to great acclaim, exposed the public, through stage designs and costumes (many by Léon Bakst), to bright colors and sharp contrasts. New art movements—Fauvism, Cubism, Futurism, the Russian Constructivism, the Kunstgewerbeschule in Weimar (Van de Velde had been its artistic director since 1902, and it continued later under Walter Gropius as the Bauhaus)—all produced new and explosive forms of expression. They were little known to the general public, which, on the rare occasions of confrontation, was not receptive to them. Nonetheless, the new aesthetics proclaimed by these movements slowly penetrated into general consciousness and, sooner or later, greatly affected design. Thus, in the last years before the First World War, abstract design, with straight lines and geometrical forms, started to appear in jewelry.

The war stopped most of the luxurious display of the *Belle Époque.* Its eventual outcome profoundly altered the structure of society. In numerous countries, the imperial and royal courts disappeared, and the nobility that supported them lost their privileged position. In Russia, the entire ruling classes, including the bourgeoisie, were wiped out. In Central Europe, many sectors of society suffered heavy losses through inflation. The void was filled by industrialists and bankers, whose preference for jewels of traditional design and high intrinsic value was a statement of their conservative beliefs. At the same time, however, women were obtaining a steadily increasing role in cultural, political, and economic life, and this was reflected in radical changes of fashion. Other cultural developments, from jazz to cars and aircraft, contributed to the formation of the new style that has come to be known as Art Deco.

Jewelry, which already had shown a trend toward geometric forms, continued along these lines. But, probably as a reaction to the grimness of the war and as an expression of the frenzied *joie de vivre* of its survivors, glittering jewels were back in fashion. Diamonds were most frequently used, together with onyx, coral, jade, or enamel, which offered sharp color contrasts and set off the sparkle of the gems.

At first, the leading colors were white, red, and black; the white was supplied by pearls, diamonds, and rock crystal, the red and black by coral, enamel, and onyx. Later, other gems—aquamarines, emeralds, and sapphires—also became fashionable, providing highlights for the diamonds. When flowers were used in the design, they were highly stylized and applied to the center of a geometric shape; small, orderly floral compositions of various stones or diamonds were set into backgrounds of jade, lapis lazuli, or enamel.

Small Oriental carvings mounted in platinum or gold and ornamented with diamonds and enamel made lapel pendants or jabot pins. After the discovery of Tutankhamen's tomb in 1922, designers adopted Egyptian motifs, which, due to their stylized character, fitted the general trend. Platinum became increasingly popular for fine settings. Stronger than gold, it enabled the jeweler to make open-backed, almost invisible mountings. The use of platinum, and what seemed an insatiable demand for diamonds, caused new types of brooches and bracelets, made mostly of a combination of large and smallish stones, to be in great demand. These pieces could be used in different ways. The bracelets were flat, flexible bands with an over-all design somewhat reminiscent of a Persian rug pattern; they could be joined to form a choker. The brooches, occasionally with some colored gems at the center of the design, could be divided into two clips or, more traditionally, could be worn as pendants. These were elegant pieces of jewelry that, in spite of all their richness, achieved a very delicate look. Finally, long earrings and long necklaces, mostly of pearls ending with a tassel, were extremely fashionable. Jewelers offered not only jewelry itself but also a variety of elegant accessories. Van Cleef and Arpels introduced the *minaudières* – tiny, fitted cases to carry make-up, cigarettes, and other small items. Boucheron, Cartier, Chaumet, Lacloche, Van Cleef and Arpels in Paris, and Asprey Ltd., and Garrard & Co., Ltd., in London were the leading jewelers at this time, supplying very beautiful pieces. Some of the better known designer-jewelers were Raymond Templier, Fouquet, and René Robert in France; H. G. Murphy in England; and Wiwen Nilsson in Sweden. Mlle Toussaint at Cartier, as well as Mme Suzanne Belperron, and Mme Jeanne Boivin were also designing important jewelry; they were the first women to emerge as recognized designers of such pieces.

Thanks to several retrospective exhibitions in France, the United States, and elsewhere, Art Deco is now regarded as a legitimate art movement, relatively short-lived but with very definite characteristics that are easily recognizable. Many of the original pieces in this style are either in museums or prized possessions of collectors. Art Deco is enjoying a widespread revival, and it is possible to recapture some of its mood in the pieces made today by many of the leading firms. However, one of the distinguishing features of Art Deco jewelry was its superb craftsmanship, which made even elaborate pieces look delicate. Today the prohibitive costs of skilled labor would make such production impractical.

The crash of the American Stock Market in 1929, with repercussions on a global scale, the monetary instability of the early thirties, and the steadily deteriorating political situation ending in the Second World War shifted interest away from luxury consumption. Jewelry, however, was in demand, mainly as a form of transferable investment in countries where restrictions on monetary transactions were enforced or expected and in those where political persecutions led to mass emigration. But imaginative design and excellent craftsmanship counted little in this type of market. As a consequence, jewelry design became coarse, showy, and repetitive, and its stylistic development came to a virtual standstill. The movements that had tried to unify the arts and crafts had also come to an end. Artists struggled as isolated individuals in this period of political upheaval, hardship, and profiteering, while the large jewelry houses continued to produce traditional designs.

The period we can consider contemporary did not begin until the mid-1950's. Great changes began to make themselves felt in almost every aspect of life, though to some extent history only elaborated or exaggerated earlier trends. The conversion of many nations from primarily agricultural into primarily industrial societies, and the consequent trend to urbanization, have been important factors in the conversion of a large segment of the working class to the habits, values, and demands of middle-class society, complete with its materialistic standard of values. The affluence of almost all classes in the Western world and Japan has produced what can well be described as an explosion in the demand for jewelry, particularly for that in the medium-price range.

In the past, only the intellectual and social elite had a keen interest in the performing and visual arts. Now, more and more groups seek active and passive participation. The popularization of the arts through exhibitions, published articles, and reproductions brings us the new styles in painting, sculpture, and decor on an almost day-by-day basis. For jewelry, a similar process has taken place. In Europe, exhibitions and competitions sponsored by various organizations of goldsmiths, jewelers, and museums are received with great interest by the public. One of the earliest, most ambitious, and comprehensive international exhibitions, "Jewelry 1890-1961," was organized by the Worshipful Company of Goldsmiths and shown at Goldsmiths' Hall in London, sponsored by the Victoria and Albert Museum, which lent the project prestige. Germany, Holland, Switzerland, and, to a lesser degree, the United States and Canada, followed suit; some of these exhibitions (for instance, one organized by the Museum of Modern Art in New York in 1967) were exclusively dedicated to jewelry designed by recognized artists. The response has been such that, in many countries, the exhibitions are now held on a more or less regular basis. The various competitions organized or sponsored by the jewelry industry itself, with the clear intention of stimulating sales, have, in the process, also succeeded in stimulating the creativity of the designers.

These exhibitions give the craftsman the necessary incentive to make pieces of jewelry that, for lack of clients, he otherwise would not make; at the same time, they bring his work to the attention of the public. Since 1954, De Beers Consolidated Mines, Ltd., has sponsored the Diamonds International Awards, in which a changing jury composed of experts of various nationalities selects thirty winning entries. This selection is then circulated throughout the world with a great deal of publicity, giving the designers the chance to become known. Thus, designers from such countries as Japan, Australia, and Brazil have recently gained international attention. Some are new to the field, others have been active for years; but, because of the reluctance of large firms to divulge the names of their designers, they had remained anonymous. Among them are Kotaku Takabatake, Hiromi Fukutome, and Takao Mitsuyau from Japan; Rex

Steele Marten from Australia; Hans Boeckh from Brazil; Gianfranco Arnold and R. Merati from Italy; E. F. Deviolles and Carl Elsener from Switzerland; Henry Dunay from the United States; and Silva and Werner Bünck from Germany. For the most part, they incline toward geometric, almost architectural arrangements. Other exhibitions and competitions that offer similar advantages are those of the Montres et Bijoux in Geneva and the Golden Rose of Baden-Baden, both organized by the watchmakers' industry. One of the important consequences of the attention and publicity produced by such exhibitions has been that private galleries have started to specialize in jewelry designed by artists or artist-craftsmen.

Primary jewelry, that is, jewelry of high intrinsic value, is for the most part still supplied by major jewelry firms. Here, less attempt is made to promote truly new design, particularly in the United States. Most firms are content with offering beautiful gems and exquisite workmanship. They ignore the developments in the major arts, which they consider passing fads. Most of their clients undoubtedly share these ideas; they expect "good jewelry" to be of conservative design, buying most frequently for sound investment or, often, to prove their status. This reinforces the jewelers' idea that contemporary design is not a paying proposition. Thus, lack of creative imagination can be hidden by the thesis that jewelry, to be lasting, should be of "classic" design. In many cases, such design is very baroque indeed. The only items for which these jewelry houses are willing to be daring are shown in their boutiques. Here, they use young designers, whose new concepts of form they probably accept as a concession to some of the younger and less conservative members of their clientele.

Of course, there are exceptions. In London, the old and highly respected firms of Asprey Ltd., Cartier, and Garrard & Co., Ltd., are very much interested in developing new designers. To this end, they actively support the program of grants and exhibition-competitions organized by the Worshipful Company of Goldsmiths and by the Design and Research Centre for the Gold, Silver and Jewellery Industries. Non-traditional primary jewelry is offered also by more recently established firms: Roy C. King, Ltd. has featured prize-winning designs by Roger King, who unfortunately seems not to have been active in the firm for several years. Another firm, Andrew Grima, Ltd., has proved that precious stones can be set in fresh, unusual designs with economic success.

Grima, who has won many prizes and several Diamonds International Awards, is even considered by many to be one of the major forces in the revitalization of British jewelry design. Throughout the years, his style has undergone changes, though it has remained consistently modern. His most recent pieces are large, three-dimensional, and very assertive. The favorable atmosphere in England has encouraged many young designers and permitted them to develop. Interesting work is being done by Jane Allen, John Donald, Barbara Cartlidge, Gillian Packard, Wendy Ramshaw, and David Thomas. Their styles cover the full range of expression in the medium.

In Italy, too, the conservative character of primary jewelry has been somewhat disturbed, although, in general, it remains very strong. The firm of Fürst in Rome has attempted special exhibitions to promote jewelry that reflects the mood of Abstract Expressionist paintings. Bulgari, also in Rome, is famous for its collections of Oriental carvings, antique silver, and gems of high quality. It is the firm's policy to offer its clientele the opportunity to select according to taste, rather than steering them firmly toward traditional designs. Therefore, besides the usual large-sized gems surrounded by diamonds or similar arrangements, it offers more contemporary pieces. Some lance-shaped or octagonal emeralds and diamonds, mounted as rings, are shown to their fullest advantage in designs of remarkable restraint and purity. Other pieces, somewhat more elaborate, try through a sharp geometric composition to convey a contemporary feeling, even when the subject matter is as traditional as a bouquet of flowers.

Faraone in Milan recently presented a collection in steel and gold; the contrast of the two metals produces a subtle and interesting effect. In Florence, a city rather accustomed to pleasing the tourist trade, Torrini features contemporary designs in which the work of Alberto Giorgi, a young sculptor, shows great individuality. His three-dimensional kinetic pieces are reminiscent of a complicated mechanism; his work, however, falls more in the category of artists' jewelry.

In Switzerland, the great watchmakers also handle much of the fine jewelry. Through their active interest in the "Montres et Bijoux" exhibition-competition (which has been held since 1942 as a national, and since 1950 as an international, show in Geneva), they have almost revolutionized the field. Watches have been divested of their purely functional character and have become, especially the wristwatch, ornaments that complement the costume and even the personality of the wearer. Art Deco started this trend, with ladies' watches enriched with small diamonds. When large gold bracelets became fashionable in the fifties, watches were hidden in the bracelet and usually well integrated into the design. In recent years, the dial has again been in view, and many attempts are made to make it part of a free-form, often elaborate bracelet.

The watches range from the very sporty variety, large, and stainless steel to the novelty type with case and strap in acrylic, and finally to the elegant watches in which the most effort at elaborate design is concentrated.

From time to time, the firms employ designers outside their regular staff. The collaboration of Patek Philippe with Jean Lurçat is well known. Omega recently has produced a collection by Andrew Grima, in which the highly simplified face of the watch is semi-hidden under a large thin gemstone; strong, bold lines and ribbed or textured gold are recurrent features. Jean Paolini recently designed a beautiful piece in white gold and diamonds for Movado. Among the interesting pieces offered by Gübelin is a ladies' watch in white gold and diamonds, in which the watch, its face in pavé diamonds, is beautifully integrated with the wristband; this was designed by Flory, who also designs free-form three-dimensional brooches in gold.

Other modern pieces are designed by Martha Widmer, chief designer at Gübelin; one, of beautifully simple design, is an evening parure for men – wristwatch, cufflinks, ring, and a clip to wear instead of the tie. The design is three-dimensional, the geometric lines in the foreground are in shiny white gold, their counterparts in the back in pavé diamonds. Gilbert Albert, for many years chief designer at Patek Philippe, is still one of the leaders in his field. Others are Max Fröhlich, who often uses gold wire for his circular compositions; Ingrid Hansen, whose works are often geometric-kinetic; Pavel Krbalek, a Czech now working in Switzerland, who designs airy arabesques in precious metals; and Othmar Zschaler, who creates collage-like pieces in white and yellow gold, lapis lazuli, and other opaque stones of geometric design.

These few examples illustrate the direction taken by the more progressive designers of primary jewelry. However, there are certain changes that are noticeable everywhere. Some are the result of technological developments, others are due to the normal evolution of styles. A general trend toward more color has brought about a transition from platinum and white gold to yellow gold in fine settings (although at the present moment a countertrend seems imminent) and the widespread use of colored diamonds (both natural or atomically treated to obtain the desired shade). There is also an almost universal attempt to create three-dimensional ornaments. This is a characteristic shared with much of the secondary jewelry. Rings, which in the last decade have become extremely popular, show this trend better than any other ornament. No matter at what price level, they are large and protruding, often worn on two or three fingers. Rough stones have been used extensively by craftsmen because of their low cost and their intrinsic beauty; this trend seems now to be spreading into primary jewelry. Rough diamonds sliced instead of cut are mounted in gold, often with diamond baguettes for contrast.

Today's main demand is not for jewels of great monetary value. Symbols of wealth have lost ground to a variety of objects used purely for personal adornment. These are supplied by the mass-producing centers of the industry and by artist-craftsmen who work independently. The latter, a new and steadily growing group, often use experimental techniques and approaches and are very much attuned to the other arts; their pieces are seldom suited to mass production, but they constantly supply new, provocative ideas.

Germany and Italy have for centuries been leading jewelry-making centers. Denmark has been known for its jewelry for some time, and Finland and Spain have recently joined the market. They all operate on the basis of rather small workshops that are highly organized and united like the old-time guilds. Faced with the dilemma of choosing between manual and mechanical work, the centers are successful in supplying the large international market with objects that are designed and finished by craftsmen but turned out in the intermediate stage of production by means of advanced technology.

Engraving of textures is obtained by an engine-turning process, which creates beautiful light effects, and especially bright ones when the metal is diamond-milled. Ultrasonic drilling and engraving are used widely to save working time and to allow for greater precision. Centrifugal casting permits exact replicas to be made without the need for highly skilled craftsmen in the finishing stage. Electroforming (rarely used in commercial centers) allows for the production of large pieces that before would have been too heavy to wear.

The largest German center is Pforzheim, with more than a thousand jewelry manufacturers (its connection with Art Nouveau and Art Deco has already been mentioned). In Pforzheim's factories, completely rebuilt after the Second World War, the production of jewelry in the most contemporary designs is vast, ranging from gold and precious gems to the simplest ornament. Much credit must be given to the Pforzheim Schmuckmuseum for inculcating in the German public a receptivity to new concepts in jewelry and for having provided this local industry with the necessary support and inspiration. The city's original art museum was completely destroyed in the war; responding to the needs of the community and to local tradition, it reopened its doors in 1961, dedicated exclusively to the art of jewelry. The museum houses an impressive collection of jewels dating from 3000 B.C. to the present and has an extensive exhibition and acquisition program. Further impetus has been given the German jewelry industry by several important international exhibitions, among them the ones held at the Hessisches Landesmuseum in Darmstadt and at Nuremberg ("Gold, Silver, Jewels, from Dürer to the Present Day," 1971).

A large number of German artist-craftsmen work on their own in a variety of styles. Friedrich Becker makes kinetic rings and bracelets in white gold and gems, his compositions organized within a circular form.

Max and Jutta Wilpert use ribbed and textured gold, the severity of the line lightened by rows of tiny pearls in some of the ridges. Jens R. Lorenzen uses a two-dimensional structure and graphic relief to contrast the geometric shapes of his pieces. Eberhard B. J. Schütze's jewels are very sculptural, with smooth surfaces in white gold and cabochons, and can be worn in various ways (as ring-pendants, pendant-brooches, etc.). Frank Müller combines satiny gold with semi-precious rough stones or baroque pearls in refined color juxtapositions.

An idea of the rapid development of commercial jewelry can be gained from figures supplied by the export organization of the town of Valenza Po in northern Italy. In 1959, 384 firms employed more than 4,400 workers; in 1972, there were 1,200 firms employing over 10,000 persons. Exports in 1958 were around 800 million lire; in 1967 they jumped to 56 billion lire. The production of this seemingly sleepy little town ranges from the traditional to the avant-garde, but the prospects for contemporary design are disturbing. The big orders from the important jewelry houses – which are vital for Valenza Po – are for pieces that seem modern yet are really conservative. Their most imaginative collections are admired but, unfortunately, on the whole remain unsold. This is all the more unexpected because it is in those items whose price range is moderate (necklaces, bracelets, brooches of gold without important stones) that some daring could be expected from the buyers.

The great number of firms at Valenza Po makes a detailed discussion impossible, and so we must limit ourselves to noting two. New Italian Art (NIA), with the assistance of two of its designers, Antonio Gié and Pinetto Mantella, has developed a line of individuality and elegance. Ferraris & Co., where Paolo Stalla is the designer, produces a variety of jewelry, including some with precious stones; in addition, it has developed jewels of avant-garde design, in which flat pebbles, carefully selected for color and texture, are very simply mounted in gold; an occasional hole in the pebble and small, abstract decorations in gold give these pieces the look of small-scale sculpture. Among the independent Italian designers outside Valenza Po is Domingo de la Cueva, a Cuban who has been living in Venice for many years, who seems to be influenced by the Byzantine riches and the glitter of the water in Venice and who at times attains an overtly opulent feeling in his gold jewelry. Bruno Martinazzi makes Pop-Surrealist reliefs with parts of the body as subject. Kiky Vices Vinci makes silver ornaments inspired by pure geometric forms. Ettore Sottsass brings to his rare pieces of jewelry his great designing talents.

In Spain, Barcelona has always been very active in the field of jewelry; in recent years it has been the headquarters of several young designers who have been making elegant jewelry of simple lines using gold or silver with ivory, lapis lazuli, or malachite. Manuel Capdevila, an important Spanish jewelry designer, favors a more severe and sculptured approach to his pieces.

Working in Belgium, Fernand Demaret produces geometric gold jewelry, with satiny and textured surfaces sparingly highlighted by gems. Holland has an interesting group of young designers, mostly artist-craftsmen, among them Emmy van Leersum, Gijs Bakker, Nicolas van Beek, Françoise van den Bosch, and Bernard Lameris. They all prefer a type of jewelry that might be defined as body ornament (which they call "wearable objects"). Their conception of the body is of a space for which they create small sculptures. The simple forms in bent and twisted shiny metal are striking and bold, the formative element as devoid of decoration as the minimal sculpture of the sixties.

The Scandinavian countries have had their own easily recognizable style for many years. Since the days of Georg Jensen, who made Denmark famous for silver, the spare forms and smooth finish of the metal have almost been the trademark of a style that influenced design all over the world. The firm of Georg Jensen continues to employ many fine designers, among them Torun, Nanna Ditzel, Astrid Fog, and Henning Koppel, who have been able to retain their individuality and at the same time convey the Jensen image. Others active in Denmark are Margarethe Broeken, Helga and Bent Exner, and Age Fausing. Bodil Buch and Winfelt Hansen have successfully combined silver and porcelain in their jewelry. In Sweden, Sigurd Persson is known for his pure designs. Olle Ohlsson imbeds pearls in molten gold or silver or contrasts various textures of gold in free-form ornaments. Wiwen Nilsson, a pioneer in the field since Art Deco, achieves his individual effect through simple, well-proportioned forms and unusually beautiful stones.

In recent years, designers have been moving toward more experimental work. They use non-precious materials successfully, and, when gold or silver are employed, the metal looks as if it were folded, torn, or molten, lending great variety to the jewelry. This development may in part have been influenced by Finland. Because it did not start to produce contemporary jewelry until after the Second World War, it is virtually a newcomer to the field; yet the quality of its production is attracting more and more attention. The lack of a well-established tradition in jewelry may account for the freedom of approach prevalent among its designers. Lapponia Jewelry, Ltd., has Björn Wekström as chief designer; his chunky pieces of gold or silver with unpolished surfaces, as well as his pendants and belt buckles of smooth bronze, are all diminutive sculptures. Poul Havgaard, a Danish designer with Lapponia, has been making witty body ornaments (iron breast-plates, belly sculptures), and is now designing pendants and rings in dark, smooth silver that are more sculptural than decorative. The firm of Kultateolisuus Ky employs Arno Viljanen, who makes severe bronze jewelry, and Esa Lukala, who mounts stone discs against stamped silver to achieve the look of contemporary graphics. Tapio Wirkkala — a designer who made his first jewelry for the 1961 exhibition at Goldsmiths' Hall — seems to draw his inspiration from folklore; his mask-like pendants convey a primitive tribal feeling. Matti Hyvarinen adds interest to his beautifully controlled pieces by combining gold and Finnish granite highlighted with pearls or diamonds. Laifor uses gilded bronze for his sculptural two-dimensional pendants and cufflinks. Like the other Scandinavian countries, Finland takes great pride in its designers, so that it is comparatively easy to follow their careers, even if they work for large manufacturers.

As for other countries, mention should be made of Czechoslovakia, where a nucleus of younger artists and craftsmen try to create interesting and unconventional pieces. Anton Cepka, a sculptor-jeweler, Ladislava Viznerová, and Jaroslav Kodjes are the most outstanding.

In Israel, several good designers of both primary and secondary jewelry have emerged; Maury Golan, Nissim Misrachi, and Bianca Eshel may be considered the most interesting.

The United States has lagged behind in recognizing the importance of independent designers in the field of jewelry and has failed to support or encourage them with coordinated programs of exhibitions and competitons. In contrast to Europe, few American museums have recognized jewelry as a viable form of expression; it has therefore almost never been included in their exhibition programs. The one exception is the Museum of Contemporary Crafts in New York, whose primary objective is to show the work of talented craftsmen in every field. At the same time, the high costs of skilled labor and the general trend away from the small workshop — unless it is used for the artist's own work — prevent creative activity comparable to that seen in Europe.

The market in the United States is divided between the jewelers, including the jewelry departments in the large department stores, and individual craftsmen-designers, who seldom can make a living at their trade alone. These craftsmen experiment with a freedom of approach that stresses personal expression and often has little concern for traditional aesthetic concepts. Actually, their work reflects strongly the vagaries of modern art in the United States.

Noma Copley, who lives in the New York area, is attuned to a Pop-Surrealist culture and consistently produces witty pieces. Gabrielle Kennedy, who works mainly with silver in her geometric or free-form pieces, has a style full of strength in its understatement. Albert Paley combines gold with fossils, bone, and other seldom-used materials to produce a fierce, mysterious, totemic quality. Stan Plotner converts non-precious metals into bold body ornaments of simple forms. Arthur Smith has for many years followed the Scandinavian principles of design in his understated silver arabesques.

In Philadelphia, several artists working in different disciplines have made important contributions. Stanley Lechtzin's pieces often resemble miniature sculptures, their rich imagery evoking mythical animals; he uses electroforming to make large (but light) wearable ornaments. Eleanor Moty has a very private sense of imagination. She loves the hidden image, the subtle detail, the unusual technique. In her experimental jewelry, she uses the photo-engraving process. Marci Zelmanoff creates large pieces – almost body ornaments – full of movement and airy as lace. In Kansas City, Mary Kretsinger has long been known for experimental pieces, mainly brooches of various materials, and Robert M. Pringle for his beautiful pure designs.

In California, Arline M. Fisch is interested in contrasting improbable materials – gold and feathers, for instance – and she creates her own techniques to achieve works of great individuality. Olaf Skoogfors in Philadelphia and Heikki M. Seppa in St. Louis make beautiful gold pieces highlighted by gems; they express an outspoken individualism with a more formal approach that betrays their European background. In Canada, a few well-known firms such as Roger Lucas and Victor C. Secrett are among the jewelers open to new design ideas. Craftsmen such as Daisy Bailey, Jane Huston, and Bill Reid are also contributing interesting works.

In trying to assess the development of twentieth-century jewelry design, the critic becomes hopelessly entangled with developments in the major arts and in changes of fashion. As far apart as art and fashion may appear, they both exert major influences on designers and craftsmen, who are generally very sensitive to the visual arts. To a great extent, fashion governs what most people will wear at given times. The increasing trend toward an informal way of dressing and the greater freedom in individual wear are probably responsible in part for the variety we now find in secondary jewelry.

Stylistically, the creation of secondary jewelry is divided into two major groups. In one belong those designers who, while using different approaches, seek forms of expression close to experiments in painting and sculpture of the fifties and sixties: some design brooches with contrasting textures that are closely related to a certain type of painting-relief, abstract, controlled and severe; some produce arabesques with molten metals in a way that can be associated with "drip painting"; still others use Surrealist or Pop imagery. The common trait among these designers is their belief in the importance of various degrees of ornamentation. The other group follows completely opposite principles. The way these jewelers arrived at their style is irrelevant—it could be called post-Scandinavian. Their designs are mostly of simple forms worked in shiny metals, in which polished stones are incorporated at times, continuing the smooth look. Their strength lies in the balance and purity of form. A splinter group prefers the same smooth, shiny metal but is exploring the decorative possibilities of solid geometry. The discs and spheres that are extensively used often evoke images of strange machinery. Much of this jewelry has a hard, cold look and often expresses a great deal of aggressiveness, which many feel reflects today's world. What future developments will occur is impossible to foresee; what is important is the vitality encountered everywhere.

One of the most exciting developments over the last decades is the increasing involvement of painters and sculptors in designing (and at times making) jewelry. Because their pieces tend to reflect the style of their usual work, a detailed discussion of individual pieces of such variety would be impossible here; moreover, it would constitute less a discussion of jewelry than of modern art. In this field there are no "trends"; the pieces are dictated by the artist's conception of how a piece of jewelry should look, uncomplicated by the anxiety to please a large public. Whether made of precious materials or not, this jewelry is powerful because of the strong convictions that brought it into being.

One of the first artists to make jewelry in this century was Julio Gonzalez. From 1910 to 1923, he supported himself in this way, as many other struggling artists, particularly sculptors, have done since. At the time, he had not yet found his sculptural style, but the imaginative use of materials and simplification of design was already evident. A silver bracelet in the form of a simple twisting rope has influenced many designers after him. A ring of silver and iron, unusual in shape, with a snake's head holding a large diamond, is oddly aggressive. Manolo Hugue, another Spanish sculptor and friend of Gonzalez, made some silver jewelry, mainly brooches and rings, in which the female figure—represented in powerful, sculptural form—is the main theme.

Alberto Giacometti in the early thirties made a few pieces that were meant to be mass-produced but never were. Usually made in gilded bronze, they were given by the artist to friends as gifts. The pieces, with their flowing lines, have a startling Art Nouveau air, particularly the bracelets with a woman's head, whose wavy hair forms the band. In the late thirties, Alexander Calder produced many pieces, although these were never in valuable materials. The metal is mostly cut and hammered into an arabesque or into decorative components with an ease that reveals Calder's unique skill with metal. Their importance lies in their being unconventional, witty, and bold. In feeling they are closely related to his drawings, so that it is possible to say that they are Calder's doodles in metal. Although the work of these artists later had great influence, at the time they were isolated cases without much following.

The real movement started in Italy after the Second World War. The first to recognize the validity and appeal of artists' jewelry was the old Roman firm of Masenza, which in 1946 commissioned a bracelet from Mirko. Since then, the firm has supplied an elite clientele with jewelry and objets d'art designed or modeled in wax by leading Italian artists and executed by expert craftsmen. Afro, Mirko, Fazzine, Canilla, Capogrossi, and Consagra have been outstanding contributors. In the 1950s, jewelry made by Arnaldo and Giorgio Pomodoro, two promising young sculptors, began to gain attention. Since both had been trained as jewelers, they had full knowledge of the techniques and demands of this special field. With the creative imagination that had led them to become well-known sculptors, they produced jewelry that reflected their search for new expressions in sculpture, inspired as it was by what Pollock and Kline had accomplished in painting. The pieces made by the Pomodoros have had such impact that now, almost twenty years later, pieces inspired by their early designs can often be seen. Today, the Pomodoros seldom make unique pieces, although they still design jewelry to be made in small editions.

Recently the Roman firm of Fumanti has specialized in jewelry designed by contemporary artists and made of precious metals and valuable gems. Afro, Canilla, and Consagra, who have also worked with the firm of Masenza, and Ceroli, Franchina, and Uncini are among its designers (they also work independently). Other independent figures are Umberto Mastroianni, who has created a beautiful series of gold pieces; Giulio Turcato; and the American sculptor Beverly Pepper, who lives in Rome.

In Paris, François Hugo, himself an artist-craftsman (and more recently an art dealer), has executed pieces designed by Jean Cocteau, Max Ernst, Jean Lurçat, and Picasso. Other French artists produce independently, among them Dubuffet, Hans Arp, Philippe Hiquely, Emile Giglioli, Guitou Knoop, and Alicia Penalba. In the early sixties, Baron Heger de Löwenfeld made over one hundred pieces following designs by Braque and in collaboration with the artist; all have the characteristics of fine jewelry. Yet the first two pieces Braque designed—a ring for his wife and one for himself, both now at the Musée National d'Art Moderne in Paris—are actually two cameos, subdued in tone and very simply mounted in gold.

In Switzerland Max Bill has made about fifty pieces that he himself considers miniature sculptures; unfortunately they are little known to the public. In Canada Etrog Sorel made three silver rings that were shown in the "Jewelry '71" exhibition at the Art Gallery of Ontario. In the United States David Hare, Claire Falkenstein, Ibram Lassaw, Jacques Lipchitz, David Smith, and more recently Clinton Hill, Louise Nevelson, George Rickey, José de Rivera, Paul von Ringelheim, Ben-Schmuel, and Fred J. Woell have created jewelry, most of it of great beauty and originality.

The strong appeal that artists' jewelry has for its admirers is largely based on the uniqueness of the works and the intimate link with the artists who designed them. Besides, regardless of whether precious gems and metals are used, or materials that previously had never entered the field of jewelry, the originality of the pieces allows them to compete with the most valuable but more conventional jewels. There is also, of course, a snob appeal in "wearing a Picasso," combined with the soothing feeling of not being too obvious. At a time when many people feel it is ostentatious to wear expensive jewelry – or at least are afraid that others will think so – artists' jewelry offers the distinct advantage of having its value usually hidden and understood only by the cognoscenti. Even the pieces from the firms of Masenza and Fumanti, although made of precious materials, do not emphasize their high value. The use of gems is usually limited, as is their size.

The two great exceptions are Mathieu's jewelry, very dynamic and with precious gems, reflecting his action-painting style, and Dali's jewels, which fully represent his baroque Surrealist style. Dali has designed a number of pieces—many of them kinetic—that were made by Carlos B. Alemany; most of them are in the Owen Cheatham Foundation. The jewels are an extension of Dali's concepts in painting. The selection of gems is influenced by Dali's complicated personal symbology. In pieces such as *The Persistence of Memory* and *The Eye of Time*, the Surrealist approach is simple and direct; in later pieces, many of religious subjects, the symbolism is more involved and the design includes some of the geometric lines that Dali has been using in his later paintings.

Since the early sixties, a development that has helped greatly to widen the market for the visual arts, particularly for graphics, has also affected the field of jewelry. Influenced by the favorable response of the public to works of art in limited editions (prints and lithographs in particular), some firms have started to offer jewelry designed by artists and produced in limited editions.

The idea has been accepted enthusiastically by the public, which now has the opportunity to find—and wear—unconventional designs by well-known artists, often at quite reasonable prices. The firm of Gem in Milan has an international roster of artists working for it, among them Lucio Fontana, the Pomodoros, Laura da Ponte, Man Ray, and Nikki de Sainte-Phalle. Gennari in Paris executes the designs of several French artists, which are then sold through the artists' galleries. One of the most successful of these artists is the Belgian Pol Bury, who made his first piece in non-precious materials in 1967 for the exhibition at the Museum of Modern Art in New York. Fascinated by the possibilities these materials presented, he made a series of kinetic pieces of great beauty. The sculptor Barbara Chase-Riboud originally made unique pieces in silver and recently had them manufactured by Gennari in limited editions. The jeweler Morabito in Nice has commissioned Arman and César, who have met the challenge with great success. In New York, the firm of Multiples, Inc., has led the way in the United States and has produced the Mon Levinsons, Lichtensteins, Summers, and Youngermans that have become classics.

René Lalique, French. Born 1860, died 1945, Goldsmith.
Tiara (head of a cockerel) in enamel, gold, and amethyst. Shown at the Paris Exposition 1900. Lalique, the most famous of the Art Nouveau jewelers, studied art in London and Paris and was apprenticed to the goldsmith Louis Aucoc. He opened his own atelier in 1881. Paris, c. 1898. W. 15.5 cm.

Henri Godet, French. Born 1863, Sculptor and medallist.
Necklace (one of the early kinetic jewels) of gold, enamel, brilliants, sapphires and pearls.
In the center of the necklace with leaves and flowers of translucent enamels and gems is
the figure of a winged woman. Her wings are set with sapphires and diamonds. The center
piece is removable and can be worn as a brooch. Engraved on the back "February 12,
1900." Brooch: 3.5 x 3 cm.

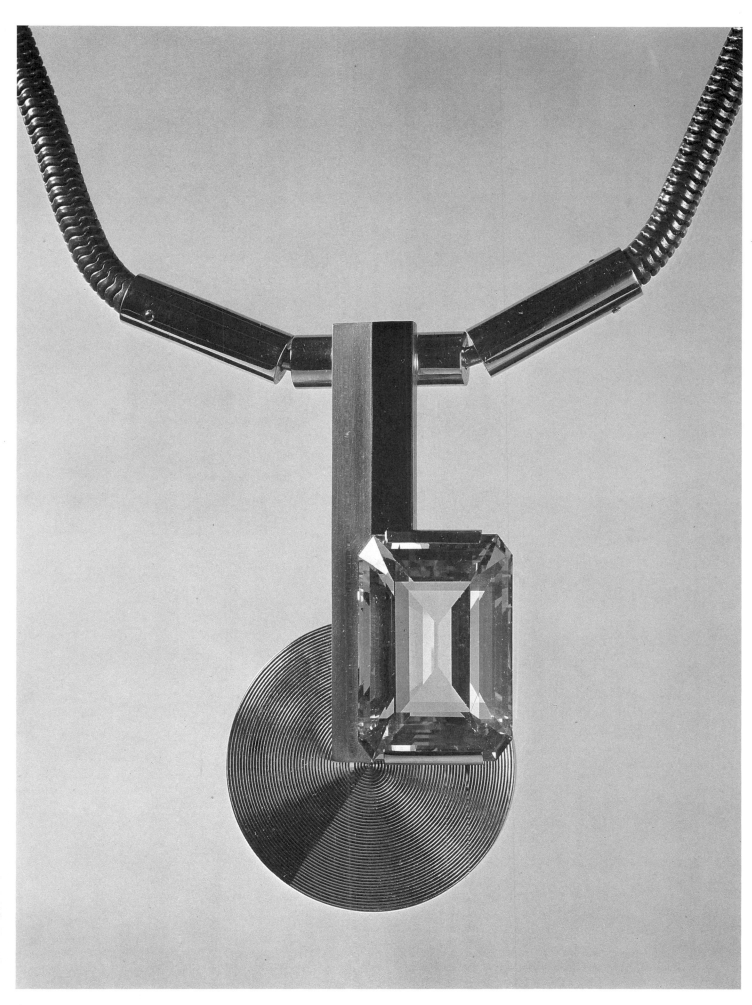

Jean Fouquet, French. Born 1899 in Paris,
Lives in Paris, Jeweler.
Art Deco necklace of white and yellow
gold, aquamarine and black enamel. In
1919, after a classical education, Fouquet
joined his father's firm. With a number of
other designers and jewelers he founded
the Union des Artistes Modernes (UAM).
Regular exhibitor at the Salon d'Automne.
Showed Brussels World Fair 1958. Paris,
1925-30. Total Ht. of pendant: 9.2 cm.

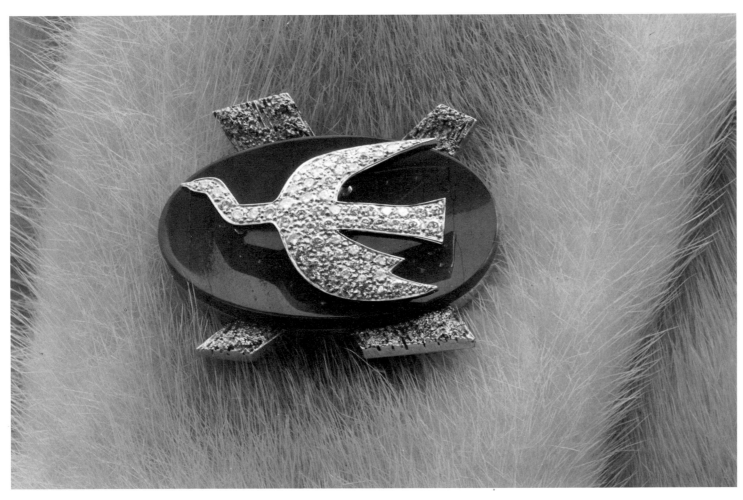

George Braque, French. Born 1882, died 1963, Painter, Sculptor.
Brooch of gold, diamonds and jasper. Icarus returns to marry the naiad Periboea in Lacedaemon. Designed by Braque and made by Baron Heger de Löwenfeld, Paris, 1963. Braque, at the age of 81, designed a series of 133 jewels. L. 5.1 cm.

Salvador Dali, Spanish. Born 1904 in Figueras, Spain, Lives in Spain, Painter. Brooch in the form of an octopus with diamonds, rubies and a large pearl. The jewels from Dali's designs are executed by Carlos B. Alemany, a New York jeweler, in close collaboration with the artist. Made in 1969. Total width: 14.4 cm.

Pablo Picasso, Spanish. Born 1881, died 1973, Painter, Sculptor.
Gold pendant photographed on a background of the enlarged signature of Picasso which appears on the back of the ornament. Picasso modeled a number of gold medallions in terracotta, some of which were cast in gold. Made in 1951.

Alicia Penalba, French. Born 1918 in San Pedro, Argentina. Lives in Paris, Sculptress.
Silver necklace of unconventional design reflecting Penalba's search for new expressions
in sculpture. Made in 1972. Total Ht. 21 cm.

Gilbert Albert, Swiss. Born 1930 in
Geneva. Lives in Geneva, Jeweler.
Long necklace of wood and gold. Made
1972. Total L. 35 cm.

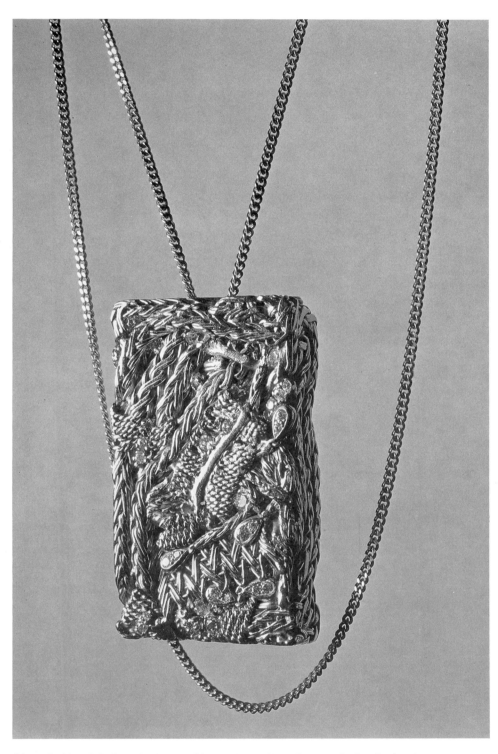

César Baldaccini, French. Born 1921 in Marseille. Lives in Paris, Sculptor.
Gold necklace, a so-called "Mini-Compression" made in 1971. In addition to his well-known auto and motorcycle compressions, César has made a whole series of "Mini-Compression" jewels. Ht. of pendant: 6 cm.

Raffael Benazzi, Swiss. Born 1933 in Rapperswil. Lives in San Vincenzo, Italy, Sculptor. Pendant of gold and Mexican opal matrix modeled by Benazzi and executed by Ingrid Hansen, Zurich. Lost-wax technique. Benazzi's jewelry is in contrast to his monumental sculptures although his newest pieces show similar features. Made in 1969. Total Ht. 6 cm.

Max Fröhlich, Swiss. Born 1908 in En-
nenda, Glarus, Switzerland. Lives in Zurich,
Gold-and Silversmith.
Necklace, brooch, and finger ring made of
wax-wire and cast in gold. Fröhlich, one of
the pioneers in the field of modern jewelry,
achieves an individual effect in his elegant
circular compositions. In recent years he
has been moving toward more experimental work. In 1964 Fröhlich received the
Gold Ring of Honor of the Gesellschaft für
Goldschmiedekunst (the highest international distinction awarded to a goldsmith). In
1966 he won the Gold Medallion at the
International Handicrafts Fair, Munich. Finger ring set with opal, 1969. Necklace and
brooch, 1970.

Sigurd Persson, Swedish. Born 1914 in Hälsingborg, Sweden. Lives in Stockholm, Gold- and Silversmith.
Finger ring of silver with gold ball. Persson, who has exhibited widely throughout the world, is renowned for his pure, architectural forms, which have had an enormous influence on contemporary jewelry. He has received numerous prizes including the Gold Ring of Honor of the German Goldsmiths' Society 1955 and in 1969 the St Eligius prize. Made in 1961. Ht. 5.7 cm.

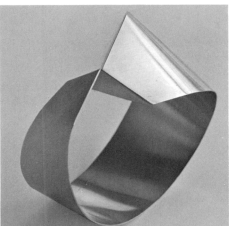

Emmy van Leersum, Dutch. Born 1930 in Hilversum, Holland. Lives in Amersfoort, Holland, Designer.
Gold bracelet of simple form which is both striking and bold. It was designed and executed by the artist who is known for body ornaments. She regards the body as a space for which she creates small sculptures. Bracelet made in 1968. 6 x 6.5 cm.

Bruno Martinazzi, Italian. Born 1923 in Turin. Sculptor and goldsmith.
Brooch – Homo Sapiens – yellow and white gold. Chisel and embossed work. Martinazzi's works have been shown in numerous exhibitions throughout the world, and he has been awarded many prizes, including the Bayerische Staats Preis in 1965. He considers his jewels to be miniature sculptures and works on sculpture and jewerly simultaneously. Made in 1973. Ht. 5.5 cm.

Yasuki Hiramatsu, Japanese. Born 1926 in Osaka. Lives in Tokyo, Goldsmith.
Finger ring of white gold. Hiramatsu, who has won several prizes, is director of the Japan Jewelry Designers Institute and the Japan Craft Centre. His creations are pure in form and of striking beauty. Made in 1971. Ht. 4 cm.

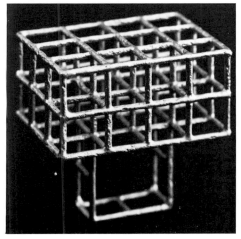

Anton Cepka, Czechoslovakiar. Born 1936 in Sulekovo, CSSR. Lives in St Jur, near Bratislava, CSSR, Sculptor, Goldsmith.
Brooch of silver and black onyx composed of geometric elements. Cepka creates jewels which are unique in character. The severity of geometric elements – the square, the oblong and the circle – is made softer by some unexpectedly asymmetrical detail. The graphic quality is preserved even when he chooses the unusual and exacting technology of sawing the silver sheet with a pad-saw, creating a frail net of simple regular patterns which grow more intricate in successive layers. the chief motif of the composition of the jewel. Made in 1967. Ht. 10.1 cm.

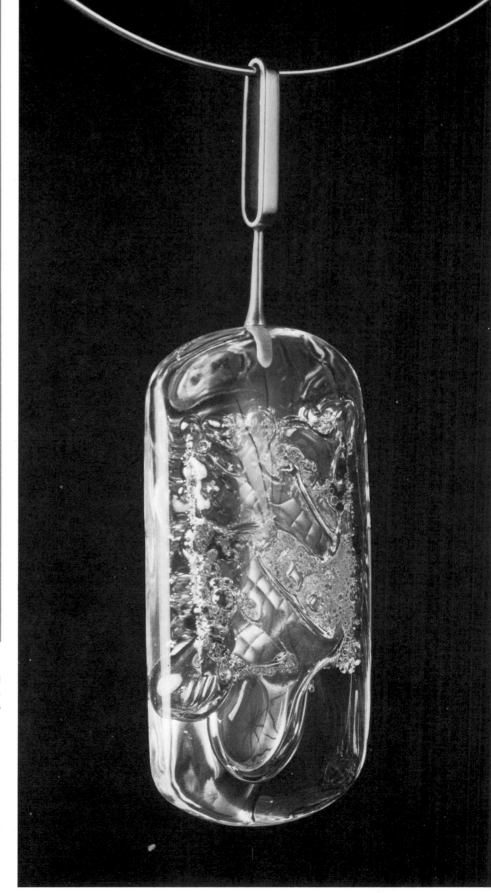

Claus Bury, German. Born 1946 in Meerholz, Germany. Lives in Hanau, Goldsmith.
Ornament, unconventional in form, of metal and acrylic reflecting Bury's search to find
new solutions in styles and materials for wearable jewels. Bury, one of the leading German
goldsmiths, feels that the wearer is the ultimate artist for only through wearing does his
jewelry comes to life. Made in 1972. Ht. c. 10 cm.

Ladislava Viznerova, Czechoslovakian. Born 1943 in Kolin, CSSR. Lives in Prague, Glass
jewelry craftsman.
Necklace of silver and crystal glass with air bubbles. Viznerova, winner of several international awards, studied at the Glass School of Kamenicky Senov, Bohemia. Made in 1967.
Ht. of pendant (glass) 5.3 cm.

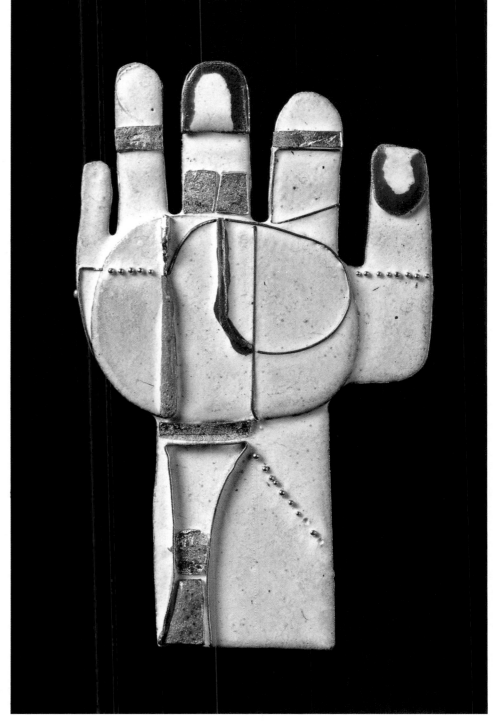

Hermann Jünger, German. Born 1928 in Hanau, Germany. Lives in Pöring near Munich, Gold- and silversmith.
Brooch in the form of a hand on gold with different colored enamels. Jünger, whose works have been seen in numerous international exhibitions, is one of Germany's leading goldsmiths. He has received various prizes. Brooch made in 1967. Total Ht. 4.7 cm.

Harry Winston, New York. Designers: Carnevale, American. Born 1909, died 1972. Koumrouyan, Bulgarian. Born 1904, died 1969.
Brooch in the form of a peacock in gold and platinum. The body is of black opal, 30.92 carats. The tail and head are richly decorated with sapphires, rubies, diamonds, and emeralds. Completed in 1967. Total Ht. 12.5 cm.

Arnaldo Pomodoro, Italian. Born 1926 in Morciano, Italy. Lives in Milan, Sculptor and Goldsmith.
Necklace of white and red gold. Pomodoro has said: "Since the middle of the 19th century up until today, a true revolution has taken place in contemporary arts, but no similar revolution is noticeable, with few exceptions in the minor arts. Therefore, it became my task to ennoble a minor art and to give jewelry a new style and a new direction." Necklace made in 1965.

Max Bill, Swiss. Born 1908 in Winterthur, Switzerland. Lives in Zurich, Architect, Painter, Sculptor.
Necklace of exceptional appeal and originality with three opals of unusual forms mounted on a gold chain. Bill brings to his rare pieces of jewelry his great designing talents. Made in 1965. (Enlarged).

Marci Zelmanoff, American. Born 1942 in Philadelphia. Lives in New York, Designer-
craftsman.
Collar of silver, forged, chased sterling with wrapped fine silver wire. Zelmanoff creates
large pieces, almost body ornaments, which are full of movement. She has exhibited in
America, Switzerland and Japan. Collar made in 1971. W. 25.4 cm.

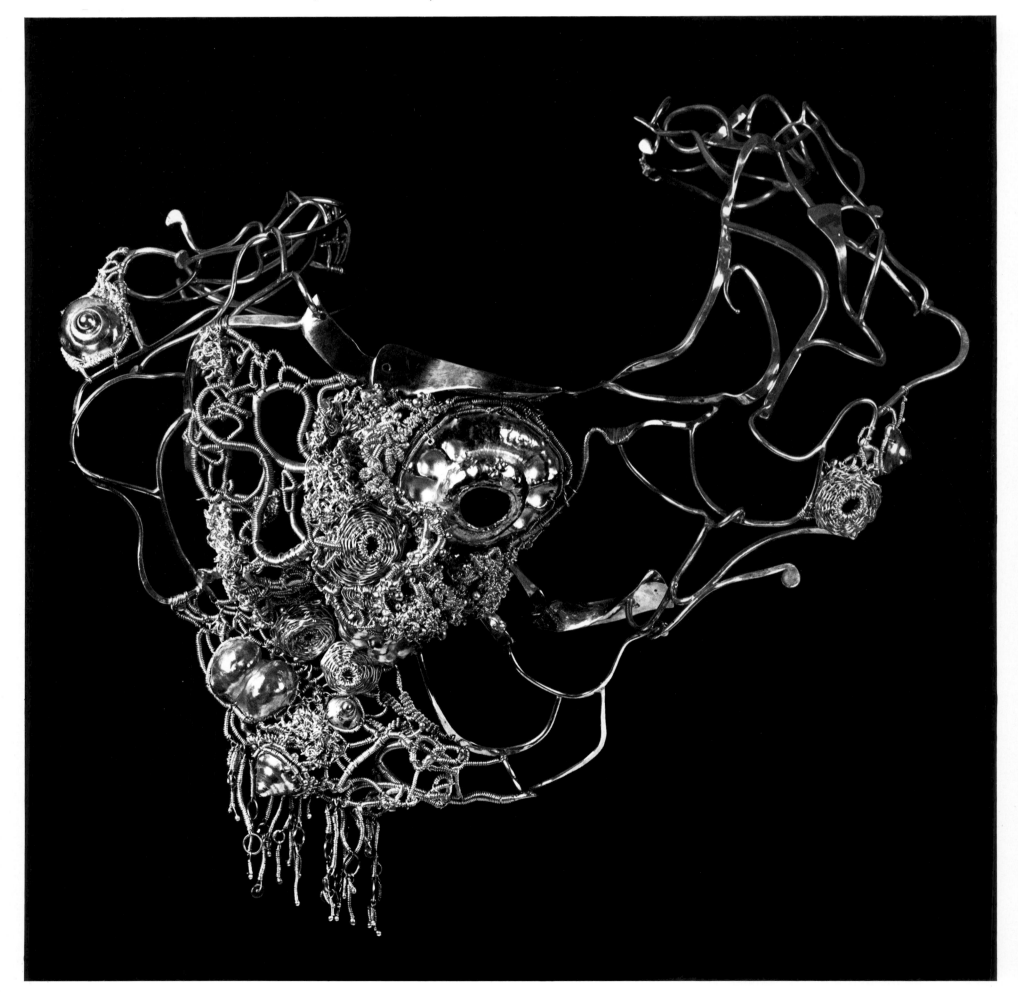

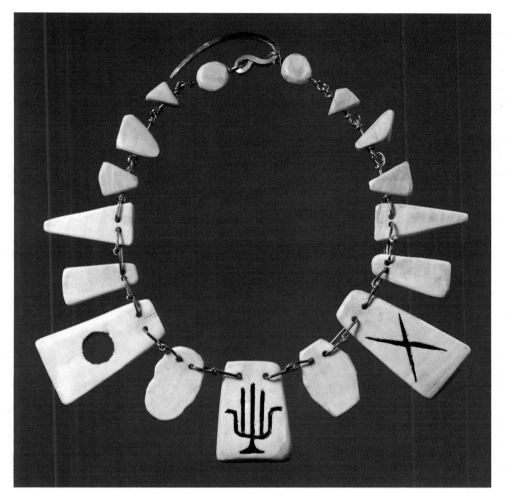

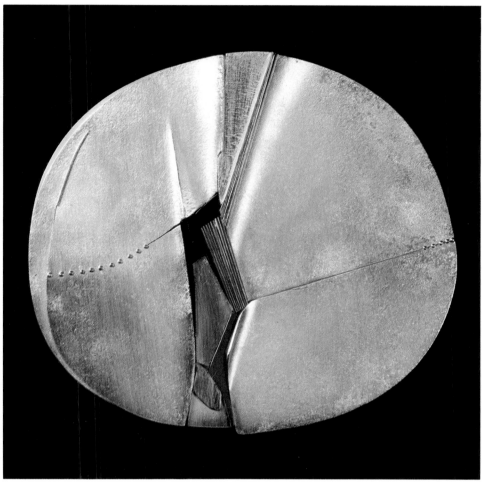

Alexander Calder, American. Born 1898 in Philadelphia. Lives in Connecticut and Paris, Sculptor.
The "Boney" necklace. Calder designed and made a small amount of jewelry, mostly for his wife, but also for Peggy Guggenheim, and a few friends during the 1930's and 1940's. This unusual necklace of bone is one of the earlier pieces, made for his wife, Louisa, c. 1935. (The photograph is slightly reduced).

Othmar Zschaler, Swiss. Born 1930 in Chur, Switzerland. Lives in Bern, Switzerland, Goldsmith.
Brooch of 24-carat gold with acryl-glass. Zschaler, one of the leading Swiss goldsmiths, has much pleasure in drawing. His works have been widely exhibited and have won him international acclaim. Honored with a one man show at the Schmuckmuseum, Pforzheim, in 1973. Brooch made in 1972. 7 x 8 cm.

Hubertus von Skal, German. Born 1942 in Jungferndorf, CSSR. Lives in Munich, Goldsmith.
Brooch of gold with a steel frame. Hubertus von Skal has participated in numerous international exhibitions, and has had one-man shows in Göppingen, Regensburg, Amsterdam. He received the Bayrischer Förderungspreis in 1972. Brooch made in 1967. Ht. 4.5 cm.

Arline M. Fisch, American. Born 1931 in New York. Lives in San Diego, California, Goldsmith.
This necklace shows an imaginative use of materials: sterling silver sheet (warp), fine silver wire (weft) and feathers. Technique: Twill weave construction, interior box clasp. Made in 1971. Diam. 11.4 cm.

Barbara Gasch, German. Born 1942 in Darmstadt, Germany. Goldsmith.
Brooch of silver with glass eye, movable eyelid, and 1 pearl as a tear. Gash often creates
jewels in surrealist style. Made in 1967. Diam. 4.5 cm.

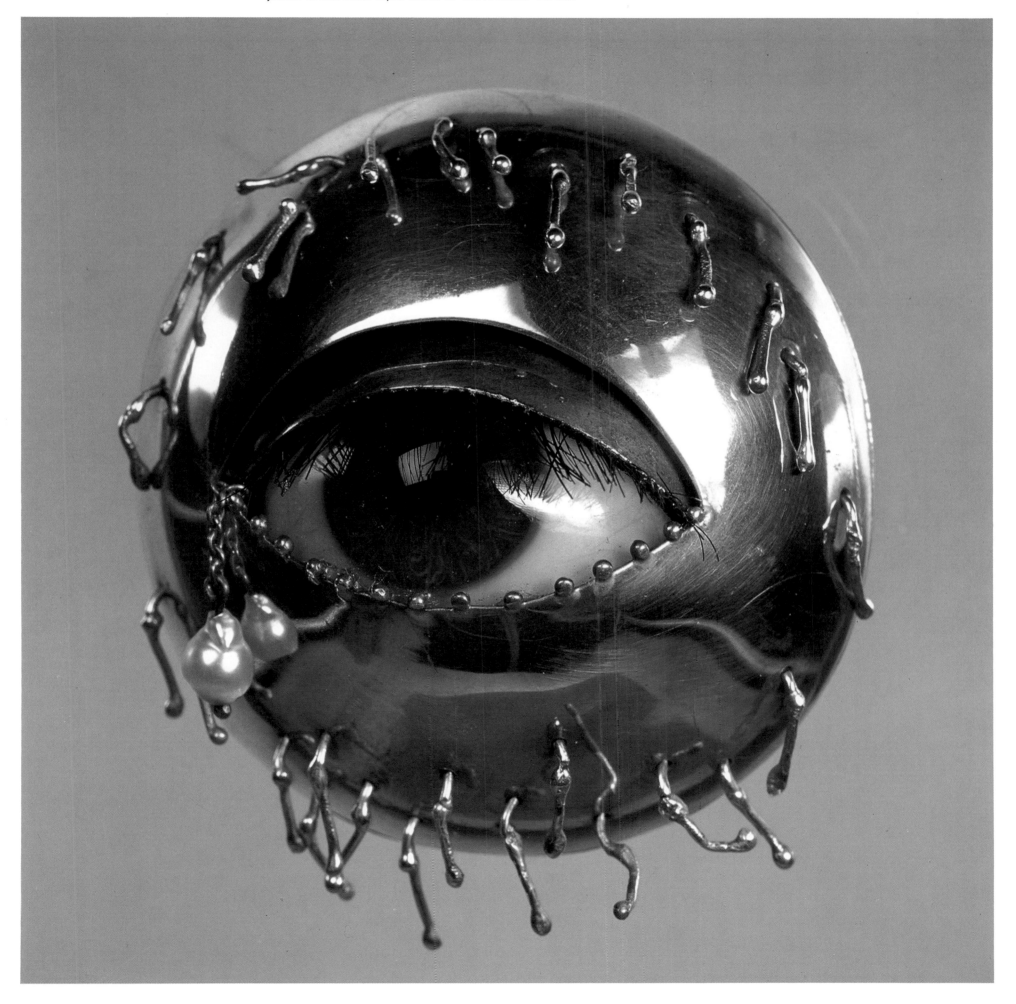

1

2

3

4

5

6

7

8

9

10

11

12

Yasuhiko Hishida, Japanese. Born 1927 in Gifu-shi, Japan. Lives in Tokyo, Goldsmith.
1 Silver brooch designed and executed by one of Japan's leading goldsmiths. Brooch made in 1970. Diam. 7 cm.

Sergi Aguilar, Spanish. Born 1946 in Barcelona. Sculptor.
2 Brooch of copper and silver, partially gold-plated. Made in 1972. Ht. 5.6 cm.

Ingrid Hansen, Swiss. Born 1931 in Basel. Lives in Zurich, Goldsmith.
3 Finger ring of 24-carat gold. Leaflet of black Australian opal. Lost-wax technique. Made in 1974. Ht. 3.2 cm.

Reinhold Reiling, German. Born 1922 in Ersingen, Germany. Lives in Pforzheim, Goldsmith.
4 Brooch of gold with brilliants. Brooch made in 1970. Total Ht. 7.3 cm.

Robert Smit, Dutch. Born 1941 in Delft, Holland. Lives in Delft, Goldsmith.
5 Brooch of white gold and acryl glass. Brooch made in 1970. Ht. 8.4 cm.

Bernhard Schobinger, Swiss. Born 1946 in Zurich. Lives in Richterswil, Switzerland, Goldsmith.
6 Two gold finger rings. Rings made in 1974. Ht. 3 cm.

Fernand Demaret, Belgian. Born 1929. Lives in Brussels, Goldsmith.
7 Necklace of gold with 2 opals and 1 small sapphire. Necklace made in 1970. Total Ht. of pendant: 10.8 cm.

Cornelia Rating, German. Born 1947 in Mülheim/Ruhr, Germany. Lives in Pforzheim, Goldsmith.
8 Brooch of silver, steel and acryl glass. Brooch made in 1972. Total Ht. 7 cm.

Beverly Pepper, American. Born 1924 in New York. Lives in Rome, Sculptress.
9 Gold cuff links which show a close affinity to Pepper's sculpture. Designed by the artist in 1970. Total width: 3.5 cm.

Andrew Grima, English. Born 1921 in Rome. Lives in London, Jeweler.
10 Bracelet of emeralds, diamonds, baroque pearls, and molten gold. Bracelet made in 1970. Diam. 4.3 cm.

Cartier, New York. Designer: Marguerite Stix, American. Born 1907 in Vienna. Lives in New York, Sculptress.
11 Ring of Marble Cone seashell from the tropical western Pacific, in a gold setting. Ring made in 1970. Ht. 3.5 cm.

Trudel Jewelry, Zurich.
12 Gold bracelet by Trudel, Zurich, a firm which is internationally known for modern designs. Made in 1970. L. 17.3 cm.

Friedrich Becker, German. Born 1922 in Ende, Germany. Lives in Düsseldorf, Gold- and Silversmith.
Kinetic brooch, inspired by pure geometric forms, of white gold set with 96 brilliants and 48 sapphires. When the ornament is worn, the wheel with the sapphires rotates. The basis of Becker's experiments for his kinetic jewels is his delight in mathematics and mechanical play. Brooch made in 1967. Diam. 6.2 cm.

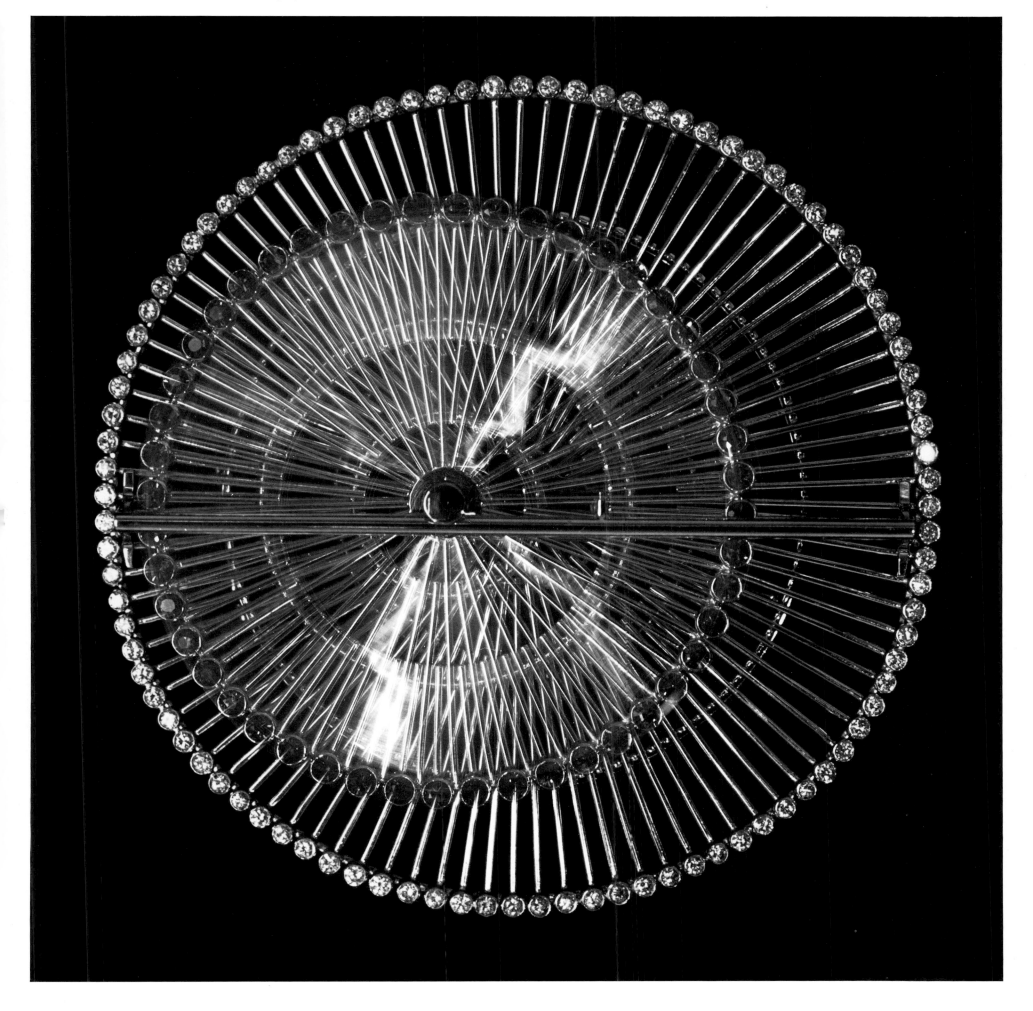

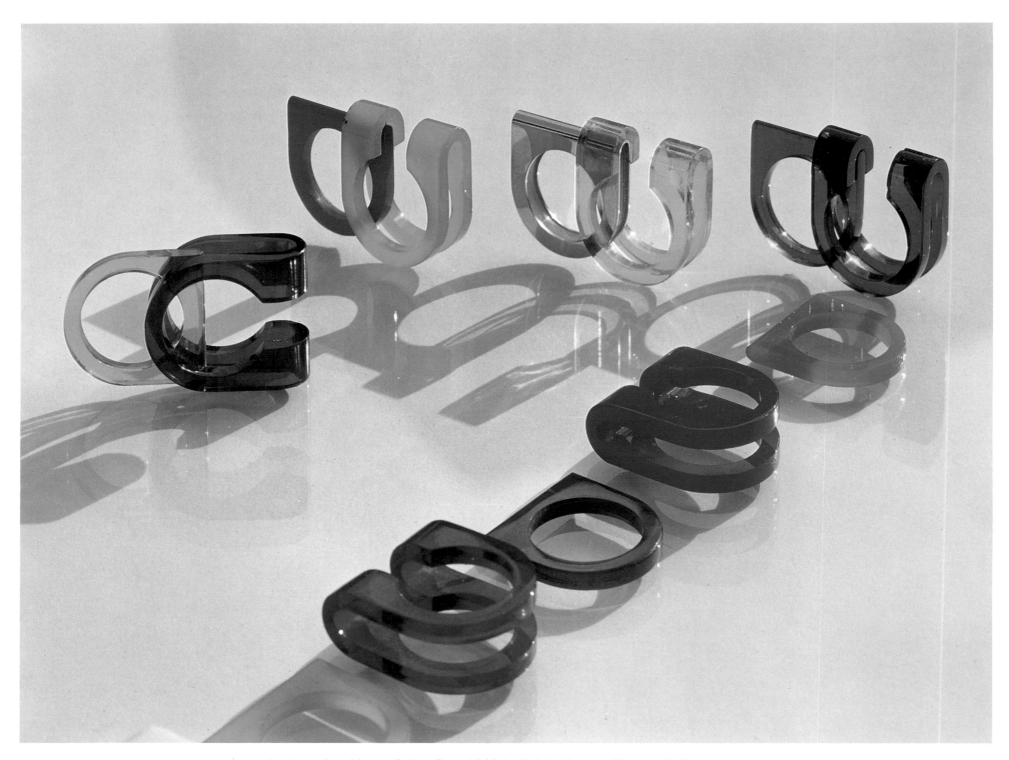

Bernhard Schobinger, Swiss. Born 1946 in Zurich. Lives in Richterswil, Switzerland, Goldsmith.
Finger rings in acrylic-glass. Although Schobinger usually creates jewels in gold, he does not hesitate to use acrylic-glass when it offers him better possibilities in forms and colors. The "Multi-rings" in ten colors consist of three interchangeable pieces, two of acryl and one of metal. According to the artist, it is possible to achieve an estimated 100,200 combinations. Made in 1972. Ht. 3 cm.

SOME
FAMOUS JEWELS
AND THEIR
HISTORIES

GEORGE S. SWITZER CURATOR, SMITHSONIAN INSTITUTION, WASHINGTON, D.C.

mine at the end of the working day after the staff had left, when he happened to glance up at one of the galleries. He noticed a large mass in one of the side walls, which he first thought was some glass embedded there by a practical joker. When the "glass" was examined, it turned out to be a huge diamond. Wells received $10,000 for his find, which was named after the discoverer of the mine, Sir Thomas Cullinan. Louis Botha, and the Transvaal Government, bought the rough stone for $800,000 to present to King Edward VII on his sixty-sixth birthday, November 9, 1907. The stone was sent to the Asscher Brothers in Amsterdam, who had successfully cut the Excelsior, heretofore the largest diamond. The huge gem was studied for months until finally, on February 10, 1908, Mr Asscher struck the steel cleaver's blade to make the first cut. The blade broke while the diamond remained intact. On the second attempt, it split exactly as planned; afterward, it was reported that Asscher was so overcome with relief that he fainted. A further cleavage produced three principal parts, and these in turn were cut into 9 major gems, 96 smaller brilliants, and 9.5 carats of unpolished pieces.

The largest gem produced, which is the world's biggest cut diamond, is a pear-shaped stone of 530.2 carats. It is now set into the head of the royal scepter as part of the British crown jewels, and is on display in the Tower of London. King George V asked that the stone be known as the Great Star of South Africa. The second largest cut diamond, Cullinan II, is a cushion-shaped stone weighing 317.4 carats, and is mounted in the imperial state crown. There are also seven other major stones in the possession of the Royal Family. During the Second World War, the stones were placed in jam jars and buried in a potato field near Windsor Castle, while the crowns were placed in old hat boxes and hidden in a secret passage in the castle. Now they are again on display in the Tower of London, having accumulated around them a considerable history despite the comparatively short time they have been known.

Darya-i-nur − the mysterious pink diamond of the Moguls

This is a great pink diamond, weighing an estimated 185 carats, and is one of the prizes among the Iranian crown jewels. It is a rectangular step-cut stone bearing an inscription in Persian, "The Sultan, Sahib Qiran, Fath Ali Shah, Qajar 1250." That date is 1834, the year of Fath Ali's death.

This is thought to be one of the diamonds carried off by Nadir Shah after the sack of Delhi in 1739. It was seen by Harford Jones in 1791, who noted its resemblance to the Great Table diamond described by Tavernier, although the weights were different. It was seen again in 1827 by Sir Malcolm Jones. The next recorded appearance was in 1902, when

Musaffer ud-Din, the then Shah of Persia, wore it on his state visit to England. In 1966, experts Dr V. B. Meen, Dr A. D. Tushingham, and Mr G. G. Waite of the Royal Ontario Museum in Toronto made a definitive study of the Iranian crown jewels. They concluded that the Darya-i-nur seen by Harford Jones was indeed the Great Table of Tavernier, that it was damaged at some time prior to 1834, and recut to its present size. Furthermore, they were able to prove that the 60-carat Nur-ul-ain, also in the Iranian crown jewels, and the Darya-i-nur could both have been cut from the Great Table.

Dresden Green

This diamond is renowned principally because at 41 carats it is the largest apple-green diamond known. It is undoubtedly of Indian origin, but nothing is known about it until its purchase in 1743 by Frederick Augustus II of Saxony.

It was exhibited along with the other crown jewels of Saxony in the Green Vault in Dresden. After the Second World War the gem was confiscated by the Russians. It was returned to Dresden in 1958.

Eureka — the first South African diamond

This 10.73-carat brilliant is not, by ordinary standards, exceptional. However, it was cut from the first diamond found in South Africa, and therefore has a great historical significance.

In 1866, a boy named Erasmus Jacobs found a pebble near the banks of the Orange River near his home. About a month later a neighbor, Schalk van Niekerk, admired the stone and the boy's mother gave it to him. Van Niekerk showed the pebble to John O'Reilly, a traveling peddler, who had it identified as a 21-carat yellow diamond and sold it for $2,500 to Sir Philip Wodehouse. The diamond was shown at the Paris Exposition in 1867 and later cut to its present form. Although Erasmus Jacobs never found another diamond, Van Niekerk was luckier. He purchased the Star of South Africa from a shepherd boy for 500 sheep, 10 oxen, and a horse. When he resold it, he received $55,000 for it.

Shah Jahan, the Great Mogul, and the Taj Mahal

This was another diamond seen and described by Tavernier during one of his trips to the East in the late 1600s. The diamond was found in the Gani mine in India in about 1650, and was presented to Shah Jahan, the builder of the Taj Mahal.

Aurangzeb, son of Shah Jahan, showed the diamond to Tavernier, who described it as "rose cut, round, and very high on one side," much like "the form of an egg cut in half." At the time Tavernier saw it, the diamond weighed 280 carats.

Nadir Shah probably took the Great Mogul back to Persia after his sack of Delhi in 1739. If he did, the stone was probably stolen after his death in 1747, and recut to conceal its identity. Its present whereabouts is unknown.

The Hope — the diamond of misfortune

This great blue diamond is perhaps the most notorious gem in history. It has left behind it a trail of so many unlucky owners that it has been popularly supposed to be cursed.

The Hope was mined in India, and the 112-carat gem was brought to France in 1668. It was said that a curse rested on it, for a thief was reputed to have stolen the diamond from the eye of a statue of the Hindu goddess Sita, wife of Rama.

Tavernier, who brought the gem from India to France, sold it to Louis XIV, who had it cut into a 67-carat heart-shaped stone and named it the Blue Diamond of the Crown. Tavernier is said to have been killed by wild dogs on his next trip to India.

Louis XVI and Marie Antoinette inherited the French Blue, as it was popularly known. In 1792, about the time of their executions, the French Blue was stolen from the Garde-Meuble together with all of the French crown jewels. Some of the gems taken in this robbery were recovered, but not the Blue Diamond of the Crown.

It is intriguing to note that a gem resembling the Hope is worn by Queen Maria Louisa of Spain in a portrait painted by Goya in 1800. There are reports that the stolen French Blue was recut to its present size by Wilhelm Fals, a Dutch diamond cutter. Fals is said to have died of grief after his son, Hendrick, stole the gem from him. Hendrick, in turn, committed suicide.

In 1830, there appeared in London a 44.5-carat deep blue oval-cut diamond the gem experts agree was the French Blue recut to conceal its identity. Henry Hope bought it, and since then it has been known as the Hope diamond.

The Hope moved on. An Eastern European prince gave it to an actress of the Folies Bergère and later shot her. A Greek owner and his family plunged to their death over a precipice in an automobile accident. The Turkish sultan Abdul-Hamid II had owned the gem only a few months when an army revolt toppled him from his throne in 1909.

Evalyn Walsh McLean, a wealthy and eccentric American social figure, bought the Hope diamond in 1911. Her son was killed in an automobile accident, her husband died in a mental hospital, and her daughter died in 1946 of an overdose of sleeping pills.

After Mrs McLean's death in 1947, New York jeweler Harry Winston purchased her jewels, including the Hope. He gave the gem to the Smithsonian Institution in Washington, D.C., in 1958, no doubt with a certain sense of relief. Coincidence or not, the diamond seems to have brought enormous troubles in its train.

The Jubilee – the world's most perfectly-cut diamond

The Jubilee diamond, weighing 245.35 carats, is the fourth largest cut diamond known. It is exceeded in weight only by the Cullinan I (530.2 carats), Cullinan II (317.4 carats), and the Nizam (277 carats). The 280-carat Great Mogul has been lost since 1739 and the 250-carat Great Table was cut into the Darya-i-nur (185 carats) and Nur-ul-ain (60 carats).

The Jubilee was found in the Jagersfontein mine, Kimberley, South Africa, in 1895. It weighed 650.8 carats in the rough and was named the Reitz diamond after F. W. Reitz, then president of the Orange Free State. In 1897, it was cut into a cushion-shaped brilliant and renamed the Jubilee in honor of Queen Victoria's Diamond Jubilee. A 13.34-carat pear shape was cut from the same rough but its identity has been lost.

The Jubilee is considered to be one of the world's greatest diamonds because of its size, its extraordinarily fine color, and because it is so perfectly cut that it balances on its culet, less than two millimeters across.

The first owner of the Jubilee was Sir Dorab Tata, an Indian industrialist, who bought it in about 1900. The second and present owner is Paul-Louis Weiller, a well-known French industrialist. The diamond has only been shown publicly twice, at the Smithsonian Institution in 1961, and at the De Beers Diamond Pavilion in Johannesburg in 1966.

The Mountain of Light – the Koh-i-noor

According to some sources, the Koh-i-noor diamond (108.93 carats) was found in the Godavari river in central India 4,000 years ago. Tradition associated with it states that its owner will rule the world, but that to possess it is dangerous for any but a woman. This, however, may have been a delicate piece of flattery to Queen Victoria, who once owned the gem.

The authentic history of this jewel begins in the fourteenth century, when it was reported to be in the possession of the rajas of Malwa. It later fell into the hands of Baber, who founded the Mogul dynasty in 1526. For the next two centuries the diamond was one of the most prized items in the treasure of the Mogul emperors throughout the years of their greatness.

In 1739, Nadir Shah of Persia invaded India, and all of the treasures of the Moguls fell into his hands except the great diamond. Nadir Shah was told by one of the emperor's harem women that the stone was hidden in the emperor's turban. The conqueror then invited the conquered to a feast, and offered to exchange turbans as a gesture of friendship. The emperor had no choice but to agree. Later, in the privacy of his tent, Nadir Shah unrolled the turban, the gem fell out, and Nadir is supposed to have exclaimed "Koh-i-noor" – mountain of light.

The stone continued in the possession of the Persian dynasty, although many attempts were made to gain ownership of it. The Persian king was assassinated, and his son, Shah Rukh, was deposed. In an effort to discover the whereabouts of the diamond Shah Rukh's eyes were put out, and boiling pitch was poured on his head, but he refused steadfastly to reveal its hiding place. Later, a Persian king fled with it to the Sikh court, and Ranjit Singh, the Lion of the Punjab, took the stone and wore it as a decoration; it was later placed in the Lahore treasury. After the Sikh wars, it was taken by the East India Company as part of the indemnity levied in 1849, and was subsequently presented to Queen Victoria at a sparkling levee marking the company's 250th anniversary. The jewel was displayed at the Great Exhibition of 1851, where it was thought to display insufficient fire. It was decided to recut it from its original Indian form, and a member of the Amsterdam firm of Coster was summoned to London to perform the operation. A steam-driven cutting wheel was set up, and Prince Albert set the stone on the wheel, while the Duke of Wellington started it. The cutting took thirty-eight days, but did not add much to the stone's brilliance; indeed, it was felt in some quarters that the historical value of the diamond was diminished by the cutting. Queen Victoria continued to wear it as an ornament, then left it to Queen Alexandra, who wore it at Edward VII's coronation. In 1911, the jewel was used in a crown made for Queen Mary, and in 1937, in another made to be worn by Queen Elizabeth at the coronation of her husband, King George VI, in 1937. The Queen Mother's crown displays the Koh-i-noor today, and is on view in the Tower of London.

An attempt to buy the love of Catherine the Great – the Orloff

Some historians believe that the Orloff diamond – 189.60 carats – was originally the Great Mogul which disappeared in 1739 (see page 285). Most authorities, however, believe it was stolen from the eye of a statue of the Hindu god Sri-Ranga in a temple in Srirangam about 1750 – though unlike the Hope, it does not seem to have brought a curse with it.

According to the Sri-Ranga story, a French soldier fighting in the Carnatic wars in southern India deserted and stole the diamond described as having "the shape of an egg." He had carefully planned his exploit, and succeeded in swimming a river while a storm raged. After he arrived safely in Madras, he sold the gem to an English sea captain, who in turn sold it to a Persian merchant named Khojeh. In 1775, an Amsterdam firm sold the diamond to Prince Gregory Orloff, for $450,000, payable over seven years.

Orloff, a former lover of Catherine the Great, gave the diamond to the Russian empress in order to try to regain her favor. Catherine was well-known as a collector of both lovers and precious stones, and she established her own private gem-cutting establishment in the Urals. Orloff's attempt to appeal to both Catherine's appetites failed. She accepted the gift but never reinstated Orloff to his former position in the Court. Catherine had the diamond mounted on top of the double eagle in the imperial scepter, and it remains in the same setting today. It is housed in the diamond treasury of the Soviet Union in the Kremlin.

From the Braganzas to the American stage — the Portuguese

This 127.02-carat emerald-cut diamond is now exhibited at the Smithsonian Institution. It was recut from a 150-carat cushion-cut stone believed to have been of Brazilian origin, and to have been owned at one time by the Braganzas, the Portuguese royal family.

For these reasons it has been assumed that the gem was cut from a 215-carat rough diamond from Brazil known as the Regent of Portugal, a stone found in the River Abatio in 1775. It later came into the hands of King John VI when he was regent of Portugal; no further historical details are available.

Before being acquired by the Smithsonian Institution in 1963 the Portuguese passed through several private hands including those of May Yohe, the American stage star, and jewelers Sydney De Yound of Boston, and Harry Winston of New York.

Murder, revolution and theft — the stormy history of the Regent

The Regent is one of the world's finest diamonds and has a long, well-documented, and interesting history.

In the rough the diamond weighed 410 carats. It was found in India in the seventeenth century, and smuggled to the coast hidden beneath the bandages covering a self-inflicted wound. The finder, despite his precautions, was murdered by an English sea captain, who sold the stone for $5,000 to a Parsi trader. In 1702, the diamond was sold to Thomas Pitt,

Governor of Madras, for about \$100,000. Pitt sent it home to England where it was cut to a cushion-shaped brilliant weighing 140.5 carats. The great diamond then became known as the Pitt.

In 1717, Pitt sold the gem to Philippe, duke of Orléans and regent of France. It was worn in the crown of Louis XV at his coronation in 1722, and was frequently worn by Marie Antoinette two generations later.

In 1792, the diamond was stolen with the French Blue and other crown jewels. Unlike many of the others, it was quickly recovered. It was given as security for a war loan in 1797 but redeemed five years later.

When Napoleon Bonaparte was crowned emperor of France in 1804 he carried the great diamond in the hilt of his sword. His second wife, Marie Louise, took it to Austria after the fall of Bonaparte, but the jewel was later returned by the Austrian emperor. Charles X wore the Regent at his coronation in 1825, and it remained in this crown until placed in a diadem designed for Empress Eugénie, wife of Napoleon III.

In 1887, the French crown jewels were sold at auction, all but the Regent, which was put on exhibition at the Louvre, and except for a period during the Second World War when it was hidden behind a stone panel at the Château de Chambord, it has remained there to this day.

A Saxon jewel still worn in the British crown today – St Edward's Sapphire

This rose-cut sapphire is perhaps the oldest stone in the British coronation regalia.

According to tradition, this sapphire was, in its original form, mounted in a ring worn by Edward the Confessor, who ascended the throne in 1042. He was the last king of Anglo-Saxon royal descent. It was probably cut to its present form in the seventeenth century, and is now mounted in the finial cross-patée of the imperial state crown.

Murdered messengers, Mazarin, and the Astors – the Sancy

The history of the Sancy is the most complicated of all famous diamonds, made so by incomplete records and because two diamonds known as Sancy have been confused in various historical accounts. It was one of the first diamonds to be cut in symmetrical facets.

Nicholas Harlai, seigneur de Sancy, bought the 55-carat pear-shaped gem in Constantinople about 1570 and took it back to France. The seigneur de Sancy later became the French superintendent of finance. His king, Henry IV, asked to borrow the diamond to use as security against a loan. A messenger was sent with the stone to Paris, but he never arrived. It is said that Sancy followed his route and found the messenger dead, slain by robbers, and the diamond missing. Knowing the messenger's loyalty, Sancy suspected he may have swallowed the diamond to thwart the robbers, and after a grim search the diamond was indeed recovered.

Sancy was later ambassador to England and apparently sold the stone to James I in 1604, for it was listed in the inventory of the British crown jewels in 1605 as "one fayre diamonde, cutt in fawcetts, bought of Sancy."

In 1644, Henrietta Maria, queen consort of Charles I of England, took many of the crown jewels to France to raise money for the royalist cause in the civil war, and gave the Sancy and the Mirror of Portugal to the Duke of Epernon as partial security for a loan. She could not repay the loan and the duke kept the diamonds.

Epernon sold the diamonds to Cardinal Mazarin, chief minister of France, and when Mazarin died in 1661 he bequeathed the two diamonds and sixteen others to the French crown, all to be known as the Mazarin diamonds. In the 1691 inventory of the French crown jewels they are so listed, with the weight of the Sancy given as 53.75 carats (55 metric carats).

There is a story of another Sancy diamond in England at this same time, and when James II was deposed in 1688 he took this Sancy with him to France and later sold it to Louis XIV. The history of the Sancy is further confused by the fact that the gem was listed as 33.75 carats in the 1791 inventory of the French crown jewels, with no mention of the 53.75-carat stone of the 1691 inventory.

In 1792, the French crown jewels were stolen, and although some were recovered, the Sancy was not specifically listed among them. In 1795, the directorate of France gave some state jewels to the Spanish Marquess of Irande as security on a loan, and among them was a 53.75-carat diamond which most experts agree was the 1691 Sancy. It was never redeemed and is said to have passed into the hands of the Spanish Bourbons.

About 1828, a diamond called the Sancy was sold by a French jeweler to Prince Anatole Demidoff and it became known as the Demidoff diamond. It was given by Prince Demidoff to his wife, the Princess Matilde, niece of Napoleon. She patronized Cartier, which ensured the introduction of the firm into court circles. In 1865, it was purchased by a Bombay merchant, and two years later was shown at the Paris Exposition by a French jeweler at a recorded weight of 53.75 carats.

In 1906, a diamond called Sancy was purchased by the first Viscount William Waldorf Astor from the Demidoff family as a gift for his son's bride, Nancy Langhorne, and it has been in the Astor family since that time. Most experts agree that the Astor Sancy is the true historical stone. Its weight, 55 metric carats, equals 53.67 old carats. It was shown as the true Sancy in the "Ten Centuries of French Jewelry" exhibition at the Louvre in 1962.

The jewel that prevented war with Russia – the Shah

The Shah is an interesting bar-shaped yellowish diamond weighing 88.7 carats, with three inscriptions that tell much of its history–a rare example of a stone carrying its own documentation.

The first reads "Bourhan Nizam Shah II in the year 1000." That Mohammedan year corresponds to 1591; the name is that of the ruler of Ahmadnagar in India. The second inscription is "Son of Jahangir, Shah Jahan, 1051," indicating the stone was in the possession of Shah Jahan, builder of the Taj Mahal, in 1641. Tavernier saw it in 1665 when he visited the court of Aurangzeb, son of Shah Jahan. The third inscription reads "Qajar Fath Ali Shah." He was the Shah of Persia in 1824, so the diamond undoubtedly formed part of the jewels seized by Nadir Shah in 1739 and taken back to Persia.

In 1829, Alexander Griboyedoff, the Russian ambassador in Teheran, was assassinated. In atonement the diamond was presented to Tsar Nicholas I and became part of the Russian crown jewels. The diamond was rediscovered in 1922, and is now part of the Soviet Union's treasury of diamonds in the Kremlin.

From a trash-heap to the sultan's treasury – the strange story of the Spoonmaker

This pear-shaped diamond, weighing 85.8 carats, is one of the principal treasures of the Topkapi Museum in Istanbul. Legend has it that it was found in a rubbish heap by a Turkish fisherman, who sold it to a spoonmaker for three spoons. The Spoonmaker may be the Turkey II, which weighed 84 carats and was last reported in 1882 in the Turkish regalia.

In the inventory at Topkapi it is recorded that the Spoonmaker is the Pigott. According to most authorities the Pigott was purchased by Ali Pasha, ruler of Albania, in 1818. Ali Pasha was an ambitious tyrant who became so powerful that in 1822 the sultan of Turkey sent an army to bring him back to Turkey. A fight ensued in which Ali Pasha was mortally wounded. After being given the privilege of dying in his own throne room, he ordered destroyed his two most precious possessions, his diamond and his wife. Another version of his story can be found interwoven in Dumas' book *The Count of Monte Cristo*. The story continues that the Pigott was then crushed to powder. The possible identity of the Spoonmaker with the Pigott has been discounted by most authorities because the weight of the latter is generally given as 49 carats. However, other records variously give its weight as from 47 to 85.8 carats, so that, in view of the statement in the Topkapi inventory, the possibility exists that they are the same.

The Tiffany – the diamond of New York

The Tiffany, a 128.51-carat cushion-cut diamond, was cut from a 287.42-carat crystal found in the Kimberley mine in South Africa in 1878. It is the largest golden yellow diamond in existence.

Tiffany and Company, the well-known New York jewelry firm, bought the crystal in 1879 and had it cut in Paris under the supervision of Dr George F. Kunz, the company's gemmologist. It has ninety facets, forty on the crown and forty-eight on the pavilion, plus a table and culet. It was shown at the World's Columbian Exposition in Chicago in 1893, and in other exhibitions, including the New York World's Fair in 1939-40. More recently, it was shown in the Kimberley mine in South Africa in 1971. The diamond has also been on almost continuous display through the years at Tiffany's in New York, where it is still exhibited today.

The Timur Ruby – the jewel that told its own story

This gem is not a ruby but a spinel, although until 1851 it was thought to be the largest known ruby. It weighs 352.5 carats and ranks second in size to the 414.3 carat spinel in the imperial Russian crown. It is not faceted, but retains its original baroque form.

The Timur Ruby has a history paralleling that of the Koh-i-noor diamond, having been seized by Nadir Shah of Persia in 1739 when he invaded India. As with the Koh-i-noor, the East India Company took possession of the gem in 1849 and sent it to England. It went unrecognized there and together with three other spinels was listed in the official catalogue as: "Short necklace of four very large spinelle rubies."

The gem remained in obscurity for 60 years before it was recognized from the inscriptions it bears. These inscriptions are among the most fascinating aspects of this gem, and give further insight into its history.

The longest inscription is in Persian, written in Arabic script. A literal translation reads: "This [is] the ruby from the twenty-five thousand genuine jewels of the King of Kings the Sultan Sahib Qiran which in the year 1153 [A.D. 1740] from [the collection of] jewels of Hindustan reached this place [Isfahan]." The remaining five inscriptions are the names of some of the emperors who had it in their possession, and the corresponding dates, the first being Akbar Shah Jahangir Shah, 1021 (A.D. 1612). It is thought that the gem once bore the dates of three earlier owners.

The long inscription tells us that this spinel is the famous stone that fell into the hands of the Tartar conqueror Timur, known to Europeans as Tamerlane, but to the Moslem world as Sahib Qiran, when he captured Delhi in 1398. The emperor Shah Jahan had the jewel from 1628-58, and he erected in Delhi the famous Peacock Throne embellished with an immense number of gems, including the Timur Ruby. Nadir Shah invaded India and captured Delhi in 1739, and took the Timur Ruby back with him to Persia, as the long inscription states. From that point, the history of the Timur Ruby parallels that of the Koh-i-noor diamond.

The "lost" diamond of Bavaria — the Wittelsbach

This 35.32-carat, deep blue, brilliant-cut diamond is of Indian origin; its early history is not known. It was part of the gift that Philip IV of Spain gave to his daughter, Margaret Theresa, on her marriage to Leopold I of Austria in 1667.

Margaret Theresa died in 1673, and Leopold married Claudia Felicitas, who died in 1696. Leopold's third wife was Eleonora Magdalena, and he gave her all of the jewelry he had inherited from Margaret Theresa, including the great blue diamond. In 1720, Empress Eleonora Magdalena died and bequeathed the diamond to the youngest of the two arch-duchesses, Maria Amelia. In this way the diamond passed to the Wittelsbach family of Bavaria when in 1722 Maria Amelia was bethrothed to Charles Albert of Bavaria. It remained among the Wittelsbach jewels until 1931 when it mysteriously disappeared.

The final chapter in the history of the Wittelsbach began in a most interesting way in 1961. J. Komkommer, an Antwerp diamond dealer, was asked by another diamond merchant for advice on how to recut a large stone that he had recently acquired. On examining the 35.32-carat blue gem Komkommer felt certain that it must be of historical significance. He therefore obtained an option to buy the stone and hurried back to his office to try to identify it. After a few minutes' search he found it described and illustrated in the diamond dictionary. The lost Wittelsbach had been rediscovered. In 1964 the diamond was sold to a private collector.

The magnificent Spoonmaker Diamond, pear-shaped, weighing 85.8 carats, is one of the principal treasures of the Topkapi Museum, Istanbul. The 49 diamonds surrounding the Spoonmaker are said to have been set by the enthusiastic gem collector, Ali Pasha, or by the Ottoman rulers (according to information obtained from officials at Topkapi in 1973). In 1822 Ali Pasha, ruler of Albania, was deposed by the Sultan of Turkey, Mahmud II, and his treasure removed to the Ottoman Palace.

Necklace with the Great Mogul Emerald, weight 362.45 carats. The discovery and history of this exquisite stone is veiled in mystery. The delicate carving of the Emerald, depicting noblemen and noblewomen of the ruling dynasty, would date this gem to approximately the 16th century.

1   2   3   4

1   This very large pear-shaped amethyst was a gift of King Charles II of Spain to the Emperor Leopold I of Austria. The gold crown-shaped mounting is set with emeralds. Spanish, 17th century. Ht. 11.8 cm.

2   The Briolette—sometimes known as the Briolette of India—weighs 90.38 carats. It is a remarkable specimen of the old form, oval in shape, entirely faceted to give clarity and brilliance.

3   The Golden Maharaja, 65.60 carats, a pear-shaped diamond of golden color, attracted international attention at the Worlds' Fair in Paris 1937 for its beauty, especially the unusual color.

4   The Nur-ul-ain, also called the Light-of-the-Eye, is a pink diamond of brilliant cut, weighing 60 carats. The Nur-ul-ain is the central stone in a platinum tiara set with 324 diamonds.

5   Detail of a pendant with enormous Ceylon rubies, emeralds, diamonds and turquoise. The pendant was sent as a present to the Prophet's tomb. Turkish, 16/18th century. Ht. of pendant: 45 cm.

5

298

The Crown of Louis XV of France. It was made by the King's jeweler, Laurent Rondé, in 1722. Above a circlet rise eight fleurs-de-lis from which eight arches develop, and the finial is a three dimensional fleur-de-lis, the central stone of which was once the famous 55-carat pear-shaped Sancy Diamond. The world-renowned Regent Diamond of 140.50 carats was set in the fleur-de-lis in the center above the headband. Ht. 24 cm.

The Sancy Diamond, a 55-carat pear-shaped stone, has one of the most colorful histories of all the famous diamonds. Purchased in Constantinople in 1570 by Sancy, the stone was brought back to France. Stolen in 1792 in the famous gem robbery of the Royal Treasury in Paris, the Sancy reappeared in 1828 and was sold to Prince Anatole Demidoff of Russia. In 1906 it was purchased by William Waldorf Astor.

The Regent, 140.50 carats, is considered to be one of the finest diamonds in the world. Originally known as the Pitt (cut from the 410-carat stone) it was found about 1701 in India by a slave. In 1717, the stone was purchased by the then Regent of France, and became part of the Crown Jewels of France. Louis XV wore it for the first time on 21 March, 1721, when the Turkish embassy visited Paris.

The Wittlesbach Diamond, 35.32 carats, sometimes called the Great Blue Diamond because of its deep blue color, guards the secrets of its origin. However, it has three centuries of documented history. It was part of the dowry that Philip IV of Spain gave to his daughter, Margareta Teresa, on her marriage to Leopold I of Austria in 1667. In the 18th century, the diamond passed to the Wittelsbach family, members of which were first dukes, then electors and finally kings of Bavaria. The Elector often wore it and, when Bavaria was made a Kingdom, the blue diamond was set in the front of the orb surmounting the royal crown. It remained in the Wittelsbach family until 1931 when it disappeared.

Emerald pendant of Sultan Abdul Hamid I of Turkey, (the pendant signifiying the sultan's strength). Gold, set with diamonds, and adorned in the middle with three enormous hexagonal emeralds. From its lower edge hangs another diamond-set pendant and at its end a tassle made of 48 rows of small pearls. The pendant is one of the gifts sent by Sultan Abdul Hamid I to the Prophet's Tomb in Medina. Turkish, 18th century. Total Ht. 43 cm.

Dagger intended as a present from Sultan Mahmud I of Turkey to Nadir Shah of Persia. One side of the handle bears three large and pure emeralds, 3 x 4cm. in size, surrounded by diamonds. The handle is topped by a 3 x 4 cm. octagonal emerald cover, in which there is a small watch marked "Clarke, London." Around the cover and on both sides of the dagger's handle there are decorations made of diamonds; the other side of the handle is of mother-of-pearl and is adorned with fruit motifs in colored enamel on gold. The sheath is of gold, decorated with enameled flowers and diamonds. Turkish, 18th century. L. 35 cm.

The Hope, 44.50 carats, the largest blue diamond in the world, is one of the most notorious of all gemstones. By speculation, the unlucky blue Hope is linked to the famous "French Blue" diamond which was brought to France from India in 1668 to become part of the crown jewels. Legend has it that this flawless gem of a rare deep blue color is jinxed because thieves plucked it from the eye of a statue of the Hindu goddess Sita, wife of Rama. In any case, it has left behind a trail of ill-fated owners.

The Timur Ruby, or the Khiraj-i-alam, (which means the "Tribute to the World"), weighing 352.5 carats, ranks second in size to the 414.3 carat spinel surmounting the Imperial Russian Crown. It is not faceted, but retains its original baroque form. This famous gemstone, engraved with the names of its successive owners, was mounted in the center of a necklace made by Garrard for Queen Victoria in 1849. The stone has a large Indian cut ruby on each side. The chain of the necklace is composed of clusters and trident-shaped links set with diamonds. Now in the private collection of Her Majesty Queen Elizabeth II.

The Tiffany Diamond is the largest and finest canary diamond in the world. It is unique among yellow diamonds, not only because of its purity and size (128.51 carats), but because it retains its fabulous color even under artificial light. Found in the Kimberley Mine, South Africa, in 1878, it was purchased immediately by Tiffany & Co., and brought to Paris where it was studied for cutting during one whole year. The diamond is valued at $ 2,000,000. It is on view at Tiffany's, New York.

Detail of the British Imperial State Crown (worn by H.M. Queen Elizabeth II each time she opens Parliament) featuring the Black Prince's Ruby and Cullinan II. The Black Prince's Ruby, the great spinel of irregular shape, is among the greatest treasures of the British Crown Jewels. Cullinan II, mounted in the circlet of the Imperial State Crown, is a 317.40 - carat cushion-shaped stone. It is the second largest cut diamond in the world.

The head of the Sovereign's Royal Sceptre with the Cross. Above the great pear-shaped Star of Africa diamond is a remarkable amethyst surmounted by a richly jewelled cross patée. The Great Star of Africa (Cullinan I) is the world's largest cut diamond. It weighs 530.20 carats and is of superb quality. Incredibly, Cullinan I and Cullinan II both came from a single crystal, an enormous diamond weighing 3,106 metric carats which was cut into 9 stones and 96 smaller ones.

The Darya-i-Nur, or Sea-of-Light Diamond, pink in color, weighing an estimated 185 - carats, is one of the greatest treasures of the Iranian Crown Jewels. Its name is associated with the Koh-i-noor as both of these jewels are said to have been first in the possession of Baber, the first Mogul Emperor of India. It is a rectangular step-cut table stone, set in a cap device, surmounted by the lion and sun, symbols of ancient origin, set with 457 diamonds and 4 rubies.

Detail of the Crown of H.M. Queen Elizabeth, the Queen Mother, featuring the celebrated diamond known as the Koh-i-noor, or Mountain-of-Light, 108.93 carats. Of Indian origin, the Koh-i-noor has a history dating back to 1304, as it is probably the large diamond reported in the possession of the Raja of Malwa. It was later owned by Sultan Baber, who founded the Mogul Dynasty in 1526, and for the next two centuries it belonged to the Moguls.

The Shah, probably found in Golconda, India, is a bar-shaped diamond, yellowish in color, of 88.70 carats. It bears three inscriptions with the names of former owners, rulers of India or Shahs of Persia. In 1829 the Persian Government presented this great diamond to Tsar Nicholas I of Russia as a "token of grief" for the assassination of the Russian Ambassador, Alexander Griboyedoff, in Teheran.

The Crown of St Wenceslas, which became the national coronation crown of the Kings of Bohemia, is one of the finest surviving examples of a mediaeval royal crown. The Crown probably owes its inspiration to French crowns. It consists of four giant gold fleurs-de-lis pinned together and is richly decorated with precious stones which are set in heavy gold funnels held in position by claws. It contains 91 gems (rubies, emeralds and sapphires) and 20 pearls. Diam. of Crown: 19 cm.

TABLE OF GEMSTONES

Name	Variety	Hardness	Coloring	Deposits	Period of greatest use
Diamond		10	transparent, colorless, blue-white, shades of yellow, green, pink, red, blue, grey, black	India, Brazil, Guiana, north and south-west Africa, Congo, Angola, Tanganyika, Rhodesia, Cameroon, Ghana, Sierra Leone, North America, Australia, Borneo	mentioned by Pliny and Marco Polo; from the 17th century onwards
Corundum	ruby	9	transparent, various shades of red, star effect	Ceylon, Burma, Siam, Kashmir, Australia, USA (Montana and North Carolina), Madagascar, Urals, Saxony, Bohemia, France	mentioned by Pliny, Marco Polo, Albert the Great; rarely used until the 16th century, more frequent from the 17th century
	sapphire	9	blue, pale blue, with star effect		from the 18th century onwards
	aquamarine oriental		pale blue		19th and 20th centuries
	amethyst oriental		various shades of violet, often tending to red		19th and 20th centuries
	topaz oriental		yellow, clear lemon		19th and 20th centuries
Chrysoberyl	chrysoberyl	8 1/2	pale yellow, pale green, from transparent to opaque	Brazil, Ceylon, USA, Madagascar	known in the Classical era; 19th century
	golden chrysoberyl or chrysolite		old gold, yellow-gold tending to greenish	usually Brazil and as above	known in the Classical era; 19th century
	oriental cat's eye		green or yellow mixed, showing streaks of reddish, bluish or violet light	Ceylon, Brazil	known in the Classical era; 19th century
	alexandrite		emerald, dark and olive green	Russia, Ceylon, Tasmania, Rhodesia	19th century
Spinel	spinel ruby	8	blood red, transparent to opaque	Burma, Siam, Brazil, Ceylon, Madagascar	Classical era and 19th century
	Balas ruby		red to reddish-violet	Balascia (Afghanistan), India	Classical era, Renaissance, 18th and 19th centuries

Name	Variety	Hardness	Coloring	Deposits	Period of greatest use
Topaz		8	translucent, yellow-gold, honey-yellow rarely: blue-green, pink, red	in antiquity: Upper Egypt, Saxony today: Brazil, Urals, Siberia, California, Utah, Australia, Mexico, Japan, Madagascar, Ceylon	from the 18th century onwards
Beryl	emerald	7 1/2-8	light green to deep green	Columbia, Upper Egypt, Urals, Siberia, Brazil, Salzburg Alps, North America, Transvaal, India, California, Madagascar, Elba	Egyptian, Greek and Roman eras; from the 17th century to 19th century
	morganite		pink, pink lilac		
	aquamarine	7 1/2-7 3/4	pale blue, transparent	Brazil, Urals, Madagascar, Elba	from the 17th century onwards
Zircon	precious zircon	7 1/2	transparent to translucent; shades of green, yellow, grey, violet	widely found: Norway, Sweden, Canada, Madagascar, Ceylon, Siam, Australia	from the 18th century onwards
	jacinth		orange-red, red, dark red, light red, violet-red	as above, Ceylon, Indochina, Siam. South Africa, Brazil	19th and 20th centuries
	starlite		blue, bluish-green, electric-blue	Siam	19th and 20th centuries
	colorless zircon or Matara diamond		transparent, colorless	same as the other varieties, Ceylon (Matara), Siam	19th and 20th centuries
Tourmaline	indicolite	7 1/2	greenish-blue, light blue	Brazil, South Africa, Urals, Colorado, Massachusetts, California, Kashmir, Madagascar, Bengal	from the 18th century onwards
	rubellite or siberite	7 1/4-7 1/2	pink, ruby-red	Russia, USA, Ceylon, Burma, Madagascar, Brazil, China	19th and 20th centuries
	green tourmaline	7 1/2	shades of green	Brazil, South Africa, Russia, Ceylon, Elba	19th and 20th centuries
	yellow tourmaline	7 1/2	shades of yellow	Madagascar, Ceylon	19th and 20th centuries
Andalusite		7 1/2	whitish, grey, green, olive, red, red-brown, violet; slightly transparent	Andalusia, Austria, Saxony, Brazil, Urals, Ceylon	19th and 20th centuries
Garnet (carbuncle)	pyrope or Bohemian ruby or Cape ruby	7 1/4	fiery red	Bohemia, Saxony, Switzerland, South Africa, Ceylon, Scotland, western USA, Brazil	infrequently used in the Middle Ages and Renaissance; much used in 19th century
	almandine or precious garnet	7 1/4-7 1/2	violet-red	India, Brazil, Uruguay, South Australia, USA, Madagascar, Greenland, Bohemia, Spain, Austria, Russia, Norway, Switzerland, Hungary, the Alps	mentioned in Pliny; used in the Classical era for engraving; from the 19th century onwards
	hessonite	7	reddish-orange, cinnamon yellow	Ceylon, USA, western Alps, Madagascar, Tyrol, Urals	from the 17th century
Quartz	rock crystal	7	very transparent, colorless	mainly: Alps and other parts of Italy, Tyrol, Silesia, Scotland, Urals, Brazil, Madagascar, Japan	Classical, Byzantine, Barbarian, High Medieval and Renaissance eras; 17th, 18th, 19th centuries; less popular in modern times

Name	Variety	Hardness	Coloring	Deposits	Period of greatest use
Quartz	amethyst	7	transparent; all shades of violet	Brazil, Uruguay, Ceylon, South Africa, Mexico, Madagascar, Russia, Australia, North America, Spain, France, Hungary, Italy	Classical and Renaissance eras, and 19th century
	rose quartz		milky rose-pink; semi-transparent	Brazil, South Africa, Japan, Madagascar, Ceylon, USA, Bohemia, Bavaria, Scotland, Ireland, Italy, Russia	Classical and Renaissance eras, and 19th century
	sunflower quartz		semiopaque, bluish-white, milky, opalescent	Brazil, India, Bohemia, Hungary, Siberia	Classical and Renaissance eras, and 19th century
	falcon's eye		opaque; greyish blue with shimmering streaks of greenish-blue light	South Africa	Classical and Renaissance eras, and 19th century
	aventurine		opaque; red-brown, and green	Russia, India, Tibet, Egypt, Australia, Brazil, Bavaria, Syria, Scotland, Spain, France, Piedmont	19th century
	jasper		white, red, green, blue, yellow, brown, black, opaque, variegated	Saxony, Siberia, Egypt, USA, Brazil, South Africa, Madagascar, Italy (Tuscany)	Egyptian, Classical High Medieval and Renaissance eras; 19th century
	chalcedony	6 1/2-7	milky, whitish, bluish-grey, greenish, yellowish	Faroe, Iceland, Brazil, Uruguay, Italy	Classical era and 19th century
	blue chalcedony		light blue, blue, opaque	Arizona, Siberia, India, Rumania, Oregon	19th century
	carnelian		blood red, various shades to yellowish-brown	India, Brazil, Arabia, Russia, Siberia, Japan, Germany	Classical era, Renaissance and 19th century
	sard		brown, black-brown, orange-brown, semi-transparent	India, Brazil, Arabia, Russia, Siberia, Japan, Germany	Classical era, Renaissance and 19th century
	chrysoprase		apple-green with white and grey streaks	Silesia, India, Urals, Austria, USA, Canada	Classical era and 19th century
	plasma		dark green, olive, opaque	India, orient, Upper Egypt, Germany	Egyptian and Classical eras
	agate		stratified, green, light blue, white, red, brown, black; semi-transparent	Germany, Brazil, India, Asia Minor, China, Madagascar	Classical era, Renaissance and 19th century
	onyx (variety of agate)		striated; white, black or black and red lines or curves		Classical era, Renaissance and 19th century
Jade or Jadeite		6 1/2-7	opaque or translucent; not uniform; basically white or greyish tending to pink or lilac-blue; specks of emerald green or light green	Burma, Turkestan, China, Tibet, Mexico, Costa Rica, New Zealand, Alaska, Greece, western Alps	Pre-Columbian era, the Far East in prehistoric times; in Europe in the 19th century onwards
Olivine	olivine or chrysolite or peridot	6 1/2-7	greenish-gold, olive-green; transparent or translucent	Brazil, Norway, Congo, Australia, Faroe, Egyptian Red Sea coast, Arizona, New Mexico, Ceylon, Burma	Egyptian and Classical eras, Middle Ages, 19th century

Name	Variety	Hardness	Coloring	Deposits	Period of greatest use
Marcasite		6-6 1/2	opaque, gold yellow, metallic	Folkestone (UK), Bohemia, Czechoslovakia, Saxony, France, Mexico, USA	19th and 20th centuries
Feldspar	orthoclase	6	gold yellow, lemon yellow	Madagascar	20th century
	adularia or moonstone	6	transparent, colorless, green, pearly, milky bluish-white	Ceylon, Brazil, USA, Australia	19th and 20th centuries
	oligoclase or sunstone	6	almost opaque, greyish-white background, flecked with gold particles	Norway, Russia, Siberia, USA	19th century
	labradorite	6	opaque, grey background, flecks of all colors	Labrador, Russia, Finland, USA, Sweden, Canada	19th century
Opal	precious opal	5 1/2-6 1/2	semitransparent, milky white tending to blue with shimmering rainbow-like colorations. Rarely: yellow, red, green, blue and black	Hungary, Mexico, Australia, Honduras, Guatemala, USA, Japan	used occasionally in the Roman era; 19th century
	fire opal		transparent to opaque, hyacinth-red, reddish-yellow, orange, wine-red, brownish-yellow. Rarely: iridescent, red or green streaks	Mexico, Faroe, Nevada, Australia	19th century
Nephrite or Jade		5 1/2-6 1/2	opaque or translucent; grey-white, grey-green, grass green, yellowish, brown, reddish	Turkestan, China, Russia, Siberia, New Zealand, North Caledonia, Venezuela, Brazil, Peru, Alaska, Switzerland	Pre-Columbian era, the Far East in prehistoric times; in Europe in the 19th century onwards
Turquoise		5-6	opaque; apple-green, green, skyblue, light and dark blue, black, brown or white inclusions	Iran, Turkestan, Tibet, Sinai peninsular, Arabia, USA (New Mexico and California), Australia, South Africa, Silesia, Saxony	Egypt (from the 3rd millennium BC), Pre-Columbian era, Renaissance, 19th and 20th centuries
Sodalite	lapis lazuli or lazurite	5-5 1/2	opaque; sea-blue, dark or light blue, tending to green or violet; specks of gold due to inclusion of pyrites	Afghanistan, Russia, Siberia, Chilean Andes	Mesopotamia, Egypt, Classical era, Renaissance, 17th, 19th and 20th centuries
Malachite		3 1/2-4	composed of copper; translucent or opaque; emerald or dark green; mottled with dark or light bands	Urals, Rhodesia, Katanga, Chile, USA, Australia, Rumania, France	19th century
Jet (fossilised wood)		3-4	opaque, brown, black	Whitby and Cleveland (Yorks), Spain, France, Saxony, Russia, Colorado	19th century
Amber or Succunite (fossilised resin)		2 1/2-3 (and 1 1/2)	transparent, semi-opaque, translucent, variegated and mottled; from clearest to darkest yellow, tending to red and brown; also blue, violet and green	Baltic coast, Friesian islands, Rumania (rumenite), Burma (birmite), Galicia, France, Spain, Russia, Canada, San Domingo	from prehistoric to modern times

SOURCES AND ACKNOWLEDGEMENTS

P.34   Smithsonian Institution, Washington, D. C.

P.35   Smithsonian Institution, Washington, D. C.

P.36   left; Smithsonian Institution, Washington, D. C.

P.38   Smithsonian Institution, Washington, D. C.

P.39   Smithsonian Institution, Washington, D. C.

P.40   below: Smithsonian Institution, Washington, D. C.

P.41   Mineralogische Sammlung der Eidgenössischen Technischen Hochschule, Zurich.

P.42   Smithsonian Institution, Washington, D. C.

P.43   Martin Bodmer Collection, Zurich.

P.44   De Beers Consolidated Mines, London.

P.45   all: Smithsonian Institution, Washington, D. C.

P.46   Polished Diamond Distributors, Hatton Gardens, London.

P.48   Paul-Louis Weiller, Paris.

P.61   Hessisches Landesmuseum, Darmstadt.

P.62   The Metropolitan Museum of Art, New York. Lila Acheson Wallace Fund, 1868.

P.63   above: The Metropolitan Museum of Art, New York. Gifts (3) of Miss Helen Miller Gould, 1910, and (1) Bequest of Mrs Mary Anna Palmer Draper, 1915.

P.63   below: The Metropolitan Museum of Art, New York. Museum Excavations, 1935-36, Rogers Fund, 1936

P.64   above: the Metropolitan Museum of Art, New York. Fletcher Fund, 1922.

P.65   above: Staatliche Antikensammlungen, Munich.

P.65   below: Archaeological Museum, Teheran.

P.66   The Metropolitan Museum of Art, New York. Fletcher Fund, 1934 and 1935.

P.67   above left: Österreichisches Museum für angewandte Kunst, Vienna.

P.67   above right: Schatzkammer der Residenz, Munich.

P.67   below: Courtesy A La Vieille Russie Inc. New York.

P.68   all: Bayerisches Nationalmuseum, Munich (Collection Kriss).

P.69   Musée du Louvre. Paris.

P.71   above left and below: E. Storrer, Zurich.

P.71   above right: Museum of Mankind, (Ethnography Department, British Museum), London.

P.72   all: Museum of Decorative Arts, Belgrade.

P.73   Museum of Mankind (Ethnography Department, British Museum), London.

P.74   1: The Metropolitan Museum of Art, New York. Carnarvon Collection, 1926.

P.74   2, 3, 7: Schmuckmuseum, Pforzheim.

P.74   4: Victoria and Albert Museum, London. Gift of Dr Joan Evans.

P.74   6, 10: E. Storrer, Zurich.

P.74   8: Ella Freidus Collection, New York.

P.74   9, 12: Museo Poldi-Pezzoli, Milan.

P.74   11: Topkapi Museum, Istanbul.

P.75   E. Storrer, Zurich.

P.76   Museum of Decorative Arts, Prague.

P.77   above: Schmuckmuseum, Pforzheim.

P.77   below: Smithsonian Institution, Washington, D. C., Collection of Mrs Marjorie Merriweather Post.

P.78   all: Schatzkammer der Residenz, Munich.

P.79   Smithsonian Institution. Museum of Technology, Washington, D. C. Gift of Mrs Marjorie Merriweather Post..

P.80   Crown jewels of Iran, Bank Markazi, Teheran.

P.81   left and right: Topkapi Museum, Istanbul.

P.82   all: Schatzkammer der Residenz, Munich.

P.83   left: Topkapi Museum, Istanbul.

P.85   above: Michel Périnet Collection, Paris.

P.85   below: Schmuckmuseum, Pforzheim.

P.86   Lillian Nassau Gallery, New York.

P.113   British Museum, London.

P.114   The Metropolitan Museum of Art, New York. Gift of Henry Walters and Edward S. Harkness.

P.115   The Metropolitan Museum of Art, New York. Fletcher Fund, 1922.

P.116   British Museum, London.

P.117   above left: National Archaeological Museum, Athens.

P.117   above right: Musée du Louvre, Paris.

P.117   below: The Metropolitan Museum of Art, New York. Purchase, 1916, Rogers Fund and contribution from Henry Walters.

P.118   The Metropolitan Museum of Art, New York. Fletcher Fund, 1926.

P.119   above left: The Metropolitan Museum of Art, New York. Fletcher and Rogers Funds, 1919-1922.

P.119   above right: The Metropolitan Museum of Art, New York. Carnarvon Collection, 1946.

P.119   below: Schmuckmuseum, Pforzheim.

P.120   The Metropolitan Museum of Art, New York.

P.121   above left: Victoria and Albert Museum, London.

P.121   above right: Musée du Louvre, Paris.

P.121   below: Hermitage Museum, Leningrad.

P.122   above: National Museum, Prague.

P.122   below: Archaeological Museum, Teheran.

P.123   British Museum, London.

P.124   Property of the Canton of Uri, Switzerland; on loan to the Landesmuseum, Zurich.

P.125   above: Bayerisches Nationalmuseum, Munich.

P.125   below: Museo Archeologico, Cividale del Friuli.

P.126   Museum of Natural History, New York. Bandelier, Heyde Collection.

P.127   above: British Museum, London.

P.127   below: Museo Archeologico, Cividale del Friuli.

P.128   left: John Wise Collection, New York.

P.128   right: Museo de Oro, Bogotá.

P.129   Museo de Oro, Bogotá.

P.130   all: John Wise Collection, New York.

P.131   above left, right: Museo de Oro, Bogotá.

P.131   below: Dumbarton Oaks, Washington, D. C.

P.132   above: Dumbarton Oaks, Washington, D. C.

P.132   below: John Wise Collection, New York.

P.133   Museum of Primitive Art, New York.

P.134   above both: Museum of Natural History, New York.

P.134   below: Dumbarton Oaks, Washington, D. C.

P.135   all: Museum of Mankind (Ethnography Department, British Museum), London.

P.136   Museum of Mankind (Ethnography Department, British Museum), London.

P.151   British Museum, London.

P.152   1 (the plates are counted from left to right, top to bottom): National Archaeological Museum, Athens.

P.152   2, 8: Schmuckmuseum, Pforzheim.

P.152   3, 4, 6, 7, 10: British Museum, London.

P.152   5, 9: Staatliche Antikensammlungen, Munich.

P.153   left: Schmuckmuseum, Pforzheim.

P.153   right: Benaki Museum, Athens.

P.154   left: National Archaeological Museum, Athens.

P.155   above: The Metropolitan Museum of Art, New York. Bequest of Richard B. Seager.

P.155   below: British Museum, London.

P.156   all: British Museum, London.

P.157   The Metropolitan Museum of Art, New York. Gift of J. Pierpont Morgan.

P.158   above left: Musée du Louvre, Paris.

P.158   above right: British Museum, London.

P.158   below: British Museum, London.

P.159   The Metropolitan Museum of Art, New York. Fletcher Fund.

P.160   above left, right: British Museum, London.

P.160   below: Staatliche Antikensammlungen, Munich.

P.161   Schmuckmuseum, Pforzheim.

P.162   Dumbarton Oaks Research Library and Collection, Washington, D. C.

P.163   left: British Museum, London.

P.163   right: Mittelrheinisches Landesmuseum, Mainz.

P.164   top: British Museum, London.

P.164   upper left, right: British Museum, London.

P.164   lower center: Dumbarton Oaks, Washington, D. C.

P.164   bottom left, right: British Museum, London.

P.165   left, top right: British Museum, London.

P.165   center right: Schmuckmuseum, Pforzheim.

P.165   bottom right: Victoria and Albert Museum, London.

P.166   1: Museo Poldi-Pezzoli, Milan.

P.166   2, 6: British Museum, London.

P.166   3: Schatzkammer der Residenz, Munich.

P.166   4, 5: Schmuckmuseum, Pforzheim.

P.166   7, 8: Museum of Decorative Arts, Belgrade.

P.167   left: British Museum, London.

P.167   right: Schatzkammer der Residenz, Munich.

P.168   Schatzkammer der Residenz, Munich.

P.169   all: Schatzkammer der Residenz, Munich.

P.170   left: British Museum, London.

P.170   right: National Gallery of Art, Washington, D. C. Widener Collection.

P.171   all: British Museum, London.

P.172   Museo Poldi-Pezzoli, Milan.

P.173   right: Schmuckmuseum, Pforzheim.

P.173   left: Marjorie Merriweather Post Collection, Smithsonian Institution, Washington, D. C.

P.173   center: Musée des Arts Décoratifs, Paris.

P.174   above: Michel Périnet Collection, Paris.

P.174   below: Hessisches Landesmuseum, Darmstadt.

P.185   Vatican Library, Rome.

P.186   Abbey of Conques.

P.187   above left: Treasury of Monza Cathedral.

P.187   above right: Kunsthistorisches Museum, Vienna, Weltliche Schatzkammer.

P.187   below: Cathedral treasury, Palais de Tau, Reims.

P.188   Kunsthistorisches Museum, Vienna, Weltliche Schatzkammer.

P.189   left: Treasury of the Abbey of St Maurice, Switzerland.

P.189   right: Treasury of Prague Castle.

P.191   Treasury of the Basilica of St Mark, Venice.

P.192   Treasury of Monza Cathedral.

P.193   above: Treasury of the Abbey of St Maurice, Switzerland.

P.193   below: Treasury of the Basilica of St Mark, Venice.

P.194   Schatzkammer der Residenz, Munich.

P.195   Musée du Louvre, Paris.

P.196   left: British Museum, London.

P.196   below: Schmuckmuseum, Pforzheim.

P.197   Musée du Louvre, Paris.

P.198, 199   Treasury of the Church of the Loretto, Prague.

P.200   St Peter's Basilica, Rome.

P.221   National Portrait Gallery, London.

P.222   Mittelrheinisches Landesmuseum, Mainz.

P.223   Museo Archeologico Nazionale, Cividale del Friuli, Italy.

P.224   all: Museo del Castelvecchio, Verona, Italy.

P.225   above left, right: Victoria and Albert Museum, London.

P.225   below: Schatzkammer der Residenz, Munich.

P.226   Kunsthistorisches Museum, Vienna, Weltliche Schatzkammer.

P.227   Kunsthistorisches Museum, Vienna, Sammlung für Plastik und Kunstgewerbe.

P.228   Prince Constantin zu Hohenlohe, Schloss Neuenstein.

P.229   above left, right: British Museum, London.

P.229   below: Kunsthistorisches Museum, Vienna, Sammlung für Plastik und Kunstgewerbe.

P.230   left: Schatzkammer der Residenz, Munich.

P.230   right: National Gallery of Art, Washington, D. C. Widener Collection.

P.231   left: By permission of the Trustees of Sir John Soane's Museum, London.

P.231   right: Schatzkammer der Residenz, Munich.

P.232   left: Schatzkammer der Residenz, Munich.

P.233   Musée du Louvre, Paris.

P.234   above: Treasury of Monza Cathedral.

P.234   below: Schatzkammer der Residenz, Munich.

P.235   all: Schatzkammer der Residenz, Munich.

P.236   Kunsthistorisches Museum, Vienna, Weltliche Schatzkammer.

P.237   Kunsthistorisches Museum, Vienna, Weltliche Schatzkammer.

P.238   Schatzkammer der Residenz, Munich.

P.239   Kunsthistorisches Museum, Vienna. Weltliche Schatzkammer.

P.240   Collection Parham Park, Pulborough, Sussex, England.

P.261   Calouste Gulbenkian Foundation, Lisbon.

P.262   Hessisches Landesmuseum, Darmstadt.

P.263   Private loan to the Schmuckmuseum, Pforzheim.

P.264   above: Gimpel and Hanover Gallery, Zurich.

P.264   below: Rebekah Harkness Collection, New York.

P.265   Collection Michèle Leiris, Paris.

P.266   left: Collection of the artist.

P.266   right: Collection Madame Olivier Thélin, Geneva.

P.267   left: Semiha Huber Gallery, Zurich.

P.268   Private Collection, Zurich.

P.269   top left: Collection Höfflin and Lüth, Pforzheim.

P.269   bottom left: Collection Mrs F. Hiramatsu, Tokyo.

P.269   upper and lower center left, right: Collection of the artist.

P.270   left: Schmuckmuseum, Pforzheim.

P.270   right: Museum of Decorative Arts, Prague.

P.271   left: Smithsonian Institution, Washington, D. C.

P.271   right: Schmuckmuseum, Pforzheim.

P.273   Collection of the artist.

P.274   Collection of the artist.

P.275   upper left: Ella Freidus Collection, New York.

P.275   upper right: Collection Egger, Ziegelhausen, Germany.

P.275   lower: Schmuckmuseum, Pforzheim.

P.276   Collection Shirley Sidnam, New York.

P.277   Collection of the artist.

P.278   1: Collection Mrs Naoko Tsuse, Tokyo.

P.278   2, 4, 5, 7, 8: Schmuckmuseum, Pforzheim.

P.278   9: Marlborough Gallery, Zurich.

P.278   11: Ella Freidus Collection, New York.

P.280   Collection of the artist.

P.295   Topkapi Museum, Istanbul.

P.297   far left: Kunsthistorisches Museum, Vienna, Weltliche Schatzkammer.

P.297   top centre right: Ella Freidus Collection, New York.

P.297   far right: The Crown Jewels of Iran, Bank Markazi, Teheran.

P.297   below: Topkapi Museum, Istanbul.

P.298   Musée du Louvre, Paris.

P.299   above left: Courtesy of the fourth Viscount Astor.

P.299   above right: Musée du Louvre, Paris.

P.300, 301   Topkapi Museum, Istanbul.

P.302   Smithsonian Institution, Washington, D. C. Gift of H. Winston.

P.304   left, right: British Crown Jewels, Tower of London.

P.305   above left: Bank Markazi, Teheran.

P.305   above right: British Crown Jewels, Tower of London.

P.305   below: Soviet Union Diamond Treasury, Moscow.

P.306   Treasury of St Vitus' Cathedral, Prague.

BIBLIOGRAPHY

ALDRED, C. *Jewels of the Pharaohs,* London, 1971

ALEXANDER, C. *Jewelry. The Art of the Goldsmith in Classical Times,* New York, 1928

ALVAREZ OSORIO, F. *Catálogo del Museo Arqueológico de Madrid,* Madrid, 1925

AMANDRY, P. *Collection H. Stathatos,* Strasbourg, 1953 et 1963 – «Le antiche civiltà mediterranee», in: *Enciclopedia Universale dell'Arte,* Firenze, 1963

ANTZE, G. «Metallarbeiten aus dem nördlichen Peru», in *Mitteilungen des Museums für Völkerkunde,* Wien, 1930

ARMSTRONG, E.C.R. *Guide to the Collection of Antiquities. Catalogue of Irish Gold Ornaments.* Dublin, 1920

N.W. AYER PUBLIC RELATIONS. *Notable Diamonds of the World,* New York, 1971

BAPST, G. *Histoire des Joyaux de la Couronne de France,* Paris, 1889

BAESSLER, A. *Alt-peruanische Metallgeräte,* Berlin, 1906

BAUER, J. & A. *A Book of Jewels,* London, 1966

BECATTI, G. *Oreficerie antiche dalle minoiche alle barbariche,* Roma, 1955

BERGSØE, P. *The Metallurgy and Technology of Gold and Platinum among the Pre-Columbian Indians,* Copenhagen, 1937

BIEHN, H. *Juwelen und Preziosen,* München, 1965

BIENKOWSKI, P. *Les Celtes dans les arts mineurs gréco-romains avec des recherches iconographiques sur quelques autres peuples barbares,* Cracovie, 1928

BING, S. *Salon de l'Art Nouveau,* Paris, 1895

BOROVKA, G. *Scythian Art,* London, 1928

BREGLIA, L. *Le oreficerie del Museo Nazionale di Napoli,* Roma, 1941

BRUNS, G. *Schatzkammer der Antike,* Berlin, 1946

BRUNTON, G., LANHUN, I. *The Treasure,* London, 1920

BRUTON, E. *The True Book about Diamonds,* London, 1961

CAIRO MUSEUM. *Brief Guide,* Cairo, 1948

CARDUCCI, C. *Ori e argenti dell'Italia antica,* Milano, 1962

CARLI, E. *Oreficerie preispaniche di Colombia,* Milano, 1957

CARTER, H. *The Tomb of Tut-ankh-amen,* 3 vol., London, 1920

CASTELLANI, A. *Antique Jewelry and its Revival,* London, 1862

CELLINI, B. *The Treatises of Benvenuto Cellini on Goldsmithing and Sculpture,* trans. C.R. Ashbee, 1888, New York, 1967

CHURCHILL, S.J.A. «The Goldsmiths of Rome under the Papal Authority», in: *Papers of the British School at Rome,* IV, No. 2, 1907

COCHE DE LA FERTÉ, E. *Les Bijoux antiques,* Paris, 1956

COPELAND, L.W. *Diamonds – Famous, Notable, and Unique,* Gemmological Institute of America, 1967

DAVIS, M.L., PACK, G. *Mexican Jewelry,* Austin, 1963

DEBO, P. *Alte Ringe,* Pforzheim, 1923

DECHELETTE, J. *Manuel d'archéologie préhistorique celtique et gallo-romaine,* II, I, *Age du bronze,* Paris, 1910 – II, 2, *Premier âge du fer ou époque de Hallstatt,* Paris, 1913 – II, 3, *Second âge du fer ou époque de la Tène,* Paris, 1914

DEGANI, M. *Il tesoro romano-barbarico di Reggio Emilia,* Firenze, 1959

DEMARGNE, P. «Bijoux minoens de Mallia», in: *Bulletin de Correspondance Hellénique,* LIV, 1930, p. 406 ss.

DOCK STADER, F.J. *Indian Art of Central America,* London, 1964

DUVAL, P.M. «Celtica Arte», in: *Enciclopedia dell'Arte Antica,* Roma, 1959, II, pp. 457-467

EDGAR, C.C. «The Treasure of Tell Basta», in: *Le Musée Egyptien,* II, Cairo, 1907/1908

EVANS, A. «A Mycenaean Treasure from Aegina», in: *Journal of Hellenic Studies,* XIII, 1893, p. 213 – «The ring of Nestor», in: *Journal of Hellenic Studies,* XLV, 1925

EVANS, J. *A History of Jewelry 1100-1870,* (second edition, revised and reset), London, 1970 – *Magical Jewels of the Middle Ages and the Renaissance,* Oxford, 1922

FLOWER, M. *Victorian Jewelry,* London, 1962

FREUD, S. *Abriss der Psychoanalyse. Das Unbehagen in der Kultur,* Frankfurt a. M. und Hamburg, 1971

GEOFFROY, G. «Des Bijoux à propos de M. René Lalique», in: *Arts et Décoration,* Paris, 1905 – «L.C. Tiffany and his Work in Artistic Jewelry», in: *International Studio,* vol. XXX, New York, 1906

GODARD, A. *Le Trésor de Ziwiyé* (Kurdistan), Haarlem, 1950

GRAHAM, H. *Modern Jewelry,* London, 1963

GRAKOV, B.N. «Deux tombeaux de l'époque scythique aux environs de la ville d'Orenbourg», in: *Eurasia Septentrionalis Antiqua,* Helsinki, IV, 1929, pp. 169-182

GREGORIETTI, G. *Il gioiello nei secoli,* Milano, 1969 – *Jewelry through the Ages,* New York, 1969

GRJAZUOV, M.P. «Pazyryskoe Kniažeskoe pogrebenie na Altae (Le tombeau d'un prince de Pazyryk dans l'Altai)», in: *Priroda,* XI, 1920, pp. 971-985

HACKENBROCH, Y. *Italienisches Email des frühen Mittelalters,* Basel, 1938

HANSMANN, L., KRISS-RETTENBECK, L. *Amulett und Talisman. Erscheinungsform und Geschichte,* München, 1966

HARRIS, J.S. *An introduction to the study of personal ornaments of precious, semiprecious and imitation stones used throughout Biblical history,* 1962-1963

HAYCRAFT, J. *Finnish Jewelry and Silverware,* Helsinki, 1962

HEIGL., C. *Gold. Silberschmuck. Gerät, von Albrecht Dürer bis zur Gegenwart,* Nürnberg, 1971

HIGGINS, R.A. «The Aegina Treasure reconsidered», in: *BSA,* LII, 1957 – *Greek and Roman Jewelry,* London, 1961 – *Jewelry from Classical Lands,* London, 1965

HOFFMANN, H., DAVIDSON, P.F. *Greek Gold,* Mainz, 1965

HOLMQVIST, W. «Europa Barbarica», in: *Enciclopedia Universale dell'Arte,* Firenze, 1958

HUBERT, H. *Les Celtes depuis l'époque La Tène et la civilisation celtique,* Paris, 1952

JACOBSTAHL, B. *Early Celtic Art,* London, 1944

JENNY, W.A. VON «Ein späthallstattischer Goldschmuck unbekannter Herkunft» in: *Prähistorische Zeitschrift,* XX, 1929, p. 115-166

JENNY, W.A. VON, VOLBACH, W.F. *Germanischer Schmuck des frühen Mittelalters,* Berlin, 1933

JENNY, W.A. *Keltische Metallarbeiten aus heidnischer und christlicher Zeit,* Berlin, 1935

JESSUP, R. *Anglo-Saxon Jewelry,* London, 1950

KAHN, G. «Dessins de Bijoux de Mucha, De Faure, Dufrene, M. Bing», in: *Arts et Décoration,* Paris, 1902

KARO, G. *Schachtgräber von Mykene,* Berlin, 1930

KAUFMANN, E., LASSEN E. *Fifty Years of Danish Silver in the Georg Jensen Tradition,* Copenhagen, 1951

LEEDS, E.T. *Celtic Ornament in the British Isles down to A.D. 700,* Oxford, 1933

LEUZINGER, E. *Wesen und Form des Schmuckes afrikanischer Völker,* Zürich, 1950

LIGHTBOWN, R.W. «Jean Petitot and Jacques Bordier at the English Court», in: *Connoisseur,* CLXVIII, 1968

MAKARENKO, N. «La civilisation des Scythes et Hallstatt», in: *Eurasia Septentrionalis Antiqua,* Helsinki, V, 1930, p. 22-48

MARGAIN, C.R. *Estudio inicial de las collecciones del Museo del Oro del Banco de la Republica,* Bogota, 1951

MARSHALL, F.H. *Catalogue of the Finger Rings... Departments of Antiquities, British Museum,* London 1907 – *Catalogue of the Jewelry... in the Departments of Antiquities, British Museum,* London, 1911

MENGARELLI, R. «La necropoli barbarica di Castel Trosino», in: *Monumenti antichi dei Lincei,* XII, 1902

MONACO, G. *Oreficerie longobarde a Parma,* Parma, 1955

Monili dell'Asia, dal Caspio all'Himalaya, catalogo Mostra a Palazzo Brancaccio, Roma, 1963

MULLER, P.E. *Jewels in Spain 1500-1800,* New York, 1972

MYRES, J.L. *Handbook of the Censola Collection of Antiquities from Cyprus, The Collection of Gold and Silver Ornaments,* p. 373-402; *The Collection of Finger Rings,* p. 405-426, New York, 1914

OMAN, C.C. *Catalogue of Rings, Victoria and Albert Museum,* London, 1930

PÁSZTORY, C., AL-CSURTI, C. *Les anciens bijoux hongrois,* Budapest, 1951

PARIBENI, R. «Necropoli barbarica di Nocera Umbra», in: *Monumenti antichi dei Lincei,* 1918

PEET, T.E. *Cemeteries of Abydos,* II, London, 1914

PEREZ DE BARRADAS, J. *80 Masterpieces from the Gold Museum,* Bogotà, 1954 – *Orfebreria prehispanica de Colombia, Estilo Calima,* Madrid, 1954 – *Viejas y nuevas teorias sobre el origen de la orfebreria prehispanica en Colombia,* Bogotà, 1956 – *Orfebreria prehispanica en Colombia. Estilos Tolima y muisca,* Madrid, 1956 – *Orfebreria prehispanica de Colombia,* 2 vol., Madrid, 1966

PETRIE, W.M.F. *The Royal Tombs of the First Dynasty,* London, 1900 – *The Royal Tombs of the Earliest Dynasty,* London, 1901 – *Arts and Crafts of Ancient Egypt,* Edinburgh, 1923

PICA, V. *L'Arte Decorativa all'Esposizione di Torino del 1902,* Bergamo, 1903

PLATON, N. «Cretese Miceneo», in: *Enciclopedia Universale dell'Arte,* IV, Firenze, 1958

POHL, H. *Gold. Macht und Magie der Geschichte,* Stuttgart, 1958

RESTREPO TIRADO, E. «Orfebreria de las tribus quimbaya y chibcha», in: *El Centenario,* Madrid, 1892

RESTREPO TIRADO, E. ARIAS, J. *Catalogo de los objetos que presenta el Gobierno de Colombia a la Exposición Histórico-Americana de Madrid,* Madrid, 1893

RESTREPO TIRADO, E. *Catálogo general del Museo de Bogotà, Arqueologia,* Bogotà, 1917

RICKETSON, E.B. *Barbarian Jewelry of the Merovingian Period, 1946-1947*

RIDDER, A. DE *Catalogue sommaire des bijoux antiques des Musées du Louvre,* Paris, 1924

RIVET, P., ARSANDAUX, H. *La métallurgie en Amérique Précolombienne,* Paris, 1946

ROOT, W.C. *Precolombian Metalwork of Colombia and its Neighbors,* Harvard, 1961

ROSS, M.C. *The Art of Karl Fabergé and his Contemporaries,* Norman (Oklahoma), 1965

SALMONY, A. «Eine chinesische Schmuckform und ihre Verbreitung in Eurasien», in: *Eurasia Septentrionalis Antiqua,* Helsinki, IX, 1934, p. 323-335

SAVILLE, M.H. *The Goldsmith's Art in Ancient Mexico,* New York, Museum of American Indian, Miscellaneous, N. 7, 1920

SCHÄFER, H. *Ägyptische Goldschmiedearbeiten,* Berlin, 1910

SCHAUSS, E. VON *Historischer und beschreibender Catalog der Königlich Bayerischen Schatzkammer zu München,* München, 1879

SCHMIDT, M. *Kunst und Kultur von Peru,* Berlin, 1929

SCHONDORFF, E. *Schmuck und Edelsteine,* München, 1955

SCHÖNFELD, J.F. *Designing and making hand-wrought Jewelry,* New York, 1960

SCOTT, N.E. «Egyptian Jewelry», in: *Bulletin of the Metropolitan Museum of Art,* New York, 1964 (new series), 22, p. 223-234

SEGALL, B. *Museum Benaki, Katalog der Goldschmiedearbeiten,* Athen, 1938

SELIGMAN, J. *L'orfèvrerie carolingienne,* Paris, 1927

SITWELL, H.D.W. *The Crown Jewels and other Regalia in the Tower of London,* London, 1953

SIVIERO, R. *Gli ori e le ambre nel Museo Nazionale di Napoli,* Firenze, 1954

STEINGRÄBER, E. *Alter Schmuck. Die Kunst des Europäischen Schmuckes,* München, 1956 – *Der Goldschmied,* München, 1966

STOTZ, J. *Kristalle, Edelsteine, Metalle. Aus der Wunderwelt des Mikrokosmos,* Heilbronn a. Neckar, 1951

STOVER, U. *Freude am Schmuck,* Gütersloh, 1965

STREETER, E.S. *The Great Diamonds of the World,* 1882

TAIT, H. «Tudor Hat Badges», in: *British Museum Quarterly,* XX, 1955-1956, p. 37 – «A Tudor Jewel, gold-enamelled Pendant», in: *Museum Journal,* LVI, 1957, p. 233

TALLGREN, A.M. «La Pontide Préscythique après l'introduction des métaux», in: *Eurasia Septentrionalis Antiqua,* Helsinki, II, 1926

TAVERNIER, J.-B. *Les six voyages... en Turquie, en Perse et aux Indes,* 1679

THOMAS, H. «The Acropolis Treasure from Mycenae», in: *BSA,* XXXIX, 1938-1939, p. 65

LORD TWINING. *A History of the Crown Jewels of Europe,* London, 1960

VERNIER, E. *La bijouterie et la joaillerie égyptiennes,* Cairo, 1907

VILIMKOVA, M. *Chefs-d'œuvre de l'art égyptien,* Prague, 1969

VILIMKOVA, M., ABDULRAHMAN, H.M. *Egyptian Jewelry,* London, 1969

VOLBACH, W.F. «L'Occidente Europeo: l'arte barbarica e l'Alto Medio Evo», in: *Enciclopedia Universale dell'Arte,* Firenze, 1963

WALDHAUER, O. «Skythische Kunst», in: *Pantheon,* 1932.

WEISS, R. *Exposition internationale des Arts décoratifs,* Paris, 1925 – *Die Wiener Werkstätte: 1903-1928,* Wien, 1929

WILKENS, M. *Das Schmuckbrevier,* Hamburg, 1960

WILSON, M. *Gems,* New York, 1967 – *Strahlende Steine. Juwelen und ihre Geschichte,* Gütersloh, 1969

WINLOCK, H.E. *The Treasure of El Lahun,* New York, 1934 – *The Treasure of three Egyptian Princesses,* New York, 1948

WOOLLEY, C.L. *Ur Excavations,* II, London, 1934 – *The Development of Sumerian Art,* London, 1935

PHOTOGRAPHIC CREDITS

All photography by Ernst A. Heiniger except:

Page 59	Charles Wilp, Düsseldorf
Page 60 left, 269	Taken from book "Parures et Bijoux" Editions Avanti, Neuchâtel 1962
Page 60 right	A. Gauvin, Musée Royal de l'Afrique Centrale, Tervuren
Page 83	Rudi Herzog/BURDA, Offenburg
Page 121 bottom	Karl Neubert, Prague
Page 127 top	Trustees of the British Museum, London
Page 185, 186, 200	Leonard von Matt, Buochs
Page 187 bottom, 299 right	Service photographique de la Réunion des Musées Nationaux, Paris
Page 266 right	Photo Wicky, Lausanne
Page 269 (3rd, left column)	Bruno Martinazzi, Turin
Page 269 bottom left	Yasuki Hiramatsu, Tokyo
Page 278 (I)	Spot Color Photo Service, Tokyo
Page 279	Walter Fischer, Düsseldorf
Page 303 top	Property of Her Majesty Queen Elizabeth II. Copyright reserved.
Page 304 (both), 305 top right	British Crown copyright, reproduced with the permission of the Controller of Her Britannic Majesty's Stationery Office
Page 305 bottom	Agence de Presse Novosti, Genève

This book is edited and published by
Edita S.A., Lausanne
under the direction of Ami Guichard,
editorial responsibility and supervision by Tim Chilvers,
and production by Charles Riesen.
The layout was designed by Ernst A. Heiniger, Zurich.

Photolithography: Actual S.A., Bienne
Printed: Grafiche Editoriali Ambrosiane S.p.A.-Milan
Binding: Maurice Busenhart, Lausanne

Printed in Italy and bound in Switzerland